D1154783

DISCERNING THE SPIRIT

Foundations and Futures of Religious Life

DISCERNING THE SPIRIT

Foundations and Futures of Religious Life

by DONALD L. GELPI, S.J.

SHEED AND WARD: NEW YORK

ORDER OF THE HOLY CROSS
WEST PARK, NEW YORK

243
G

Imprimi Potest:
John Edwards, S.J.
New Orleans Province

Biblical excerpts are from *The Jerusalem Bible,* copyright © 1966 by Darton, Longman & Todd, Ltd. and Doubleday & Company, Inc. Used by permission of the publishers.

© Sheed and Ward, Inc., 1970
Library of Congress Catalog Card Number 79–103364
Standard Book Number 8362–0197–3
Manufactured in the United States of America

to Tony Mangiaracina, S.J., Gus Coyle, S.J., and C. J. McNaspy, S.J., who had the patience to introduce me to religious living

Preface

Having written this book, I feel obliged to warn the reader ahead of time that I can in all honesty lay no claim to the skills of a professional exegete, patrologist, or theologian. I have written it not out of training but out of need, because the issues with which it attempts to deal seemed to me confused, and because, having been bookish all my life, I have the misfortune of experiencing my problems verbally. And I offer it to the public in the hope that the personal limitations which mar the following chapters will be obvious enuogh to harm no one and that the light I have found in the Spirit while writing them may in the Spirit be of help to those who read them.

For honesty's sake, therefore, I have called it an essay in discernment. By discernment I mean a personal attempt to get behind some of the facts of religious living in order to discover the purposes and ideals which motivate them and give them life. The scholarly apparatus of textual references is, therefore, included so that the reader may have some idea of the factual material which has grounded the discerning process and return to it, if so inclined, in order to see if he finds implicit there the same ideals that I do. My limited and very personal intent in writing will also help to explain the manner in which some of the factual material is handled in the pages which follow. Since my main purpose was a personal rediscovery of a sense of purpose in my own attempt to live the religious life, I have been concerned with many of the historical personages who appear in these pages merely as embodying, in this or that comment or opus, some typical ascetical attitude. My concern has been, then, with the specific ideas expressed by them in the texts dealt with rather than with doing them complete historical justice as thinkers.

I regret that the exigencies of method have not permitted a simpler exposition of the religious ideals expressed in the following pages. I regret, too, that the history of the problems which confront us is so convoluted. But responsible theological reflection demands an examination of the available and pertinent historical data whose thoroughness is commensurate both with the importance of the problem and with the limiting circumstances which surround its investigation. It also demands some critical examination of other theological alternatives than the one defended. My deepest regret is that on both counts the limits of time and talent have precluded the possibility of a more thorough treatment. Eventually, of course, the test of the theory of religious life herein offered must be the attempt of religious to live it.

I am especially indebted to many friends at Fordham University whose insights and conversations have helped make this a much better book than I could ever have made it by myself. To Robert Colacurcio, S.J., Leo Klein, S.J., Milton Gonsalves, S.J., Neil Gilmartin, S.J., Al Culliton, S.J., and Stephen Rowntree, S.J., I am particularly grateful for many pleasant evenings spent together in discussion of the topics treated in this book. I also owe a special debt to William Cleary whose thoughts and suggestions were also most helpful. I am, too, very grateful to Mrs. Astrid O'Brien and to Clyde Crews for sharing with me their insights into the celibate and the married vocations. Finally, I owe special thanks to the community of John LaFarge House in Cambridge, Mass., for their help, insights and suggestions in the final stages of writing. Joseph P. Kelly, S.J., George Brown, S.J., Richard Clifford, S.J., Michael Coogan, S.J., Donald Crosby, S.J., John Galvani, S.J., James Kelly, S.J., John L'Heureux, S.J., William Meissner, S.J., John Muller, S.J., William Russell, S.J., and John Miles, S.J., the members of that community, should not be surprised if from time to time they should encounter themselves in the following pages.

One member of that community deserves a vote of special thanks. To Frank Oppenheim, S.J., I am truly indebted for the many helpful suggestions he made for improving the manuscript prior to publication. For these and many other kindnesses and insights, I am most grateful.

In addition to many other signs of friendship and affection, I am particularly thankful to Philip Donnelly, S.J., and to C. J. McNaspy, S.J., for reading the present study and for the wonderfully encouraging reception they both gave it. With friends like these religious living can only be a dynamic experience.

Loyola University
New Orleans, La.
September, 1969

Contents

Abbreviations

Gn	Genesis	Ba	Baruch
Ex	Exodus	Ez	Ezekiel
Lv	Leviticus	Dn	Daniel
Nb	Numbers	Ho	Hosea
Dt	Deuteronomy	Jl	Joel
Jos	Joshua	Am	Amos
Jg	Judges	Jon	Jonah
1S	1 Samuel	Mi	Micah
2S	2 Samuel	Ze	Zechariah
1K	1 Kings	Mt	Matthew
2K	2 Kings	Mk	Mark
2Ch	2 Chronicles	Lk	Luke
Ne	Nehemiah	Jn	John
Jdt	Judith	Ac	Acts
Est.	Esther	Rm	Romans
2M	2 Maccabees	1Co	1 Corinthians
Jb	Job	2Co	2 Corinthians
Ps	Psalms	Ga	Galatians
Pr	Proverbs	Ep	Ephesians
Ws	Wisdom	Ph	Philippians
Si	Ecclesiasticus	Col	Colossians
Is	Isaias	1Th	1 Thessalonians
Jr	Jeremiah	2Th	2 Thessalonians
Lm	Lamentations		

1Tm	1 Timothy	MG	Migne, J.P., *Patrologiae cursus completus, series graeca* (Paris, 1857ff).
2Tm	2 Timothy		
Tt	Titus		
Heb	Hebrews	ML	Migne, J.P., *Patrologiae cursus completus, series latina* (Paris, 1844ff).
Jm	James		
1P	1 Peter		
2P	2 Peter	DS	*Enchiridion symbolorum,* H. Denziger and A. Schönmetzer (eds.) (New York: Herder, 1957).
1Jn	1 John		
Rv	Revelation		

DISCERNING THE SPIRIT
Foundations and Futures of Religious Life

1

American Religious: The Search for Identity

Not long ago the major superior of a group of American religious included in a newsletter a "problem-posting session." Slightly paraphrased, the problems posted included the following: the current tendency among religious to appeal to their subjective feelings and sincerity as the ultimate criterion of their behavior; lack of communication between older and younger religious; a feeling of futility among middle-aged religious; lack of money; lack of skilled personnel in religious-sponsored institutions; lack of trained spiritual directors; a failure of morale caused by administrative indecision in the matter of ministries; discouragement over the discontinuation of traditional ministries; confusion in the program for the formation of young religious; confusion about shared ideals; lack of communication between young religious more advanced in training and those entering now; constant pressure for the bourgeoisification of religious life; the failure of older religious to provide inspiration and guidance to the younger; despondency among young religious over their own lack of meaningful ideals; lack of agreement among religious about Christian doctrine, liturgical worship, administrative policy, and pastoral direction; disagreement among religious on basic questions of Christian morality. The superior in question, who has a fine sense of humor, might in the newsletter have ended the list with the remark: "Otherwise, everything is just fine," but unfortunately did not.

Needless to say, it is easy to play Cassandra and to cry doom and destruction over any worthwhile cause. Still, one would have to be immensely naïve not to recognize that American religious orders are today passing through an important period of crisis. Religious orders everywhere are, of course, being faced with the problems of implementing the decrees of Vatican II. But there are enough symptoms among American religious to indicate that the crisis we are now beginning to experience goes a bit deeper than that.

There seems to be a growing shortage of vocations among us. There seems to be an increasing number of defections. And according to a recent prediction of Fr. Andrew Greeley, the defections and the shortage are likely to grow greater before they will grow less. What is, however, most alarming of all, among those who defect there seem to be more and more whose sincerity, personal idealism, and dedication are beyond question.

These symptoms cannot be explained away simply in terms of the transitional phase through which the orders and the Church at large are passing, even though the process of renewal among religious is indeed producing something like a collective identity crisis. We are being forced to re-focus even our most basic goals and to re-formulate even our most fundamental commitments and most traditional modes of life. Under the circumstances, it is almost inevitable that the image which any religious group projects to its prospective candidates should be somewhat blurred by this internal process of re-evaluation and that within the order itself a certain amount of confusion should reign temporarily within the ranks. But this cannot be the total explanation of our problems.

Moreover, if to some the period through which we are passing seems more like a painful wrenching than a growth, in a sense we have no one to blame but ourselves. If the changes which are now coming about in the orders seem violent and drastic, it is because many of them are at least several generations, in some cases perhaps several centuries, overdue.

The basic question confronting us is this: Is it possible to reconcile the basic values of Christianity as they have come to find expression in the traditional structures of religious life and the values which motivate contemporary American life and culture? The problem is real, complex, and inevitable.

Focusing the Issue

One of the clichés of the American aggiornamento is that the present generation of American Catholics is both American and Catholic. This has, of course, been true in some sense of every generation of Catholics in this country. But what seems to be peculiar about the present generation is that they are both American and Catholic consciously and that in their simultaneous awareness of both their Americanism and their Catholicity they are inwardly conscious of a commitment to two sets of values whose complete compatibility is far from being immediately obvious. It is, moreover, in the religious life that the problem of reconciling these conflicting values becomes most acute. What, then, concretely are some of the values which are at stake? There is a dark and a light side to almost every national tradition, and America is no exception. In its more demonic aspect the American mind is materialistic, money-grabbing, and egotistical. Needless to say, there is no question of reconciling ideals such as these with Christianity, much less with the religious life. But the problem of reconciliation does become a pressing one when we consider the more idealistic side of the American genius. For the better half of the American spirit has consistently repudiated our native materialism and has done so in a tradition that has been culturally and literarily articulate.

First of all, the American idealist has traditionally felt no irrevocable commitment to any historical institution as such. As a people, we are conscious of having fashioned and framed our own national and state governments. And we have endorsed the democratic principle that these governments exist solely for the common good and must be adapted according to circumstances to meet that good. But even when they have failed to function properly, the institutions themselves have remained, in principle at least, mere means whose sole justification for existence has been their ability to meet the common need. Ideally their end has been man himself and the protection of basic human rights.

Second, the American idealist has traditionally placed immense value on human creativity. Part of this insistence has been polemic: an angry and often futile effort to protect our human resources from the ravages of a cheaply commercialistic society. But part of it has had deep religious motivations as well and can be traced back through pragmatism and transcendentalism to the evangelical piety of the eighteenth and early nineteenth centuries. One enduring theme in American thought has, for instance, been the need of man to overcome his selfish individualism precisely in and through his spontaneous creative response to the world in which he lives. Viewed in this light, the democratic community becomes ideally one which is mediated not by laws but by creativity itself, by each individual finding fulfillment through contributing what he can best do in order to enrich the community of which he or she is a member.

Third, the American idealist has traditionally affirmed the value and religious significance of the material universe. Much American thinking is motivated by the more or less conscious repudiation of a Calvinistic doctrine of inner human corruption and by the rejection of a rigid and unyielding puritanical ethic. Men like Franklin, Emerson, Thoreau, James, Dewey, and Santayana found the admittedly limited meaning available to them through personal dedication to nature, to society, or to "the human" preferable to the "retailed" religion of the church establishment. Out of their thought and the thinking of like-minded men, there has emerged in the American tradition a deep sense of the goodness of the material creation, together with a firm feeling that man is fully at home in his body and in the world of matter, and a conviction that human fulfillment must be sought in the effort to subdue this material creation to the benefit of humanity at large.

The Conflict of Ideals

Now, if these three interrelated values—democratic detachment from specific institutions, the conscious cult of creativity, and a sense of the religious significance of the material universe—are enduring factors in the world-view of the typical idealistic American, it is not difficult to see why Catholics who are consciously both idealistic and American would find great difficulty with those structures and attitudes in the religious life which have been inspired by an excessively ritualistic and authoritarian version of Christian ascetism.

For instance, our American detachment from specific institutional structures and insistence on the necessity of subordinating those structures to human needs has in the past run head on into the notion that the rules and regulations of the religious life are the concrete embodiment of the absolute will of God. Accustomed as he is to measuring institutions by human needs, the idealistic American is at best ill prepared to cope with such a speculatively ambiguous interpretation of the rule. In the past he has all too often been tempted, rightly or wrongly, to conclude that in the religious life one seems expected to endorse the principle that the institution as such assumes priority over the concrete human needs and aspirations of its members. As one religious superior I know of once put it in a moment of self-righteous absolutism, "The only right a religious subject has is to a decent burial."

Imbued with an American cult of creativity, a young idealistic religious will be equally inclined to conclude that in an ascetical world formed by authoritarian presuppositions holiness itself is actually identified with the conscious cult of external uniformity and mediocrity. And, indeed, there is no lack of evidence that in a superficially ritualistic version of religious living, life in community is not for all intents and purposes mediated by the spontaneous creative gift of oneself to the community but by sterile external conformity to regulations for their own sake.

Finally, in any excessively authoritarian version of asceticism the world at large ceases for all practical purposes to be a potential vehicle of grace. For where the "religious" are arbitrarily identified exclusively with what is sanctioned, the unsanctioned tends to be dismissed as "secular" and "profane." Moreover, when holiness is conceived in such narrowly legalistic terms religious life can all too easily fall victim to a false and humanly destructive brand of pseudo-mystical asceticism, despite the fact that in a truly Christian view of the world, the only thing completely profane is the malice and unbelief of men. Everything else is at the very least potentially holy.

The Danger of Oversimplification

Nevertheless, we must be on our guard against the temptation to resolve this conflict of values within American religious life into a simplistic choice between remnants of an authoritarian, decadently ritualistic asceticism and an American idealism. Our problem is much more complex than that. It is rather to distill from either set of values whatever in it is seen to be valid in the light of Christian revelation and to embody that result in a way of life and in an institutional structure which is simultaneously American, Catholic, and religious.

To be a bit more specific, all three values here suggested as being enduring elements in the American idealistic tradition have historically been subject to serious distortions. There has been the tendency, for instance, for our American lack of commitment to any specific institutional structure to degenerate into a repudiation of the institutional as such. And unless it is balanced by a hard-headed realism and a willingness to accept the unadorned fact of human limitations, this same lack of commitment to the institutional can easily take the form of an egotistical cult of a "personal integrity" which refuses to become involved in any movement or organization which is not already humanly perfect. At its worst such an attitude is a refusal to love as Christ did, not only creatively but redemptively. And in its more self-centered forms it easily runs down into various manifestations of anti-social behavior.

Americans must also beware of a tendency in our cultural tradition to identify creativity with total spontaneity. To do so is not only false; it is ultimately to undermine the possibility of any genuine creativity by a failure to recognize that any significant creative achievement must emerge from the mastery of an often painfully acquired discipline.

Finally, there has been the tendency for our American sense of the religious significance of the material universe to degenerate into mere naturalism and hence either into a denial of any ultimate value in human living or into the naïve affirmation of man's ability to achieve ultimate salvation on his hook.

On the other hand, there is no need to catalogue the distortions, the spiritual dryness, the dehumanization, the pharisaism which arise from a rigidly authoritarian approach to the religious life. Hence, both attitudes, both humanly limited sets of values, are in need of a radical reassessment, which can be accomplished only by measuring them against the event and the person of Christ.

Thus, it is in the confrontation of Christ risen that every naturalistic humanism must be forced to acknowledge the full extent of man's utter need for redemption. It is ultimately in an openness to the Spirit of Christ that we must discover that the graced fullness of creativity is one with the prophetic experience and that the prophetic experience is linked irrevocably with fidelity to the community and to the cross.

At the same time the event of Christ illuminates and fulfills everything that has been truly valid in the aspirations of the American idealistic tradition. For even the permanent sacramental structures of the Church exist for the sake of man and for the fulfillment of his enduring need for salvation. Moreover, the event of Christ has taught us once and for all that justification before God cannot be achieved by mere external conformity to religious rules and practices, that justification demands of us a radical response to the redeeming love of Christ, a response which assumes responsibility for the needs of those whom he loves.

Moreover, judged in the light of the new creation inaugurated in Christ, the whole mission and purpose of a religious community can only be to foster the creative gift of each of its members to one another and to the fulfillment of the needs of the Church at large. Our love must be a participation in the creative love of God himself. And our service should ideally be full of the zest and the joy and the imagination which rightly marks the children of the new creation.

Finally, it is in the universal redemptive love of Christ that we discover the extent to which all things are truly holy in God's eyes. Flight from the "world" must not be distorted into flight from people, from the twentieth century, or from reality. Flight from the world is flight from egotism, from selfishness, and from unbelief. Therefore, it is also flight from the "world" which authoritarian or merely ritualistic living can all too easily create *within* the religious community itself, the world of selfish and egotistical attachment to particular pious practices and modes of life as though they themselves were God.

In brief, the crisis which we are currently facing in the religious orders in this country consists largely in fact that we have in the course of our historical development allowed ourselves under the influence of an exaggerated ritualism and authoritarianism to lose our grip on an authentic and realistic sense of purpose. Our nominalistic logic has led us all too often in the past to convert means into ends, to absolutize things which are not absolutes, and as a consequence to substitute a rigid regularity and a formalistic piety for the creatively adaptable love of Christ. We have all too often allowed ourselves to become inordinately attached to specific pious practices and modes of living and in the process have become partially blind to the human needs which cried out and still cry out to us on every side. And to the extent that we have done so, we have lost contact with the living reality of Christ, who is present in those we meet and longing for our response. Hence, too, we have inevitably lost full clarity of purpose and direction in the mission of service to God's people which is ours as religious men and women. If, then, we are to regain that sense of purpose, we must be willing to detach ourselves from the "world" we have created within the religious life and renew within ourselves Christ's own redemptive love and attachment to the real world which surrounds us. We must dedicate ourselves anew to the work of using all of the gifts of God available to us to mediate by our imaginative, spontaneous, and creative response to every human need a truly Christian community of love.

The issues, then, seem quite clear. If we are to meet the present crisis in religious life, we can do so only by re-discovering in its concrete fullness our Christian sense of mission and of purpose.

And we can re-discover our sense of purpose only by asserting the primacy in our daily living of those enduring redemptive needs of the people of God which call us into existence as an order or congregation, which justify our continued existence as religious in the Church, and to whose fulfillment we have totally dedicated our lives. Moreover, unless the legitimate values which motivate young idealistic Americans, values of which democratic adaptability, creativity, and an incarnational approach to the material universe are only selected examples, are explicitly endorsed and effectively embodied in our rules and actual manner of living, then we can make no claim to having truly re-discovered a Christian sense of purpose, granted the society in which we live. For it is values such as these which put purpose into our lives as Americans and which we as Christians and as religious must learn to sanctify and consecrate to God.

Thus far we have spoken a great deal of creativity and adaptability and said little explicitly of the cross. But in a deeper sense we have actually spoken of nothing else but the cross. For a totally flexible and creative dedication in the name of Christ to meeting the needs of a mankind still desperately in need of redemption will make far greater demands upon us than any rule book ever could. Still, like Christ himself, our goal is not the cross but the new creation. Like him, we hope to be able to embrace the cross when our mission demands it. But we must acknowledge as religious that our mission seen in its fullness is not the cross alone but the creative mediation under God's saving and strengthening grace of a Christian community of love.

II

Gratuitous Sharing

To the extent that it occurs at all, the question of the purpose of poverty arises relatively late in the development of Old Testament thinking. For the devout Jew of the time, financial success was, in the normal providence of God, the expected outcome of virtuous living.[1] Well he knew that fear of the Lord was the beginning of wisdom, but he also expected it, ideally at least, to be the beginning of a comfortable life.[2] In fact, one of the principal tasks of the Old Testament sages in their reflections on poverty and wealth was their attempt to explain to the devout why things did not always work out in exactly that fashion.[3]

The Burden of Wisdom

The problem was a prickly one; and the effort of the wise men to resolve it, groping and tentative.[4,5,6] For what after all could they say of the virtuous poor? What of the innocent who are gulled and oppressed by the rich and powerful? A sage named Agur, son of Jakeh, found in the very problem a lesson worth his prayerful reflection. He concluded that though riches may be the crown of virtuous living, they are no guarantee of virtue and may in the last analysis be incompatible with true fear of the Lord. Agur gave formal expression to a significant advance in Old Testament thinking when he prayed to Yahweh: "Give me neither poverty nor riches, grant me only my share of bread to eat, for fear that surrounded by plenty, I should fall away and say, 'Yahweh—who is Yahweh?' "[7]

Agur seems to have pondered long the deeper meaning of both the law and the prophets. From the Torah he had learned that innocent poverty creates specific rights before the law and that any violation of the rights of the innocent poor constitutes contempt for the very covenant that binds Yahweh to his people.[8-13] For the covenanted Jew, therefore, economic oppression of the innocent carried with it a triple malice. Not only was it a violation of basic justice and an act of contempt for God in the creature who shared his image, but it also deprived the innocent of the promised blessings of God which they by their fidelity to the covenant had rightfully deserved.[14-19]

The Plight of God's "Little Ones"

Thus, in the Old Testament, the cry of the innocent poor mounts up to God with a threefold efficacy. For they are his creatures and the work of his hand; and to contemn the work is to insult the maker. They are his covenanted faithful enjoying the guarantee of the law's protection; and for the rich to spurn the law is for them to defy the divine authority. Finally, the innocent poor are those who by their fidelity have earned the blessings promised the covenant; and for the rich and powerful to deprive them of those blessings is maliciously to thwart the divine plan of salvation.[20-22]

Still, in spite of his suffering, if he is to remain innocent in the sight of Yahweh, the poor man has no choice but to wait upon God. His attitude in the face of his own misery and of God's silence becomes, therefore, one of total inner self-abandonment into the divine keeping. In spite of all, he will be faithful and await the day of his vindication at the hands of God.[23]

Reflection on the plight of the innocent poor who remain faithful to the covenant in spite of every injustice gives rise to two significant developments in Old Testament thinking. For perplexing as the problem was for the devout believer, three things at least were absolutely clear to him: first, the strict right of the innocent poor on the basis of the covenant to divine vindication; second, the fact that as a result God hears the prayers of the innocent poor with favor and pity; and third, that God will somehow be faithful to the covenanted divine word.[24-26]

At the same time, the wise men taught, inner poverty of spirit is a virtuous religious attitude which need not be accompanied by actual financial hardships.[27,28] Granted the whole context of Old Testament belief, the inconsistency here is only apparent. For if one's fidelity to God and to his covenant does reach an intensity of inner abandonment to him and to his will, what would be more natural than that God should respond in kind with the blessings he had promised to those who heed his law? Of course, the wise men presupposed that the truly humble and poor of spirit would, like the heroic mother of Maccabees, be ready to sacrifice all for fidelity to God: "for wisdom and instruction mean fear of the Lord, and what pleases him is faithfulness and gentleness."[29-33]

Tensions in Old Testament Thought

There seems to be, then, a genuine tension in Old Testament thinking about the meaning of poverty, a tension which is, moreover, never wholly resolved. On the one hand, poverty is pictured as a social abomination explicable only in terms of the sinfulness of man; on the other, it is seen as a providential means of preserving inner detachment of heart and abandonment to God. By the same token, riches are presented both as a reward for virtuous living and as an illusion which can all too easily entice the human heart from the God who is the only source of its peace.

Almost inevitably, then, Old Testament thinking about the purpose of poverty suffers from the same ambiguity. Initially, the purpose of poverty is conceived in terms of retribution: God sends poverty on men as a fitting punishment for sloth, arrogance, and selfishness. But the plight of the innocent poor necessarily complicates the issue. Old Testament thinking never loses the conviction that innocent poverty is indeed a blight in the eyes of God which must be eradicated from human society. Moreover, the basis of this conviction is the very covenant through which God had revealed himself to his people; for by that covenant he had promised that the blessings of a good life would rest upon all who are faithful to him.

At the same time, reflection on the meaning of poverty of spirit gradually uncovers a sense of purpose in the experience of poverty itself: God uses the very injustice of the rich for the express aim of binding the hearts of the oppressed to him with longing and complete self-abandonment. Moreover, this inner attitude, this "poverty of spirit," is seen to be an ideal to which every covenanted Jew is ipso facto committed. Finally, the willingness to share one's wealth with one's covenant brothers who are in need is recognized as an obligation binding upon all. For it makes no sense to profess belief in a God who wills to bless with the good things of this life all who serve him well and at the same time to cast an indifferent eye upon the misery of the innocent. Generosity to the innocent poor among God's people is, then, a work especially pleasing to God; for it furthers his revealed purposes in making the covenant. Moreover, granted the fact of human sinfulness, such generosity takes on the aspect of an act of religious atonement, of reconciliation with God through one's reconciliation with one's covenant brothers. In the words of Ben Sirah, "water quenches a blazing fire, almsgiving atones for sins."[34]

Teachings of Jesus

In his preaching as it is recorded in the books of the New Testament, our Lord seems to have been determined to dispel some of the ambiguity found in the observations of the Old Testament sages on the meaning and purpose of poverty and wealth.

On one point Jesus is quite clear: Money is no assurance whatever of divine favor and is in fact a serious hindrance to accepting the revelation of God which is present in his own person.[35] His astonished disciples must learn that only with great difficulty can the rich man hope to enter the kingdom of God,[36] that money is "tainted" by human sinfulness,[37] and that God's vindicating justice threatens the idle and indifferent rich. In the ultimate analysis, however, the problem lies not with money itself, which must be used by all men, the disciples included. The problem is rather with man, who allows the all-absorbing pursuit of wealth to deprive him of the center of his soul, a center which he can find again only by acknowledging the God who reveals himself in the person of Jesus as the only reality worthy of man's ultimate concern.[38] "If you cannot be trusted with what is not yours, who will give you what is your very own?"[39,40]

For in the last analysis either ultimate concern with God or ultimate concern with wealth is constitutive of the kind of person one gradually becomes in the course of living out one's days. Thus, the choice every man must make in giving basic orientation to his life is posed by Jesus in radical terms: "You cannot be the slave both of God and of money."[41]

But for those who desire a more intimate association with the master even more is required. As a preliminary to joining his company, they are expected to perform the atoning act of selling their possessions, giving them as an alms to the poor,[42] and being content thereafter to live on their share in a common fund.[43] And they must perform this act of generosity with the full realization that they are joining the company of one who is himself financially indigent. To the young man who offers to follow Jesus wherever he goes, the master's reply is the blunt warning: "Foxes have holes and the birds of the air have nests, but the Son of Man has nowhere to lay his head."[44]

Moreover, the purpose of this external renunciation is the disciple's personal initiation into the mystery of the master's own inner poverty of spirit: "Shoulder my yoke and learn from me, for I am gentle and humble in heart, and *you will find rest for your souls*."[45] Thus, the sum and substance of the wisdom sought by the Old Testament sages in their reflections on poor man's abandonment to God has become nothing less than the lesson of the master's own inner abandonment to his Father.[46,47]

At the same time this very lesson of inner abandonment implies the further lesson of accepting the gratuity of God's love for us as the norm of our own dealings with one another. As a result, self-abandonment to God becomes inseparable from dedication to the task of establishing his kingdom on earth; and it presupposes in the devout believer the same quality of love as that which motivated the divine impulse which sent Jesus into the world as author and founder of God's kingdom. Thus, the close follower of Jesus, by sharing gratuitously and universally what he has with others, seeks to imitate the perfection of a loving God who cares tenderly for every man, even for those who abuse and repudiate his love.[48]

Dedication to the work of the kingdom, however, also creates specific rights and duties both for those who consecrate their lives to the task of bringing to others the good news of salvation and for those to whom they minister. For the disciple it creates the obligation of working with dedication for the spread of the kingdom. For the people to whom he ministers, it creates the obligation of providing for his material support as a workman for God; for the laborer in the kingdom is "worthy of his hire."[49]

At the same time, the work of the kingdom must not be conceived as though it were some sort of financial agreement between the close disciple of Jesus and those to whom he ministers. There are no "charges" for the labor of spreading the good news; for the work itself is from first to last one of gratuitous love and must be carried on in such a way that this fact is manifest to all.[50,51]

Thus, under the master's example and tutelage, the universal and gratuitous sharing of the good things of this world as an expression of inner abandonment to God is gradually revealed to be inseparable from the heart and soul of religion itself. It is useless and hypocritical to utter long prayers before God while keeping from others those very necessities which will fill their material wants[52] or to exact from oneself and others external conformity to the ritualistic prescriptions of religious laws while the justice, mercy, and sincerity which these laws are meant to embody are left ignored.[53]

Moreover, in the master's eyes, it is crucial that this sharing be genuinely gratuitous and truly unrestricted. Even though one may foresee that there will in fact be no return made to him in this life, the true disciple of Jesus, who has learned the meaning of the master's own abandonment to God, is to remain content to receive his reward in the world to come. And as a sign of that trust he must be willing to share *most* readily with those who *cannot* respond in kind.[54] Moreover, he must constantly remind himself that in God's eyes the measure of the generosity of any gift is not the amount given but the actual sacrifice and risk which results for the giver himself.[55]

The Scandal of the Cross

However well the close disciples of Jesus may have learned these lessons, the full scope of that abandonment to the Father to which they had committed themselves remained concealed from them until the passion and death of Jesus.

The master had taught them that he considered any act of gratuitous generosity to those in need as directed to himself.[56] As a result his rebuke to Judas during the supper at the house of Lazarus shortly before the passion is filled with meaning. John is careful to link the betrayal of Jesus with Judas's objection that the expensive oils which Mary uses to anoint the master at table might have been put into the common fund for distribution to the poor. But, the evangelist adds, "he said this, not because he cared about the poor, but because he was a thief; he was in charge of the common fund and used to help himself to the contributions."[57] The master's rebuke is direct: "Leave her alone; she had to keep this scent for the day of my burial. You have the poor with you always, you will not always have me."[58] The passage suggests that at the heart of Judas's betrayal of the master was his failure to learn the meaning of the life of selfless sharing which Jesus had lived with his closest followers, that Judas had chosen instead to use the generosity of his companions to line his own purse, and that this failure, in all that it implied, was the *inner* betrayal of Jesus which made possible the final overt act of treachery.

But it is as he hangs on the cross that the master gives his disciples their last terrible lesson in the meaning of poverty of spirit. Utterly abandoned and alone, he prays the prayer of the innocent poor man: "My God, my God, why have you deserted me?"[59] and dies stripped of everything, even of the clothes upon his back.[60] All that is left to him in his agony is his own total abandonment to his Father and his offer of love and reconciliation in spite of everything.[61]

But it is in the final revelation of the divinity of the risen Jesus that the disciples finally begin to realize that the master's call to a life of common sharing with him possessed a dimension which exceeded everything they could have possibly imagined. Perhaps Paul gives best expression to the insight:

> In your minds you must be the same as Christ Jesus: His state was divine, yet he did not cling to his equality with God but emptied himself to assume the condition of a slave and became as men are; and being as all men are, he was humbler yet, even to accepting death, death on a cross. But God raised him high and gave him the name which is above all names so that *all beings* in the heavens, on earth and in the underworld *should bend the knee* at the name of Jesus and that every tongue should acclaim Jesus Christ as Lord, to the glory of God the Father.[62]

In other words, the master's own human longing to share the good things of this life unrestrictedly and gratuitously with others is seen in the light of the Resurrection not only to have been the human embodiment of a love which was in its very nature divine but also to be a permanent and constitutive element within the new and irrevocable covenant of grace concluded between God and man upon the cross. For that same inner abandonment of Jesus to his Father, that inner poverty of spirit, which during his life had led him to share whatever he possessed with his disciples and in the passion took the visible form of his total and unconditioned self-offering to the Father in death, is revealed, through the Father's irrevocable response of love in raising Jesus from the dead as the historical embodiment of the new and everlasting covenant of grace which found God's promised kingdom. As a result, the relationship of Christian sharing to the covenant becomes clear; for since the inner abandonment of Jesus to his Father upon the cross is only the culmination of the same inner abandonment to God which found expression in the life of gratuitous and unrestricted sharing which he lived with his disciples, henceforth such a life of sharing, grounded in one's faith in Jesus as Lord, is by that very fact a sign and a quasi-sacramental expression of that same new and irrevocable covenant of grace which was concluded between God and man in the crucifixion and exaltation of the Son of Man.

Moreover, in the unrestrictedness of its gratuity, the new covenant significantly corrects the old: The offer of membership in God's covenant with men is no longer restricted by race but only by the willingness of each man to risk reliving in faith the unrestricted and gratuitous offer of divine love revealed to men in Christ. Thus, each Christian's selfless sharing of the good things of this world with anyone who is in need comes to be seen as his own personal share in the *kenosis,* the revelatory self-emptying, of the Word made flesh and as his profession of faith in the final fidelity of the God who has raised Jesus from the dead. Especially is this so when it is a question of sharing with those most in need and least able to respond in kind.

Nevertheless, by its very relationship to the covenant, Christian sharing is also an expression of the belief that mere human sharing is of itself incapable of effecting any final and definitive reconciliation among men. Ultimate reconciliation, of which gratuitous sharing is only a foreshadowing, must await an intervention of God in human affairs as decisive as the resurrection itself: It must await the second coming. But in the meantime, gratuitous sharing in the name of Christ, which seeks to mediate a non-exclusive community of faith and of love, must remain the quasi-sacramental anticipation of our final salvation, a symbol whose ultimate efficacy must depend upon the saving power of the God whose love for men has evoked from them this kind of selfless concern for one another. Thus, as a sign and expression of faith, Christian sharing also has as its purpose and function to initiate every believer gradually into the full meaning of filial belief and trust in his heavenly Father.

The Experience of the Apostolic Community

Predictably enough, the apostles, in organizing the first Christian community at Jerusalem, attempted to continue the life of common sharing which they had lived with the Lord when he had walked among them. Thus, their life in common is presented in *Acts* as an expression of their unity of spirit through their abandonment in faith to almighty God,[63] as a source of profound harmony and joy,[64] and as an expression of mutual concern in Christ for one another's need.[65-68]

The agape of the gentile Christians and the collection organized by Paul for the needy in Jerusalem were similar manifestations within the apostolic Church of the same belief which motivated the life of common sharing at Jerusalem, namely, that the Lord, by the life he had lived in common with his disciples, had revealed to men the manner in which they must use the material goods of this world in order to mediate to one another the reconciliation offered them in the new covenant.[69-74]

It is also clear both from Acts and from the letters of Paul that the administration even of considerable sums of money was regarded as compatible with the office of an apostle, provided that the funds in question were well administered and administered for the benefit of the community rather than for the personal profit of the apostle himself.[75] It is also clear, however, that from the viewpoint of their specific pastoral mission within the community, the apostles regarded such purely administrative tasks as secondary in importance to their life of prayer and to the preaching of the word.[76]

The Constitutive Tradition

In sum, then, the first Christians seem to have meditated faithfully the teaching of both testaments concerning the meaning and purpose of poverty and wealth. They were conscious of belonging for the most part to the poorer classes of society[77] and tended to see in this very fact confirmation of their belief that the all-absorbing pursuit of wealth is indeed a snare and a delusion.[78,79]

The first Christians were also quite aware that the active concern for others and especially for the poor demanded by faith in Christ is capable of imposing genuine sacrifices on the believer.[80] Moreover, any Christian's selfish repudiation of others in their need was taken as evidence of his own liability to the ultimate repudiation of an angry God.[81,82]

The Patristic Tradition

In the course of the patristic age, most of the basic biblical teachings on the meaning and purpose of poverty are both reiterated and embellished. Patristic catechesis repeatedly confronts its auditors with the same fundamental option as confronted the disciples of Jesus themselves: Ultimately one must choose between the service of God and the service of money.[83,84] On the one hand, both degrading poverty and indulgent affluence are repudiated as incompatible with the Christian ideal;[85] and, on the other hand, frugality and genuine concern for the material needs of others are presented as marks of a truly Christian life.[86-89]

Pastoral Perplexities

In the process of repeating such basic biblical teachings, however, the Fathers also manifest in their catechesis a great sensitivity to the particular spiritual needs of the people of their time; and they are constantly concerned to exclude misinterpretations and abuses from the traditional practice of truly Christian sharing.

The problems vary from generation to generation and from one community to the next. The *Didache,* for instance, written toward the end of the first century, repeats faithfully the basic principle enunciated by Jesus that all Christians must share with one another in imitation of the generosity of their heavenly Father. But it then goes further and rebukes those members of the community who accept alms without being in actual need of help. By their greed and hypocrisy they deprive the truth indigent of the support which the latter desperately need.[90]

Preaching several centuries later, however, St. John Chrysostom finds himself confronted with a very different kind of pastoral problem. The difficulty is no longer that over-generous Christians are finding themselves taken advantage of by professional con-artists, but that the practical generosity of many of the faithful leaves much to be desired. Chrysostom, therefore, uses all his eloquence to rebuke members of his congregation who come to offer long prayers to God in their church, but coldly refuse to spare an alms for the poor and the needy who congregate upon its steps in the hope of finding a spark of charity in people who are externally so devout.[91-95]

A significant portion of patristic catechesis concerning Christian sharing and inner poverty of spirit seems to have been directed at the rich. Not only did the Christian community of the first centuries share the basic economic structure of the age, with its sharp division between "haves" and "have-nots"; but there are also some indications that in moments of persecution and crisis it was the wealthy Christians who more frequently reneged on their baptismal commitment than did the defenseless poor.[96,97] In addition to this backsliding, however, some of the Fathers also seem to have been frankly appalled by the self-indulgent debauchery of the rich so common in an increasingly decadent pagan society.[98,99]

There is, then, in patristic teaching a growing insistence upon the need for moneyed Christians to detach themselves from their superfluous possessions in order to put such superfluities to charitable uses. Moreover, as the preached message seems in large measure to have fallen from generation to generation on deaf ears, the catechetical emphasis shifts gradually from active sharing itself to the need for inner detachment and actual renunciation.[100]

Since, in addition, the Fathers were preeminently men of their time, their preaching on the Christian's need for inner detachment understandably and inevitably borrowed some of its vocabulary from the thinking of their period. Side by side with biblical phrases and concepts, therefore, Stoic and neo-Platonic terms and concepts begin to creep into their proclamation of the Christian message. One encounters an increasing tendency in the patristic texts to speak of man's need to cultivate greater inwardness, to seek a transcendent openness to the divine reality through inner spiritual detachment from all merely material goods and through calculated withdrawal from the distractions of everyday living.

Clement of Alexandria, for instance, insists in the *Pedagogus* that real riches consist in gradually silencing one's inner desires for material goods. The desires of which he speaks are, of course, selfish, avaricious desires; for he warns elsewhere that for a Christian there is no question of complete renunciation of all possessions, that one should rather look upon material goods as instruments given by God for effecting right order in human society. Still, to speak of poverty as "indigence of desire" and as inner "contempt" for riches sounds to the uncautious reader like something very close to Stoic apathy. And it would take a discriminating audience to make the necessary qualifications that Clement would, no doubt, himself have made, if pressed to do so.[101,102]

This tendency to identify authentic Christian living with an inner cultivation of virtuous attitudes occurs with increasing frequency as the patristic age proceeds. And though the accents vary from writer to writer, still the basic message is the same.[103] Gregory Nazianzen, for instance, in a letter to Basilissa includes among his spiritual counsels the warning: "To be genuinely rich does not consist in possessing many things, but in not wanting them."[104,105] And Ambrose argues that any good man can be rich in his own eyes and in the eyes of God if he measures his riches by his longing for eternal and imperishable goods and by his mercy, simplicity, wisdom, and knowledge.[106-110]

Another important development affecting the patristic understanding of the meaning of poverty was the growing institutionalization of the Christian renunciation of property. Many generations had passed since the master had invited the rich young man to sell all his possessions, give the proceeds to the poor, and come join the company of his intimate disciples. The master's invitation had been to a life of common sharing, of prayer, and of labor together for the establishment of God's kingdom on earth. But much had happened since that far-off day in Palestine: The little band of disciples had grown in spite of persecution into a complex ecclesial structure, large enough to embrace both classes of a basically two-class society. In the changed circumstances of the patristic age, the renunciation of property became less and less a prelude to pioneering work for the establishment of the kingdom and more and more a dramatic public gesture, not unlike the dramatic gestures of the Old Testament prophets, by which an individual Christian spurned the life of riches and luxury enjoyed by the baptized "haves" of the community and cast his lot instead with the baptized "have-nots." Inevitably, then, the renunciation of one's property became a prelude to living a life of financial dependence upon more affluent Christians. As a result, religious poverty assumed more and more the character of passive indigence rather than that of an active and concerned sharing. Under the circumstances, sharing seemed to be rather the rich man's duty, while religious men and women came to be expected to cultivate the virtues more proper to their social class, viz., quiet patience and confidence in their need that the Lord would care for them as he cares for the lilies and the sparrows. Granted the economic structure of the patristic Church, this logic was inevitable; and inevitably, too, the spread of monastic discipline gave permanent institutional expression to these diverse social and ecclesial roles.[111]

Along with the tendency to reduce the meaning and purpose of religious poverty to passive indigence, there is also a growing inclination among the patristic writers to speak of riches as somehow contemptible in themselves. And it is in the fifth and sixth centuries, just at the moment when monasticism is beginning to become a dominant force in the West, that the texts dealing with the subject begin to take on a peculiar vehemence. Typical of this strain in late patristic thought is the reflection of John Climacus in his *Ladder to Paradise* that the goal of religious poverty is the acquisition of an inner tranquility of spirit resulting from one's ability to regard all the goods of this life as mere dung.[112-115]

Reaping the Whirlwind

St. Francis of Assisi brought to the religious practice of poverty a unique combination of medieval lyricism and almost Spartan austerity. Francis's initial vision was like the man himself of deceptive simplicity and spontaneity: he sought to gather around him a group of men who would re-live in medieval Italy the same life that Jesus and his apostles had lived centuries before in Palestine. Needless to say, Francis's enthusiastic vision of what the life of the Lord and his disciples had been was inevitably filtered through the traditions of the intervening centuries. In any case, what he found at the heart of the gospel account of that intial Christian experience was an inner detachment from self and an external detachment from creatures.

As far as Francis himself was concerned, his simplicity and deep humility tempered his austerity with a warm sense of the goodness of God's creation and of his own solidarity with even the lowest of God's material creatures. The order which resulted from his vision was, moreover, destined to enrich and deepen not only the Church's spiritual life but also her best philosophical and theological traditions. From it would come the eloquence of an Anthony of Padua and the vision of an Alexander of Hales, a Bonaventure, a Duns Scotus.

Even before the death of Francis, however, bickering factions were beginning to form within the order, which would one day provoke some important papal pronouncements concerning the meaning of Christian poverty. On the one side stood the Zelanti or Zealots, later known as the Spirituals or as the Fraticelli. These were the self-appointed watchdogs of the faithful observance of holy poverty according to the mind of St. Francis. Rigorists with a penchant for religious enthusiasm, they sought through literal fidelity to the original rule of their founder to preserve the practice of Franciscan poverty in all of its primitive austerity; and they fought doggedly against the Relaxati or Laxists, who favored in the name of a realistic approach to the order's growth and institutionalization many modifications and mitigations of the original Franciscan rule.

St. Bonaventure spent much of his generalate trying to mediate between these two factions and in fact produced a revision of the Franciscan constitutions approved by the general chapter of 1260, which sought to adapt the true spirit of St. Francis to the institutional needs of the rapidly expanding order. But apparently not even another saint could satisfy the Spirituals; for after the death of Bonaventure trouble erupted again. Alarmingly, the Spirituals began to manifest a tendency to claim direct divine inspiration for their rules in the form originally set down by Francis and to question the right of Church authority to change a jot or tittle of the original text. The first major crisis came in 1283 when Pope Martin IV issued a bull establishing the office of apostolic syndic, which would be legally empowered to act in the name of the Holy See in accepting and spending money for the needs of the friars. Predictably enough, the Spirituals were outraged at this latest insult to Lady Poverty; and in their indignation, they severed all ties with the Laxist community, repudiated the authority of their provincials, and retired to a life of solitude, austerity, and prayer. But they were not allowed to pray in peace very long. Repressive measures were quick to follow, measures which, moreover, only aggravated the Spirituals' ordinary ecstatic tendencies. But however comforted they may have been by this latest outpouring of heavenly visions, the Spirituals found themselves in an awkward position indeed. Their desire had been to hold fast to Francis's initial vision of recreating in medieval Europe the life of the original apostolic community. And they were bewildered to discover that the times had indeed changed and changed in the direction of complexity. As a result, their only reward for their stiff-necked pursuit of austerity was the accusation of heresy, rebellion, and contempt for authority. Some of them had been forced into imprisonment and exile; others were excommunicated.

The Spirituals, however, did not lack for champions, the best known, perhaps, being Peter John Olivi. And in 1312, the same year that the Council of Vienna condemned a number of Olivi's theses, Pope Clement V attempted to patch up the rupture between the Spirituals and the Laxists with the papal bull *Exivi de Paradiso.*[116] To the Spirituals, however, the document smelled of legal compromise; and in 1317 their dissatisfaction became vocal once again. But the new pope in Avignon, John XXII, had apparently had enough of their squabbling; and ordered these latest stirrings quashed. Four Spirituals were burned as heretics; and the whole matter was handed over to the Grand Inquisitor. This reverend gentleman was a Dominican named John of Belna. His preliminary investigations of the Franciscan controversy convinced him that the Zealots' defense of "spiritual poverty" stood on very shaky dogmatic ground indeed; and he said so in an official condemnation of their position. When an appeal against his decision was made to Pope John, the pope, by now quite weary of the whole matter, upheld the verdict of his Inquisitor; and his papal constitution *Cum inter nonnullos* of 1323 sounded the death knell of the Spirituals as a force within the Franciscan order and, indeed, within the Church at large.

Cum inter nonnullos is an illuminating document. For, though it refrains from giving any positive definition of the meaning of religious poverty, it helps even a modern reader understand some of the things that poverty certainly is *not*. The document condemns as heretical the suggestion of the Spirituals that Jesus and his apostles neither possessed material goods, whether individually or in common, nor had the right to use them, sell them, give them away, or acquire them. Read in the light of the historical development of Christian asceticism, such an imaginative reconstruction of the life of the first apostolic community might indeed fit the demands of a stoicized or platonized theology of the vow of religious poverty. But unfortunately (and the pope is at pains to note the fact) such a theory fails to fit the scriptural accounts of what had actually taken place centuries before in Palestine.[117]

Seen in retrospect, the sincerity and zeal of the Franciscan Spirituals is certainly beyond question; not only were they men of penance and of prayer, but many of them were willing to face the fagot and the stake for their beliefs. At the same time, their cult of visionary enthusiasm, their flight from the body, and their contempt both for the material universe and for the human hazards inherent in a sacramental system give solid historical support to Pope John's judgment that their movement was nothing else than a medieval resurgence of Donatism.[118-120]

The Wisdom of Vatican II

Official pronouncements of the magisterium on the meaning of religious poverty are hard to come by; and one must jump from the Middle Ages to the documents of Vatican II in order to find an important statement of the magisterium dealing with the problem.

The bishops at Vatican II were careful to distinguish in their decrees between the traditional ideal of Christian poverty and degrading economic destitution. They insisted that far from being an ideal, the latter is a disease on the body politic that cries out for a cure.[121]

More specifically, the bishops call upon Christians everywhere to become actively involved in programs which will foster sound socio-economic development and to fight for the principles of charity and of justice in society either as individuals or in association with other men. They also praise lives thus lived in the pursuit of social justice as "permeated with the spirit of the beatitudes, notably with a spirit of poverty."[122]

The bishops point out in addition that a Christian's moral and social obligations do not stop with the frontiers of his own nation. Rather, those who profess to believe in Christ must show active concern for and involvement with the problems of world poverty. The Council Fathers, therefore, also give warm praise and encouragement to those men and women who volunteer to help the people of countries poorer than their own and go on to encourage Christians everywhere to be willing to meet their social and international obligations in the manner traditionally expected of true believers, "out of the substance of their goods, and not only out of what is superfluous."[123]

In addition to these general reflections on the need for a Christian response to the contemporary challenges posed by widespread economic destitution, the Council Fathers also attempt to spell out in some detail the positive Christian meaning of "poverty of spirit." They remind all Christians that those who are baptized and who profess belief in both the cross and the resurrection should neither remain enslaved to wealth nor aspire to riches for their own sake. Instead, all the faithful of Christ should dedicate their lives to the spread of God's kingdom by fashioning and perfecting the world in which they live; by doing good to all men, especially to those of the household of the faith; and by seeking to draw all men to Christ. "Following Jesus who was poor they are neither depressed by lack of temporal goods nor puffed up by abundance. Imitating Christ who was humble, they have no obsession with empty honors but seek to please God rather than men, ever ready to leave all things for Christ's sake and to suffer persecution for justice's sake."[124]

In the case of priests, the Council Fathers become more specific and enunciate some definite and wise directives regarding the clerical use and management of material possessions. After affirming that priests have a right to a "decent livelihood," the bishops indicate that priests should use their superfluous possessions in order to promote their own personal apostolic endeavors as well as those of other apostolic and charitable groups within the Church. Moreover, priests should scrupulously avoid anything that would give rise to the charge that they have taken advantage of their pastoral office for the sake of their own personal financial gain or that of their families.[125]

Similarly, after praising the vow of poverty, the bishops caution religious against any attempt to reduce the living of their vow to a mere "inner detachment" which finds no visible correlate in their external manner of living. Rather, one who publicly professes to follow the poor and humble Christ should *be* poor in fact as well as in spirit and so live that men may clearly recognize him as one who does indeed keep his treasures with Christ in heaven.[126]

Finally, in reaffirming the right of religious communities to possess "whatever is necessary for their temporal life and mission," the bishops note two important restrictions: those demanded by the rules and constitutions of the community in question and those demanded by the obligation binding upon all religious to "avoid every appearance of luxury, of excessive wealth, and accumulation of possessions."[127]

The Manual Tradition

The kind of systematic asceticism found in manuals of ascetical theology is the distillation and codification of the fruits of centuries of Christian reflection on religious living. In such manuals the spiritual struggle for perfection is often couched in militant, aggressive terms: The Christian soul is armed to go out and do battle against its three deadly enemies, the world, the flesh, and the devil.

"The world" is peopled by unbelievers, by those who are indifferent to religion, by hardened sinners, and by the spiritually tepid and lukewarm. These enemies of Christ seek to seduce the true Christian with maxims opposed to the gospel, with a false show of vanity and pleasure, and with their own bad example. They terrorize the devout with mockery, threats, and sometimes with open persecution. "The world" is, therefore, both an enemy to be resisted and an apostolic field for zealous activity. The Christian soul may resist its wiles by reading and meditation on the gospel, by avoiding dangerous occasions of sin, by countering bad example with good, by organizing to resist persecutors, and by refusing to compromise its religious principles. Moreover, according to manual catechesis, one of the most effective weapons against the wiles of "the world" is the religious vow of poverty, for this vow curbs one of the world's most characteristic vices, namely, the worldling's inordinate love of riches.

Manual asceticism also distinguishes two main sources of a religious's obligation to strive after perfection: the vows and the rule. By the solemn vow of poverty, we are told, a religious renounces the right to ownership of property, so that any act of ownership performed under the vow is canonically void. By a simple vow of poverty, a religious does not renounce the right of ownership (he can, for instance, still inherit property) but binds himself not to perform acts of ownership without the approval of his superiors. Moreover, the rule of the order or congregation of which he is a member serves as the concrete norm for interpreting the limits of the superior's authority to grant such approval.

All of this sounds legalistic in tone; and indeed it is. But manual asceticism hastens to insist that the vow of poverty is only a means to the cultivation of the virtue which corresponds to it. Since the vow of poverty is opposed to the vice of avarice, which is the inordinate love of riches, the virtue which corresponds to the first vow of religion is Christian detachment. Avarice is a vice which prevents one from truly placing his whole confidence in the God who feeds the sparrows and clothes the lily. It supplants the love of God with love of riches and pleasure and thus nourishes pride, which is opposed to obedience and to submission to God in addition to being the source of all vice. The vow of poverty, on the other hand, through the renunciation and dependence to which it binds a religious teaches the soul not to place absolute value on the passing goods of this world (whose purpose is, after all, to fill man's material needs) but to seek instead the things of God and the riches which await one in the heavenly kingdom. Detachment from riches through the abandonment of one's will to the will of superiors in the ownership and use of material possessions thus becomes a spiritual deposit in the bank of heaven and a promise of the riches that are to come.

The manual explanation of the meaning of poverty is not without its positive values; but as we shall see, religious in search of an understanding of the purpose of religious living would do well to measure this "traditional" explanation of the vow against a more thorough reading of the entire Christian ascetical tradition. The manual explanation, for instance, speaks, on the one hand, of the vow of poverty primarily in terms of its legal and canonical consequences upon individual acts of ownership and, on the other hand, of the virtue of poverty in terms both of inner personal detachment from material goods and of dependence in the ownership and use upon the will of others who speak in the name of Christ. In other words, the optic of the manual explanation of poverty tends to be legalistic, individualistic, static, and negative. That is to say, even though the legal dimensions of the vow of poverty are unavoidable and religious would indeed do well to be thoroughly informed concerning the canonical consequences of all three vows before they actually take them, and even though the manual explanation of poverty recognizes a need to go beyond mere legal extrinsicism to a consideration of the spiritual motives which ground the vow and give it purpose, nevertheless, the manual explanation of poverty presents those motives almost exclusively in terms of the individual cultivation of inner attitudes and of personal habits of soul. As a result, apart from an explanation of the legalities of poverty, the explicitly ecclesial dimensions of the vow tend to be overlooked or at least underplayed in the manual tradition, while the inner dispositions of heart which constitute the virtue of poverty are reduced to terms which, precisely because they look primarily to one's individual vertical relationship with a transcendent God, remain socially and ecclesially negative and static. To live poorly, a religious is taught that he need only *renounce* his possessions, and detach himself *from* the world by letting *someone else,* who is in authority, assume responsibility for deciding what material things will be at his disposal.

Unfortunately, however, in the traditional explanation, little or nothing is said about *how* or *for what purpose* these same material possessions which are at the disposal of religious should be *used.* Moreover, in a manual account of poverty, what goes by the name of "common life" comes to be mediated bureaucratically by the simple expedient of centralizing the control of material goods under the single will of the superior and of his official representatives, who become in virtue of their office both the "guardians" of their community's poverty and its unique source of supply. At the same time, the community's own poverty is measured in terms of external non-possession, of inner absence of desire for possessions, and of willingness to abide passively by the superior's dispositions of the available material goods—all socially negative and static attitudes.

Malaise at the Grass Roots

For some time now American religious have experienced a certain malaise with this manual explanation of poverty. Fr. C. J. McNaspy in his book on religious renewal,[128] has, moreover, articulated with admirable clarity some of the major sources of that uneasiness. Does, he asks, a poverty of inner detachment and dependence on the will of others perhaps tend to breed moral and spiritual irresponsibility toward material possessions on the part of religious, who are thus relieved both of the maturing experience of financially supporting themselves ("the superior will provide") and of learning the responsible Christian use of material goods ("the superior will decide")? In other words, when decision and provision are left solely or primarily to the responsibility of the superior does the passivity which results in subjects encourage the presence of community "drones," of emotionally infantile people who are quite content to sponge off their order but monumentally disinclined to lift a finger to justify in any significant way their financial support? Does a poverty of dependence tend to produce people who are indifferent to the plight of the economically poor and of the laboring classes because superiors are indeed such good providers that subjects go through life without ever having really experienced what it means to earn one's bread by the sweat of one's brow? Or again does the sort of poverty presented in the manual tradition encourage "tokenism"? That is to say, does it encourage religious to be satisfied that they are living like "poor" men if they merely perform the painless ritualistic and symbolic act of legally renouncing their property only to have their every need subsequently fulfilled on the formalistic condition that they are willing to perform the equally ritualistic and symbolic gesture of asking the superior's permission to use the goods they initially renounced? In other words, does not the ritual of legal renunciation and permission tend all too easily to become a charade of self-delusion which rationalizes and masks with a formalistic gesture the absence of genuine poverty in a community? Moreover, might not something similar be said of our American cult of "efficiency"? How often do we American religious use "efficiency in the apostolate" as a motive for securing the soothing sanction of superiors for our self-indulgent enjoyment of superfluities? If poverty means not having things, then it is by definition immensely inefficient; can, then, religious be both poor and apostolically effective in a technological age?

These and similar questions have been troubling the consciences of American religious for quite some time. We are, moreover, haunted by the feeling that in all too many instances most of the questions raised above can in fact be answered affirmatively.

The Theological Dimension

Needless to say, the real problem is not that the manual explanation of poverty necessarily leads to passivity, irresponsibility, and formalism. Nor is our intent to pass judgment on any man or woman who has felt the generosity to consecrate himself and his life to God. The problem being raised here is purely conceptual, namely, that there seem to be no speculative elements in the manual explanation of poverty which logically exclude the possibility of passivity, irresponsibility, formalism, and sloth. Our problems here are verbal, not moral; and hopefully the reader will join in an attempt to approach them at that level.

Our problems are, moreover, speculatively complex. For the reflective reader, for instance, they can actually be increased by some of the admonitions of Vatican II. Thus, on the one hand, the Council Fathers warn us that religious poverty involves more than "limiting the use of possessions to the consent of superiors," that inner detachment is not enough, and that religious should be poor in fact as well as in spirit. The bishops also warn us that poverty is not passive, that there is a close connection between poverty and ordinary human labor. In a word, a careful reading of the documents of Vatican II suggests that the bishops were concerned to exclude from the understanding of poverty some of the less desirable consequences of an uncritical acceptance of a manual explanation of the first vow.

On the other hand, there are real difficulties raised for the reflective reader by the text of the conciliar decree on the religious life. For when is a religious poor in fact as well as in spirit? Is it when he is socially identified with the poorer classes in society? Possibly, but then again, is the ideal of Christian poverty a "class" concept? Or is it rather aimed at the abolition of classes? Does a religious measure his de facto poverty by an economic yardstick comparable to that used in ex-President Johnson's war on poverty? Possibly, but is the ideal of Christian poverty really an economic concept? Or does it involve something deeper and more dynamic than economics? Finally, if the economic, the sociological, or the traditional ascetical notion of "poverty" are all inadequate to express the ideal embodied in the first vow of religion, then isn't it possible that we would be better off abandoning the term "poverty" altogether? Could it not be that much of our present confusion about the meaning of the first vow has semantic roots and that the inevitably misleading connotations of the very word "poverty" demand that we search for a less confusing substitute?

Grass-roots discontent with the limitations of the manual explanation of poverty has, moreover, found echoes in the more intellectually sophisticated reflections of some outstanding theologians. The late John Courtney Murray, for instance, voiced eloquently the growing discontent when he suggested that the first vow actually deprived religious of any meaningful encounter with the elemental force of "earth," i.e., with God's material creation. He suggested that since by taking a vow of poverty religious enter a life of financial security which relieves them of the responsibility of creating the conditions for their own physical survival, they run the dangerous risk of living comfortably off the collectivity while suffering a spiritually destructive emotional impoverishment never intended by the vow.[129]

In an article on the problems of living religious poverty in the context of contemporary society, Karl Rahner cautions against the double error of simply identifying the ideal of Christian poverty with programs of social reform and of reducing poverty in practice to mere interior detachment. He insists that as the expression of an act of faith in God's grace as the only ultimate fulfillment of human existence, evangelical poverty loses its meaning unless it finds embodiment in the actual renunciation of material goods. Rahner notes, too, the relative and "situational" character of poverty: To be "poor" means different things in different epochs and in different regions.[130]

Both of these eminent theologians, however, raise more problems than they answer. Is it possible, then, to elaborate an explanation of the meaning of the vow of poverty which will incorporate within it the challenges inherent in a meaningful encounter with "the earth" or one which will be more than a "flaccid and miserable compromise between monastic and modern living"?

Fr. Ladislas Orsy has suggested an approach to the vow of poverty which supplements the conceptual inadequacy of the manual explanation. He insists that one cannot understand the meaning of poverty without having had an "experience of the kingdom of God." Within the context of such an experience, to be poor means for Fr. Orsy four things: to live on gifts and to give gifts to others; to sacrifice material goods, and to use created things.[131] Orsy's approach is certainly an important advance of a manual explanation of the vow largely because it draws additional inspiration from a reflective reading of Scripture and the Fathers. But as a conceptual articulation of the meaning of the first vow, it is not beyond some criticism. How, for instance, does one actually go about having an "experience of the kingdom of God" and how precisely does the experience relate to the vow of poverty? Also, is it possible to interrelate the four elements implied in such an explanation of poverty under a single unifying concept? As it stands, the antithetic character of the explanation is undeniable. To give is not to receive: how then can the same ideal of poverty comprehend both giving and receiving? To renounce material goods is not to use them: how then can the same ideal of poverty comprehend both renunciation and use? And if one should argue that poverty means sometimes to give, sometimes to receive, sometimes to use things, and sometimes to sacrifice them, then what criterion does one employ to decide what will be the appropriate expression of poverty for each given occasion? Finally, what possible common conceptual factor can one find which will successfully unite all of these antithetical options under the single rubric of "poverty"?

Let us see if we can possibly pick a clear path through this maze of conceptual perplexities.

The Redemption of Matter

Christianity never lost its Hebrew feeling for the goodness of the things of this world. But in Christianity the basis of that belief ceased to be primarily an experiential one. The typical Hebrew had believed the material universe good largely because he found fulfillment and joy in the world in which God had placed him and because he believed that from a good and benevolent God only good things could come. A Christian attitude toward the material universe was, however, considerably more complex. Typically, the Christian believed the world to be good partly for the same reasons as the devout Hebrew; but the ultimate ground of his belief went much further. The Christian believed the world to be good because God had died to prove his love for it and because, like Paul, he believed that all things have been divinely destined to redemptive transformation in the likeness of the risen Christ, whom most Christians have never in fact seen or experienced directly.

To the extent, however, that the man of the new covenant retained and expanded old covenant convictions about the actual goodness of matter, he was in fact able to appropriate many of the beliefs and practices of the old law in his attitude toward the material world and toward his own body. He could, for instance, retain a prophetic concern for the lot of the poor, that they be given their fair share in the blessings granted men by the God who saves. He could also retain the wise man's mistrust of riches, which can harden a man in an illusion of self-sufficiency and close his heart both in pride to the God who had made him and in arrogance toward the "little ones" of this world. The Christian could also espouse the sapiential ideal of the "innocent poor man" whose heart is set not upon possessions but upon accomplishing the will of God in the minute details of life, even though the Christian would be more likely to find that ideal embodied in the person of Jesus than in the pages of the Old Testament. The Christian could retain his belief that his obligation to share the good things of this world with his fellow men is rooted in his covenant commitment to God even though the different character of the two covenants necessarily demanded certain modifications in the basis on which such sharing would be practiced in the new. For as Paul clearly saw, the old covenant, as it had developed historically, was fundamentally law-oriented; the new covenant, primarily love-oriented. To be sure, love of God and love of neighbor were an integral factor in ancient Hebrew belief; but whereas under the Sinai covenant the meaning of love tended to be reduced to fidelity to the compassionate prescriptions of the law, under the Christian covenant, love became a force which included legal prescriptions while simultaneously transcending them and going far beyond their specific norms. Similarly, the Sinai covenant was first tribal and only gradually and hesitantly became universal in its orientation; the Christian covenant was universal in its scope from the start. The Sinai covenant approved the *lex talionis;* the Christian covenant demanded an atoning and forgiving love for all men regardless of whether they deserved one's love or not.

Moreover, as a revelatory anticipation of the shape which the material universe would assume at the second coming, the new covenant in the risen Christ illumined Jesus' insistence that the possession of riches is in fact no certain sign of God's favor. For the Christian, the only true definitive sign of that favor had become one's own resurrection in Christ, a resurrection whose preparation in time demands of each man the willingness to live his life in the image of the Savior who had come among men as one of God's "little ones," one of his humble poor, a Savior who had cast his whole care upon God and who had lived only to accomplish the Father's will.

Moreover, what God had in fact willed in the mission of his Son was the active redemption of the material universe he had created. As the revelation of the new creation, the passion and resurrection of Jesus was in effect God's revelation to men of the extent to which the material universe had indeed become "tainted" by human egotism and selfishness. For on the one hand, in confronting the utter abandonment of the master to his Father on the cross, the disciples were forced to confront the extent of their own sinfulness and selfish attachment to the good things of this world. On the other hand, in confronting the glorified flesh of their risen Lord, they were also forced to recognize the extent to which the material world as men experience it still groaned for the glory for which God had destined it. In other words, they came to see that the redemption of the material world, tainted as it had become through the sinfulness and selfishness of men, demanded that it be used in the work of selflessly and lovingly spreading the kingdom whose fulfillment was promised in the glorification of Christ, by actively sharing with others, as Jesus had done, whatever material goods they possessed, as a sign of their belief in the salvation God had wrought in lifting up the Lord Jesus and in sending his Spirit of love and of faith into their hearts. In other words, in the time between the resurrection and the parousia, the redemption of the material world demanded that men of faith actively use the good things of this life in order to mediate a community of men and women whose unrestricted, gratuitous sharing of the good things of this life would be a lived sign of their faith in the wonders God had accomplished in Christ and of their confidence in the ultimate triumph of divine love on the last day.

Broadening the Context

Moreover, implicit in the active, dynamic ideal of gratuitous sharing are all of the values demanded by a manual asceticism of poverty—and more. Manual asceticism does indeed demand detachment from the "tainted" material things of this world; but as the course of patristic and medieval reflection on the meaning of poverty clearly testifies, by insisting too exclusively upon a flight from material contamination, it also tends to ally itself with a denial of any goodness whatever to the world in which we now live.

The ideal of gratuitous sharing, on the other hand, is the expression of a balanced belief both that material things are in fact good but that they are not the ultimate good. It is precisely because they are good that the believer is willing to share them with others as a sign of his love for them in Christ's name. At the same time, precisely because the believer is convinced that material goods are not ultimately valuable, he is willing to part with them in order to share them, and specifically in order to share them with those who are, because of their need or disposition, least able to respond in kind. In other words, unless detachment from material goods is also detachment for sharing, for love, for use, for a purpose, it runs the serious risk of degenerating into a negative attitude toward material things which is ultimately incompatible, by reason of its partiality and incompleteness, with an integral Christian faith. Thus, detachment from material goods becomes integrally Christian when it ceases to be static and negative and becomes instead the precondition for a positive, loving, dynamic, gratuitous sharing of material goods with others in Christ's name.

Moreover, manual asceticism also tends to become preoccupied with detachment as an individual, personal, attitude. It tends, as we have seen, to relegate the ecclesial dimensions of poverty to the careful observance of the juridical aspects of the vow, namely, to securing proper permissions and to the observance of rules governing the use of material things.

The ideal of gratuitous sharing, on the other hand, makes it quite clear that "individual" detachment in a Christian context can never be purely individual. It cannot just be the solitary cultivation of an inner attitude toward the material universe with no reference whatever to other men; nor can its ecclesial dimensions be purely legal and canonical. Christian detachment is one's willingness to share with others, not simply by obeying some predetermined rule which ensures one's individual canonical right to use some material object (however necessary or useful such permissions may on occasion be), but by being concretely sensible to the actual needs of those with whom one deals. It demands, therefore, of its very nature a positive ecclesial orientation, an active concern to use the good things of this world in order to mediate a community of mutual and gratuitous love and concern in Christ's name.

Negative Conclusions

Moreover, the identification of evangelical poverty with the ideal of Christian sharing helps to clarify a number of difficulties in understanding the vow of poverty. For one thing it helps us to understand what the vow of poverty is not.

First of all, evangelical poverty is not the pursuit of non-possession of material goods for its own sake. That is to say, non-possession is not in the normal course of events the purpose of sharing. In a Christian context, non-possession is not an ideal; it is at best the unavoidable consequence of sharing that is genuinely gratuitous, i.e., oriented to need, not to merit. The purpose of evangelical sharing is ultimately always a positive one, namely, the use of material goods in such a way as to mediate a community of people actively and gratuitously concerned for one another in Christ's name. At the same time, when non-possession is accepted in faith and love as a consequence of my active and gratuitous concern for others, it does take on positive value to the extent that it embodies an expression of confidence on the part of the one who shares, in the faithful God who rewards those who serve him selflessly in his adopted children. But here too, it is the graced faith and confidence of the believer who shares freely with others in the name of Christ which gives positive value to the non-possession, not the non-possession which is valued for its own sake.

Second, evangelical poverty is not the effort merely to identify with a particular social class. We shall have occasion to return to this problem in a later chapter; but here it suffices to note that the purpose of gratuitous sharing is not the perpetuation, but the obliteration, through the effective sharing of goods, of economic class distinctions within both the Christian and the human community. What the command of Christ to share freely and gratuitously with others means, therefore, is that as long as distinctions between haves and have-nots continue to exist within the Church and within society, those who possess property are seriously obligated to use the material means at their disposal in order to put an effective end to such distinctions, just as those who lack material goods are obligated to do what they can to support themselves so that they too can share with others more needy than themselves. By the same token, religious who would seek closer identification with the poor must never make the mistake of conceiving such an identification as an end in itself. For unless "identification with the poor" is approached as a means—as an effective means to oppose social injustice in the name of the poor; as a means to help those in society most in need of help; as a means to earn the right to preach the ideals of Christian sharing to those who have very little; as a means of mediating to those in need the effective love of Christ; as a means to end class distinctions, not to perpetuate them—such identification is at best a romanticized idealization of an attitude of upper class condescension for the poor. At the worst, it is the rationalization of one's acquiescence in social and economic divisions which one is as a Christian dedicated to oppose.

Third, evangelical poverty is not a flight from the enjoyment of material things. The person who is opposed in principle or in practice to the enjoyment of material things is not likely to want to share them lovingly with others. Needless to say, the ideal of Christian sharing does indeed presuppose active retrenchment in one's personal use of material goods. But the retrenchment should always be an act of love; that is to say, it should have as its purpose the facilitation of active sharing with others in Christ's name. The purpose of retrenchment or of "mortification" should not be perverted into the simple avoidance of what is pleasurable because it is pleasurable. Rather, it must embody an effort to curb that selfishness which prevents one from sharing with others freely and joyfully the truly good things of life. Hence, in place of the solitary multiplication of private acts of self-denial, joyful, gratuitous sharing with the sacrifices it involves could, if taken seriously, itself constitute a religious's most basic practice of "mortification" and "retrenchment." For the poor religious in the Christian sense of "poor" is not necessarily the religious who merely gives up material pleasures; one can give things up in solitary abnegation and remain basically closed-hearted toward one's brothers and sisters in Christ. Rather, the truly poor religious is one who is actively and creatively concerned to share whatever is at his disposition lovingly, freely, and spontaneously with others, because he (or she) enjoys life itself enough to enjoy also, even at the cost of personal sacrifice, the very sharing of its pleasures with others, especially with those whose life is otherwise drab and pleasureless. The mortified religious is, then, one who truly loves life, but not so much as either to seek its pleasures at the expense of others or to imagine that those pleasures can ever be a source of one's ultimate satisfaction.

Fourth, poverty of spirit has nothing to do with stoic apathy toward the goods of this world. The person who is apathetic toward the material universe is also apt to be apathetic toward the material needs of others and to rationalize his lack of concern under the rubric of seeking to teach the needy the "spiritual" benefits of his own unchristian attitudes. The Christian cannot be apathetic toward the material universe because he is convinced not only that the God who created it and destined it for transformation in Christ loves his material creation but also because the true follower of Christ is deeply concerned to cooperate in the redemption of matter from human sinfulness by using it to mediate a community of faith and love through the concerned practice of active and gratuitous sharing.

Fifth, evangelical poverty is not a mere means to cultivating the inner virtues or facilitating one's contemplative ascent to God. To be fully Christian, it should also have an explicitly ecclesial orientation. Needless to say, the active practice of gratuitous sharing is in fact humanly impossible without real strength of character and the prayerful cultivation of the motives which will sustain one in the personal sacrifices which are integral to selfless sharing. For gratuitous sharing is an expression of faith; and faith is an openness of the human spirit to a God who is the goal of human longing, an openness which must be sustained through prayer and the cultivation of generosity. But Christian faith terminates in a God who is neither purely immanent nor purely transcendent but in a God, who though by nature transcendent, has freely chosen to become incarnationally and sacramentally involved in the transformation of the world he has made. The person who seeks salvation exclusively in a vertical ascent to God is, therefore, dangerously apt to overlook the divine descent into matter; and in the process, such a person may all too easily substitute for God's plan of salvation his neoplatonized version of the redemptive process. In other words, although the ideal of gratuitous sharing includes an element of immanence as well as an element of transcendence, by its explicitly ecclesial orientation it keeps the quest for inwardness from degenerating into a species of loveless egocentricity and continuously reminds one that the God we seek has so loved the world that he freely and gratuitously chose not to remain completely transcendent but to share our human life, our pleasures, and our material joys and sorrows in a community united by its confidence and love for his Father.

Not, of course, that the Christian God has become completely immanent either. But the advantage of gratuitous sharing lies in the fact that it demands a transcendent openness to God in the very use of material things. Or, to put the same notion a bit differently, as the expression of belief in an incarnate God and in the transforming presence of his spirit, the ideal of gratuitous sharing presupposes as its practical pre-condition a transcendent openness to an incarnate God which includes as an element integral to it an openness and a concern for the material needs of others.

Finally, it is clear that poverty of spirit is not the cultivation of contempt for material creation. The Christian does not consider the material universe, as John Climacus suggested he should, to be mere dung; though a Christian does, as Paul did, acknowledge the world's need for redemption and should be ready to sacrifice any personal material advantage for the spread of the kingdom of Christ.

Positive Corollaries

More positively, then, sharing is the use of material goods for the purpose of mediating a community of faith and of mutual love and concern. Gratuitous sharing is sharing on the basis of need, not of merit, as Christ did, without pre-conditions, whether the one with whom one shares deserves one's concern or not, as an expression of one's belief that it is in this way that God has shown his love and grace to us in the mission of his Son.

The identification of the ideal of gratuitous sharing with the ideal of evangelical poverty also makes sense out of a number of statements of the magisterium whose meaning remains obscure when read in the light of a typical manual asceticism of non-possession or of passive dependence. The condemnation of the Fraticelli, or Spirituals, was in effect the medieval Church's repudiation of a gradual drift in patristic thought toward the identification of a genuinely Christian ideal of poverty with an ideal of passive indigence or with a neo-Platonic flight from the material universe. *Cum inter nonnullos* affirmed in effect that the Christian ideal of poverty as practiced by Jesus and his apostles does not exclude the possibility of using, selling, giving away, or acquiring material goods, whether this be done individually or in common. Once one recognizes, however, that to be poor in the gospel sense means to share freely and gratuitously with others in Christ's name, it also becomes clear that when one vowed to poverty acquires property, then it must be with a view to mediating by these material means a community of people gratuitously concerned for one another in Christ—with a view, that is, to sharing these material goods more effectively with those who most need them. The speculative deficiencies of a poverty of "non-possession for its own sake" or of "total passive dependence" become apparent when one reflects that there is, in fact, no unavoidable theoretical conflict between such an explanation of poverty and the poverty of the Franciscan Spirituals.

The explanation of Christian poverty in terms of gratuitous sharing also makes it clear how the bishops at Vatican II could, on the one hand, condemn economic poverty as a social blight and, on the other hand, praise work in the pursuit of social justice as "permeated with the spirit of poverty." Christian poverty is not simply identical with economic poverty. Economic poverty is not a moral ideal; it is factual. It is measured by the amount of material goods one actually possesses or does not possess. Christian poverty, on the other hand, is precisely an ideal to be achieved; and it is measured by the active willingness of a person to share whatever he has with others, to labor selflessly to obliterate social injustices and immoral economic imbalances, and to spend his personal and human resources in order to see to it that each man shares equitably in the good things of this world. There are, however, no explanatory elements in a poverty of "non-possession" or of "passive dependence" to motivate such social involvement.

The implementation of the ideal of gratuitous sharing also explains the bishops' special concern that Christians come to the active help of the developing nations. To foster the material growth of nations who stand most in need of economic and social assistance is clearly both an appropriate concretization of the ideal of gratuitous sharing and a challenge to greater generosity on the part of those who are moved to offer them their assistance in Christ's name. Once again, however, there is nothing in the ordinary manual explanation of the first vow to motivate active involvement in the problems of world poverty.

The ideal of gratuitous sharing also explains the bishops' insistence that Christians must share with others from the very substance of their possessions, "and not only out of what is superfluous." Since an important measure of gratuity in any act of sharing is the degree of sacrifice it entails, to share with others merely out of the superfluity of one's possessions, with no financial risk or insecurity, demands no faith or confidence in the God who cares for those who care for his "little ones." Moreover, to place personal financial security over the needs of others is ultimately to trust in money rather than in God—a dubious course at best for those who profess to believe that they cannot serve both God and mammon.

The identification of the ideal of gratuitous sharing with the ideal of evangelical poverty helps explain, too, why the bishops regard active dedication to the work of spreading Christ's kingdom as an expression of "poverty of spirit"; why, too, they demand that priests dedicate their superfluous possessions to the spread of God's kingdom and avoid all semblance of using their office for their own financial advantage; and why, finally, religious cannot be content with mere "inner detachment" as a measure of true poverty while simultaneously living in what appears to be comparative luxury and wealth. In the first place, gratuitous sharing demands not only detachment from this world but the active use of material goods to mediate the spread of Christ's kingdom of atoning love. Hence, members of the hierarchy who possess a leadership function in the community, should lead it above all in the selflessness and generosity with which they share of what they have with others for the sake of the kingdom. Religious, who make a public profession, then, of dedication to the pursuit of the ideals of gratuitous sharing in service to the community cannot be truly poor if their poverty is purely interior. On the contrary, their lives must be characterized by constant and active sharing of whatever they possess with those needier than themselves. Theoretically, however, there is nothing in a poverty of non-possession or of passive indigence which demands such active dedication to the spread of Christ's kingdom.

Some Theological Conclusions

If we understand the ideal of gratuitous sharing as the real meaning of Christian poverty, then it becomes clear why poverty must involve both giving and receiving gifts. Gratuitous sharing is the use of material goods in order to mediate the love of a community of people whose concern for one another does not depend on their individual merits or deserts but on a belief in the revelation in Christ of God's gratuitous and unconditioned love for every man, even in his sinfulness. But obviously, since to share gratuitously in the Christian sense is to mediate love through the use of material things, it demands a willingness on the part of the members of the community both to give and to receive, both to offer love and accept it.

Similarly, gratuitous sharing necessarily demands both renunciation and use. In sharing I must actively use what is at my disposal to mediate a community of faith and of love; but by using material things for others, not simply for myself, I must also renounce any use of material things which confirms me in my selfishness and unconcern for others or which inhibits my freely sharing with them. In other words, religious should stop feeling guilty about actually having things and should become instead actively concerned to use, to share, or even to give away the things that are at their disposal when circumstances demand it in order to mediate a community of genuine Christian love and faith.

At the same time, an explanation of the ideal of poverty in terms of gratuitous sharing makes it clear that the eschatological dimensions of poverty do not look exclusively to the world to come. Renunciation alone, dissociated from active gratuitous sharing, is not an adequate existential sign of the covenant of love concluded between God and men in Christ. Evangelical poverty in the full Christian sense becomes a fully adequate sign of the kingdom only when it is the active and self-sacrificing embodiment of a concerned effort to mediate a believing, loving community of gratuitous sharing. That is to say, though the selfless renunciation integral to gratuitous sharing is an eschatological sign of one's hope in the final coming of Christ's kingdom, it becomes such a sign in the full and proper sense only when it is integral to the very act of sharing lovingly with others in Christ's name.

Similarly, an explanation of poverty in terms of gratuitous sharing makes it clear that the evangelical ideal of poverty does not, as Murray feared, automatically deprive a religious of a meaningful encounter with "the earth," even though a manual poverty of "non-possession" or of "passive indigence" might well tend to do so. As we shall see in more detail later, dedication to the ideal of active and gratuitous sharing not only does not exclude labor, it demands it. It demands, too, as we shall see, that every Christian in the Church and especially those vowed to gratuitous sharing do whatever is within his or her power to become financially self-supporting so that he or she may share more effectively and more gratuitously with others in Christ's name.

Finally, the very fact that the term "poverty" has become situational, as Rahner has observed, the fact that its meaning in the minds of most men has economic or sociological rather than Christian connotations indicates that the time has come to find a new name to express the evangelical ideal which corresponds to the first vow. For that ideal is not situational. And as an ideal it is timeless and unchanging in a peculiar sense precisely because it derives from the immutable historical facts surrounding our salvation in Christ, although needless to say the active implementation even of timeless ideal must of necessity take cognizance of what are the concretely available material means to achieve its realization. But since the evangelical ideal corresponding to the first vow does in fact remain the same and is not an economic concept, nor a class concept, nor a sociological concept, nor even the static, negative ascetical notion of non-possession or of passive indigence sought for their own sakes, and since the term "poverty" is in fact situationally conditioned and connotes to the modern mind all of these misleading interpretations, we shall hereafter, with the reader's indulgence, replace the term poverty with one already frequently used in this chapter, namely, "gratuitous sharing."

The ideal of gratuitous sharing also illumines the meaning of the religious vow of poverty and the place of religious authority in the regulation of material goods. Correctly interpreted, the purpose of the first vow is not simply an act of renunciation; nor is it an attempt to identify symbolically with the poorer classes as an end in itself. It is the public dedication of one's material resources to the service of the Christian community, an active dedication which implies as well one's willingness both to depend when necessary upon that community's response of love for one's financial support and to labor personally in the future in the service of that community and most particularly in the service of those members who are most in need. Although such a public self-dedication to the dynamic ideal of gratuitous sharing does indeed create a certain right on the part of the one who makes it to support by the community in certain circumstances (we shall discuss later in more detail what those circumstances might be), the relationship established by the vow is not one of mere justice but rather one of mutual and gratuitous love. That is to say, the vow is not a mere financial contract in the normal sense of that term; it is the free and loving gift of oneself and of one's possessions to the service of others with the hope and confidence that their love will lead them if and when the necessity arises to respond to that gift in kind, but without such a response being a condition for one's initial gift. At the same time, just as in the case of St. Paul, there is nothing to prevent one vowed to gratuitous sharing and to the service of the community from becoming independently self-supporting, when this is practically possible, in order that the gratuity of his service may be better manifested. Nor is there any reason why one so vowed should not be allowed to administer large sums of money for the sake of the common good and for the help of those in need, provided he is held publicly accountable to the community for his administration and provided he makes no effort to turn his administration to his own personal advantage.

Such an interpretation of the meaning of the first vow of religion also helps clarify in the matter of gratuitous sharing the difference between the publicly vowed and unvowed lay person; for a religious is simply a lay person who has taken certain vows which change his ecclesial status within the living, worshipping community. This change is largely one of active function. As baptized Christians, both vowed and unvowed lay people are in fact dedicated to the same ideal of gratuitous sharing. Nevertheless, through the vow, a believer's practice of gratuitous sharing achieves a new ecclesial dimension and direction and a new and public kind of social visibility. That is to say, the gratuitous sharing of the baptized lay person is the expression of a personal act of piety undertaken on private initiative. If the lay person in question is married, he is, moreover, committed to making his own family the primary object of his Christian desire to share the goods of this world, the rest of the community being a concern, but as a result of the special ecclesial status which accrues to marriage vows, of necessity a secondary concern. The layman with religious vows, on the other hand, dedicates his property and labor in the first instance to the service of the believing, worshipping community as such, and most especially to those members of that community who are in greatest need. To the extent, then, that the latter's vowed practice of gratuitous sharing has as its express purpose to share with those in greatest need and least able to respond in kind, its gratuity is more explicit and to that extent is in itself more "perfect" than the commitment to gratuitous sharing implied in nuptial vows, although the very word "perfection" is a misleading one, since it seems to imply both an automatic holiness and an elite privileged character proper to vowed Christians which smacks of pharisaism and spiritual pride.

Moreover, gratuitous sharing which is publicly vowed and has upon it the sanction and blessing of the worshipping community ceases to be a mere personal profession of faith. The public acceptance by the community acting in the person of its official leader and ordained representative of a promise before God by one of its members to live a life of gratuitous sharing and service of the needy means that the one who pronounces the vow is committed to try to live in such a way that the rest of the community will be able to find in the manner in which he uses material goods an exemplification as nearly perfect as possible of the ideal of gratuitous sharing to which each Christian is by his baptismal vows committed. In other words, viewed in its ecclesial dimensions, the vowed gratuitous sharing of the religious seeks to manifest with greater social clarity and less ambiguity than is ordinarily possible in the life of most lay people that the Christian community's practice of sharing springs ultimately not from merely humanistic or humanitarian ties nor exclusively from ordinary social and familial ties but from a concern in faith rooted in one's belief in a risen Christ. We can only broach the problem of the difference of the ecclesial commitment of vowed and unvowed Christians; a full resolution of the problem must await an investigation of the other two vows of religion. But for the present we must be content.

Once, then, we interpret the first vow of religion in the dynamic, positive terms of gratuitous sharing rather than in the static, negative terms of manual asceticism, the purpose, the limits, and the necessity of the exercise of some measure of authoritative control upon a religious community's use of material goods becomes manifest. It becomes clear, for instance, that there is no "tokenism" necessarily involved in the first vow of religion. One does not by one's vow simply make a token renunciation of material goods and then take back what one has renounced by the simple legal expedient of blessing it with a permission, no more than does the constitutive role of authority in the use and disposal of material goods consist in a superior's acting as the single source of supply for a community of drones. On the contrary, by vowing in faith to follow the way of gratuitous sharing in the name of Christ, a religious commits himself to actively using material goods in a special way and for a specific purpose, namely, to share them as effectively as possible with those in greatest need as a mediation to them of the love he bears them in Christ. It is, moreover, a purpose which is shared publicly by all of the other members of the community to which he belongs. But the common pursuit of such a purpose presupposes unified direction; and unified direction presupposes some mechanism within the community to decide authoritatively disputed issues in the community's concrete disposal of its available possessions. Hence, in the context of gratuitous sharing, permission-getting ceases to be an end in itself; it is instead justified only to the extent that it is concretely necessary to secure the effective sharing of material goods with those who are in greatest need. The precise form that the decision-making apparatus in a community will take must also depend upon the makeup of the community and upon its concrete material circumstances. Hence, though superiors continue to have an important role in the disposition of the community's resources, they cease to function as one who passes out token permissions, carfare, and toothpaste. Rather in the context of gratuitous sharing, the superior is challenged to play a positive leadership function within his or her community by creatively directing the most efficient sharing possible of the community's material possessions with those whose need for them is greatest.

The Contemporary Challenge

At the same time, contemporary religious cannot help but confront the ideal of gratuitous sharing with a certain amount of malaise. For there can be little doubt but that many of the "traditional" practices of the religious life, whatever their original purpose, have been transformed in the course of time into institutional buttresses for an asceticism of ritualistic non-possession and of passive indigence. The challenge which the first vow poses to contemporary religious is, then, the discovery of new structures for religious living which will truly express the ideal which that vow seeks to embody, structures which will allow religious to actually pursue a life of active, selfless sharing with those whose need is greatest. For where rules and permission-getting inhibit such active sharing, it is clear that, whatever their seeming legitimacy, they are opposed to the true purpose of the vow and must be replaced by structures which foster rather than discourage genuine religious living.

At the same time, the elaboration of such structures will demand that religious approach the problem of renewal with a new kind of logic significantly different from the one that has characterized ascetical thinking in the past. That logic corresponded to a poverty of non-possession and of passive indigence and was, in fact, the a priori deductive logic of the Franciscan Spirituals, who sought to deduce both their own conduct and that of Jesus and his disciples from the neo-Platonic presuppositions which grounded many of their ascetical ideals. Since, however, gratuitous sharing is precisely a way of using things, it demands of today's religious a *logica utens,* a practical logic capable of factually discerning existing needs, of proposing alternatives to meet those needs, of selecting the proposals most likely to succeed, and of evaluating the success of each means chosen.

Inner Poverty

But even if one should grant all of these suggestions, sharing and labor for others is in its own way an external thing; it need not necessarily touch the heart. One can share grudgingly, one can be forced to labor at a task and for people one despises. If, then, gratuitous sharing is to be truly an expression of deep religious faith, it must actually come from the heart and not merely from the hand. Implicit, therefore, in the first vow of religion is the second vow; for that vow looks directly to the heart. We refer, of course, to the religious vow of unrestricted love.

Notes

1. Ps 1:3.
2. Ps 112:3.
3. Jr 12:1–2.
4. Pr 19:1,22;28:6;Qo 4:13.
5. Pr 6:6–11;10:4;13:18;21:17.
6. Pr 22:1.
7. Pr 30:9.
8. Ex 22:21–24.
9. Ex 22:24–25;Dt 24:10–13.
10. Dt 23:15;25:19–15.
11. Ex 23:6.
12. Dt 15:3.
13. Dt 26:12–15.
14. Dt 6:1–3;Ex 16:26.
15. Ex 19:15–17;Pr 17:5.
16. Jb 24:2ff;Ez 22:29–30;Mi 2:1–3; Is 10:1–3;Jr 22:18–19.
17. No 5:1–15.
18. Jr 22:18–19.
19. Am 8:7.
20. Ps 55:23;9:9.
21. Ps 69:3.
22. Ps 10:12–13.
23. Ps 37:10–11.
24. Ze 2:3.
25. Is 66:1–2.
26. Ps 18:28.
27. Pr 22:4.
28. 2M 7:1ff.
29. Si 1:27.
30. Ws 2:21–3:8.
31. Is 11:1–4.
32. Ps 72:12–13.
33. Ze 3:11–13.
34. Si 3:30.
35. Mt 13:22;Lk 8:14.
36. Mt 19:6ff.
37. Lk 16:9–16.
38. Lk 16:11–12.
39. Lk 16:11–12.
40. Lk 12:15;Mt 16:25–26.
41. Mt 6:24.
42. Mt 19:16–30.
43. Jn 12:6.
44. Mt 8:20
45. Mt 11:29.
46. Jn 4:34.
47. Mt 6:31–33.
48. Mt 5:43–48.
49. Mt 10:9.
50. Mt 10:8;Ac 8:18–25.
51. Lk 4:18–21;Is 61:1–2;Jn 14:9;Mt 11:4–5.
52. Mk 13:38–40.
53. Mt 23:23.
54. Lk 12:33–34;Mt 6:19ff;Lk 14:12–13.
55. Mt 13:41–44.
56. Mt 24:31–46.
57. Jn 12:6.
58. Jn 12:7–8.
59. Mt 27:47;Ps 22.
60. Mt 27:35.
61. Lk 23:34.
62. Ph 2:5–11.
63. Ac 4:32.
64. Ac 2:46.
65. Ac 2:44–45.
66. Ac 5:3–4.
67. Lk 14:28–33.
68. 2Co 8:9.
69. Ac 3:6.
70. 1Co 9:4–5.
71. 1Co 9:13.
72. 1Co 9:17–18.
73. 2Co 1:7–9.
74. Ph 4:11–13.
75. 2Co 8:20.
76. Ac 6:3–6.
77. Lk 14:21.
78. Jm 2:6–7.
79. Jm 2:8–9.
80. Heb 10:34;Rv 2:9;3:17–18.
81. Jm 5:1–6.

82. 1Tm 6:17–19.
83. MG 2,903;ML 2,439C;4,533B;26, 88C;38,1461.
84. MG 9,617C;ML 4,454A;38,413;76, 1098B.
85. MG 8,608B;37,3850.
86. F 1,10;MG 8,605A,608B;14,1122B; ML 22,549.
87. MG 35,909B;ML 15,1676A.
88. F 2,204;ML 4,604B.
89. MG 8,437C;MG 37,385D.
90. F 1,1;F 1,10.
91. MG 51,300.
92. ML 38,413.
93. ML 39,1579.
94. ML 38,1461;32,1190;33,960.
95. ML 33,960.
96. MG 2,903.
97. ML 1,677B.
98. MG 3,608B.
99. MG 47,337.
100. MG 8,608B;9,616A,617C;13, 1300A;ML 4,449A;26,841B;31. 881B;37,385D;22,549;82,425C; MG 6,581C;88,937B.
101. MG 8,437C;9,616A;617C.
102. MG 8,605A;608B.
103. MG 13,1300A.
104. MG 37,385D.
105. MG 47,366.
106. ML 16,147B;14,750B.
107. ML 22,444.
108. ML 22,549.
109. ML 22,1075.
110. MG 31,881B.
111. ML 4,449A;540A;MG 26,841B; ML 22,878,1122.
112. MG 82,425C.
113. MG 65,81C.
114. MG 65,228A.
115. MG 88,928B.
116. DS 908.
117. DS 930–931.
118. DS 486.
119. DS 1087–1089.
120. DS 1090–1094.
121. *Pastoral Constitution on the Church in the Modern World,* 31.
122. *Ibid.,* 72.
123. *Ibid.,* 88.
124. *Decree on the Apostolate of the Laity,* 4.
125. *Decree on the Ministry and Life of Priests,* 17.
126. *Decree on the Appropriate Renewal of the Religious Life,* 13.
127. *Ibid.*
128. C. J. McNaspy, S.J., *Change not Changes: New Directions in Religious Life and Priesthood* (New York: Paulist Press, 1968), pp. 123–129.
129. John Courtney Murray, S.J., "The Danger of the Vows," *Woodstock Letters,* xcvi (Fall, 1967), p. 422.
130. Karl Rahner, S.J., "The Problem of Poverty," in *Contemporary Spirituality,* R. Gleason, S.J. (ed), (New York: Macmillan, 1968), pp. 45 ff.
131. Ladislaus, Örsy, S.J., *Open to The Spirit* (Washington: Corpus Books, 1968), pp. 99ff.

III

Unrestricted Love

Had a devout Old Testament Jew been asked to explain exactly what made the God of his father so different from the Baals of the Gentiles, his answer might well have been that the God of Abraham, of Isaac, and of Jacob is a living God.[1-3]

As source of life, God is also the source of human fertility.[4] It was almost inevitable, then, that sterility, the absence of life, should appear in Old Testament belief as a sign of abandonment by the living God.[5,6]

Understandably, then, the writers of the Old Testament were hard put to find any purpose or positive meaning in a celibate life.[7,8] Jeremiah, it is true, is prophetically called to choose a celibate life for a specific purpose; but it is a dark and ominous one. His childless life serves to remind the parents then living in Jerusalem that for their sins and their idolatry they, too, are doomed by God to die childless "unlamented and unburied."[9]

To the extent, then, that it appears as a positive concept in the Old Testament, virginity implies, not celibacy, but supreme marriageability, a marriageability which is characterized by innocence and by undivided love. By the Levitical code, for example, the high priest was obliged to take a virgin of the priestly tribe to be his bride so that her innocence might assure the ritual purity of his descendants.[10,11]

Consecrated Widows

Some theologians have thought that the Old Testament makes something like an approach to later Christian reflections on the purpose of celibacy in its apparent acknowledgement of widowhood as a state of life in which one can be wholly occupied with the things of God; but this aproach is, at best, a rather distant one.[12]

The textual material relevant to widowhood is, moreover, meager, so that if one is to find an Old Testament basis for Christian reflections on the purpose of celibacy, one is forced to seek it in a different line of thought. Perhaps the most promising lead can be found in the recurring notion that the Sinai covenant is indeed a covenant of love, a marriage contract concluded between God and his people. By its betrothal to Yahweh the people of Israel deliberately commits itself to God with a love that is, at least initially, virginal—that is, both innocent and single-hearted.[13]

Theology of the Covenant

The image of the covenant as a marriage contract is first introduced in the writings of Hosea;[13] but thereafter it becomes a constant theme of the prophets and even finds echoes in the Deuteronomic code.[14] In the prophets, the image is frequently used polemically. The love of Israel for its God was indeed *once* virginal; but by yielding to the seduction of the surrounding pagan fertility cults, the people of God has long since abandoned its former innocence and single-hearted devotion to the living God.[15-18]

The people of Israel were, however, first and last the creation of Yahweh, to the extent that they are anything at all. Since, then, the virginal integrity of their first self-offering to Yahweh was itself a divine gift, in spite of the tragedy of its loss, what Yahweh has once given Yahweh is powerful enough to restore.[19]

Inevitably, then, the eschatological longing of God's people for final deliverance from their own sinfulness gradually took the form of a deep longing for restoration to the lost innocence of its first virginal betrothal to Yahweh, a yearning to return to its former single-hearted consecration to the Lord, to a consecration which would, indeed, be an enduring one.[20] But conscious now of Israel's former sinfulness, the prophets are all the more insistent that such unshakeable fidelity to God must truly be the saving work of God himself.[21,22]

Teaching of Jesus

In writing to the Corinthians, Paul affirms that he has "no directions from the Lord" concerning any obligation to live a celibate life.[23] And indeed in the recorded teachings of Jesus, explicit reference to the question occurs rarely. In one instance, it seems to appear obliquely in a discussion, not of celibacy, but of marriage.[24] The master's repudiation of Jewish divorce practices and insistence that no merely human authority is competent to dissolve the marriage bond provokes a dismayed objection from his disciples: "If that is how things are between husband and wife, it is not advisable to marry." Far from retracting his stand, the master is more emphatic: "It is not everyone who can accept what I have said, but only those to whom it is granted. 'There are eunuchs born that way from their mother's womb, there are eunuchs made so by men, and there are eunuchs who have made themselves that way for the sake of the kingdom of heaven. Let anyone accept this who can.' "

The passage is filled with exegetical complexities; but one thing must have been immediately clear to the disciples. Acceptance into the kingdom demanded of them a willingness to rethink their basic position on the meaning and purpose of married love. For, interestingly enough, the metaphor of the eunuch would seem to apply to those disciples who enter into married union and not simply to those who opt for celibacy.

Still a further source of astonishment for the disciples was, no doubt, the master's apparent willingness to let pass without objection a proposition whose absurdity, as seen from their viewpoint, had initially motivated them to propose it as an objection to the master's own teaching, namely, that celibacy *is* indeed an acceptable mode of life. In fact, the only restrictions that the master seems to place, at least implicitly, upon the choice of celibacy is that one embrace it freely and "for the sake of the kingdom."[25] For the disciples, such innovations, whatever their ultimate explanation, must have seemed initially troubling at best; and the master's intransigence may well have provoked more than one crisis of faith among them.

If any were troubled, they may, however, have found further glimmers of light in the master's debate with the Sadducees concerning the resurrection of the body.

The master refutes the Sadducees by appealing to their faith in the living God; and his answer offers some further clarification of the place which the sexual expression of love occupies in the eschatological kingdom he had come to found.[26] Once the day of the Lord has finally and definitively arrived, men will express their enthusiastic love for one another in ways other than sex. Hence, until the kingdom of God is definitively established, the love which founds the kingdom does indeed find legitimate expression in the relationship of the sexes; but on the other hand this same founding love is broader in its scope than mere erotic love. Perhaps, then, the celibate life could become a way of expressing the larger dimensions of love.

The New Covenant of Love

But as in the case of inner abandonment to God, the full revelation of the meaning of the kingdom of love and of mutual concern preached by the master had to await the shattering events of his own death and glorification. For if the cross was a lesson in the depth of the master's own inner abandonment to the Father, it was also a lesson in the incredible immensity of his love. "A man can have no greater love than to lay down his life for his friends."[27]

But in the master's love for his disciples there was more at stake than the love of mere human friendship; for what he was asking his disciples to believe as he spoke to them on the eve of his passion was that his own human love for them was the concrete embodiment of the eternal love of his heavenly Father for a sinful and loveless world. "To have seen me is to have seen the Father."[28]

Even more, he was asking them to believe that in the death he was about to undergo, mankind would be made to witness the final test, the ultimate proof, of God's love for them, a test which would itself *be* the new covenanted betrothal of mankind to God.[29]

Here, then, was the final explanation of the master's own parables of the bridegroom,[30] of the miracle at Cana,[31] of the Baptist's joy at being chosen as the bridegroom's friend,[32] of the longing of Israel to rediscover the virginal integrity of its first commitment and self-abandonment to God. For what the disciples came to understand at last in the dawn of Easter, as they saw and touched the risen flesh of their master now made Lord, was the Father's own irrevocable ratification of the unshakeable love revealed to men in the agony of his own divine Son. The death and glorification of Jesus is, then, his revelation to men as the eternal bridegroom, as the Lord who has loved men with an everlasting love and who has longed and longed for the glimmer of a human response. The new covenant sealed in Jesus' blood is itself the new betrothal of mankind to God, in the worship of service of the Word made flesh.[33]

Most staggering of all, in the person of their risen Lord, the disciples began to glimpse both the unthinkable breadth of divine love and the extent of its gratuity. For they began to see that God's offer of love and reconciliation tested and revealed in the brutal death of their master and eternally ratified in the risen person of the Lord Jesus is not only utterly universal in its scope but also by its very irrevocability goes before any merely human response of love. The living God loves every man who breathes, loves him even in his sinfulness, loves him even when he fashions a cross to torture the living God with death. The challenge of the cross, the challenge which faces every man who comes into this world, had suddenly become simply this: somehow to find the means to respond to such a love.

A Community of Love

One senses in reading the books of the New Testament that the first Christians were conscious of the fact that they had both responded and failed to respond to God's latest and final offer of loving union with mankind. They had responded by their first faith in Jesus and by what efforts they could make to live in the image of the master; but they also recognized that those same efforts were fraught with human imperfection.

Their longing for the Lord's second coming, for the final conclusion of the nuptials between the risen Lamb and the Church he had created by his love, was also an expression of their awareness that much was still wanting in their own love of God and of one another. The virgin bride of the Lamb described in the book of Revelation appears, then, not merely as an image of a church triumphant in its integrity and single-hearted consecration to the Lord but as a sign also that the true believer's achievement of the full integrity of love must await the day of the Lord, the day of his own personal resurrection.[34]

Moreover, in their longing in spite of failure to live up to the virginal consecration of mankind to God accomplished seminally in the glorification of Jesus and mediated to men in their personal baptismal consecration to Christ, the first Christians seem to have turned to the virgin mother of the Lord for inspiration and example.[35] Luke, for instance, is careful to link the virginity of Mary with her *fiat* of faith, to her unique acquiescence to the living God in love and fidelity, an acquiescence which had mediated redemptively to the world the saving person of Jesus himself.[36] Thus, for Christian reflection, Mary's virginal surrender to God in love came to be the archetype of Christian belief, a surrender which found, it was realized, both its meaning and fulfillment in the virginal love of Jesus, who had freely chosen a celibate life as a means of revealing to men the unlimited scope and gratuity of divine love.

The Pauline Insight

For it was in the confrontation of the infant Church with the risen Christ that the full implications of the master's teachings concerning marriage and celibacy began to dawn on Christian consciousness. He had demanded of his disciples the willingness to rethink their position on the meaning and purpose of married love. What the early Christians came to realize in the light of Easter was that the very death and glorification of Jesus had provided them with the leading principle which must guide that reassessment in faith. For the Christian call to faith is nothing less than a call to share in the final revelation of God's love for sinful men by learning to love other men with the virginal integrity of Christ himself—that is, unconditionally and without exception. With his habitual depth of insight, Paul was quick to see that the summons to such a faith involved a double consequence for Christian living. It not only transformed the meaning and purpose of married love, but also made positive sense out of a Christian's free choice of celibacy "for the sake of the kingdom."

Thus, Paul insists that through the Christ event, the purpose of married love has become not merely the engendering of offspring but the mutual sanctification of the married couple in and through their experience in marriage of the full meaning and scope of Christian love.[37] Moreover, what is crucial in Paul's eyes is that for the Christian couple to find that meaning their own human love for one another must be transformed into an embodiment of their faith in Christ's love of them. In other words, their love of one another must become a particularization of their own baptismal commitment to love all men gratuitously in the name of Christ. Thus, what Paul had seen clearly is that, paradoxically, the revelation to men of the meaning and purpose of Christian marriage is radically dependent on the meaning and purpose of Christ's own celibate love for mankind.

It is true that particularly in his early preaching Paul seems to have had a greater sense of the imminence of the second coming and that this feeling that the day of the Lord is truly near inevitably lent color to his teaching concerning marriage and celibacy.[38]

But the fact that Paul's apparent timetable for the second coming was considerably off does not dim his insight into the meaning of celibacy as an enduring factor in the Church of the latter days. His concern is with the consequences of Christ's love upon human conduct in the last age of salvation rather than with predicting the "day" or the "hour" of the parousia. And in this context, he insists that the purpose of celibacy lies in the first instance in freeing a Christian to follow his conscience and the promptings of the Holy Spirit in the concrete living out of his baptismal commitment to a life of non-exclusive and gratuitous love of others in the name of Christ. His experience told him that the obligations involved in the task of building a family must in many instances take precedence over matters which are intrinsically more important when viewed in the light of the Easter event. A married Christian's family problems, he felt, must rightly and inevitably prevent him from assuming the risks which total dedication to the work of the kingdom involved.[39] As far as Paul was concerned, then, the commitment to universal love and to zeal for the kingdom involved in celibacy is not in any way a withdrawal from life, but is on the contrary a way of becoming involved with others at a level which is deeper and more urgent than private family affairs, business, the simple enjoyment of life, or even personal grief, namely, through the work of preparing the second coming by spreading the good news of God's kingdom on earth.[40-46]

To sum up, then, the people of the Old Testament were hard put to find any positive value in a life of celibacy, though Jeremiah transformed it into a prophetic sign of divine doom and destruction. For the Christian, however, celibacy does take on a positive meaning to the extent that it is the reincarnation of the same sense of purpose which motivated Jesus' own celibate option: His celibacy was, however, nothing else than the revelatory incarnation of a divine love for men which is not only unrestricted in its scope but utterly gratuitous. Since, then, the same love of God which was revealed to us in the virginal love of

Christ became fully manifest as human history in the eternal covenant of love sealed between God and man in the death and glorification of Jesus, not only is Christian celibacy a profession of faith whose lived expression must take the form of that sort of concerned involvement with the needs of others in the name of Christ which maintains one in a constant state of existential openness to the saving reality of the God who has revealed himself as love in the mission of the Word; but as a dynamic, ecclesially visible way of life embodying a universal and gratuitous love of others in Christ's name, celibacy is also a Christian prophetic gesture. For not only does it seek to prolong the lived reality of Jesus' own celibate option, because it was the means he chose prior to his own passion and glorification to reveal to men the universal and gratuitous character of divine love; but Christian celibacy is also, by reason of the very continuity of Jesus' virginal love with the divine love revealed to men in his passion and glorification, a consequence and an existential sign of the new and everlasting covenant itself. In other words, just as the virginal love of Christ anticipates the full revelation of divine love in the events of the paschal mystery, so Christian celibacy which takes the form of a vital concern for others reflects the universality and gratuity of divine love and is a Christian's participation under grace and after the event in Jesus' own loving surrender to his Father upon the cross.

The Patristic Catechesis

As one might almost imagine, the relative meagerness of scriptual references to virginity is reflected in two ways in patristic catechesis. On the one hand, explicit biblical allusions seem to appear less frequently in discussions of virginity; on the other hand, when references do occur they are sometimes apt to be a bit contrived.[47,48]

Athanasius, for instance, remarks in commenting on the parable of the sower that those symbolized by the seed which bears fruit a hundred-fold are consecrated virgins, whose life is superior to the world and more difficult.[49]

The sparseness of biblical material also inclines the Fathers to rely heavily on the relatively few texts in the New Testament which raise the issue of virginity directly. One encounters, for example, considerable insistence on Pauline teaching that the virginal life must be freely chosen in response to a special grace from God and that such a choice does not involve the repudiation of marriage as something wicked or vile.[50,51]

Most of all, however, the Fathers seem to insist upon the "angelic" character of the virginal life, alluded to in Luke 20:36. But in attempting to give meaning to this aspect of virginity, different patristic commentators are hard put to agree on the precise implications of the Lord's teaching that in the resurrection of the body the just will neither marry nor give in marriage, but be instead like the angels of God. Cyprian of Carthage, for example, draws two conclusions from the text: First, that in some mysterious way consecrated virgins already possess the glory of the resurrection even during the present life; second, that they should, therefore, be most careful to pass through this world without sharing its degradation and corruption.[52] By the time of Gregory Nazianzen, however, this same avoidance of worldly contamination has already begun to be conceived in somewhat anti-corporeal terms.[53-56]

Example of Jesus and Mary

The Fathers also appeal to the lived example of Christ and his mother as manifesting God's special predilection for the virginal life.[57,58]. And in the course of time, Mary gradually assumes greater and greater prominence as the model for those who practice virginity. Ambrose, for instance, elaborates eloquently the theme of God's free choice of a virginal mother. "See, then," he writes, "how great are the merits of virginity. Christ existed before the virgin, Christ is born of a virgin. Indeed, he was born of the Father before the ages, but was born of a virgin for the sake of the ages. The former birth pertains to his nature, the latter to our advantage. The former always was; the latter, he chose."[59]

Appeal to the example of Mary in order to edify holy women

who have themselves opted for a virginal life sometimes leads the patristic writer to embroider his account of Mary's life with the taboos imposed on the consecrated virgins of his own day, For example, in the same tract on virginity just cited, Ambrose also tells us not only that Mary lived a life of fasting but also that "she never knew what it meant to go outdoors, except when she would go to church, and then only in the company of parents and relatives."[60-63]

The Meaning of "Virgin"

Partly for historical reasons not too difficult to discern, the Fathers show a clear tendency to associate virginity with a life of seclusion, contemplation, and prayer. In so doing, they are, to be sure, in part following the lead of St. Paul. But a number of other concrete historical influences ground this association as well.

First of all, in the writings of the Fathers the term "virgin" is reserved almost exclusively for *women* consecrated to God. Second, although the general disintegration of Greco-Roman society seems to have allowed the fair sex more social liberty in the patristic age than in earlier times, the writings of the Fathers give ample evidence that such liberties were certainly not allowed to consecrated virgins. For all practical purposes, then, apart from the domestic duties proper to her sex the only activities socially possible for a woman leading a virginal life were prayer, fasting, almsgiving, and the cult of the interior virtues.[64-66]

Philosophical Influence

As in the case of gratuitous sharing the Fathers inevitably came to speak of virginity not merely in biblical terms but also in the common philosophical language of their day. One can, therefore, discover in the pertinent texts a tendency to present the Christian ideal of a virginal life in terms that suggest a Platonic soul-body dualism quite foreign to biblical thought.

Origen, for example in his homilies equates virginal consecration to God with segregation from the rest of men who "live carnally" and are "bound to worldly tasks," so that one ceases to be concerned with such ephemeral matters, seeks only the things of heaven, and renounces forever subjection "to human uses and actions."[67]

St. Cyprian, in his *De Habitu Virginum,* warns against vanity about physical beauty or concern with fancy hair-dos. Their concern in life should rather be to struggle against the flesh and to conquer their bodies.[68-71]

It would be a gross caricature of patristic teaching even to imply that the whole optic of the Fathers with regard to virginity is colored by such Platonic dualism. Such is certainly *not* the case. At the same time, that such an optic is present in many texts is certainly undeniable.[72-77]

In their efforts to foster the practice of virginity, the Fathers are inevitably led to compare virginity and matrimony. Moreover, by expanding the germinal thrust of Pauline thinking, they always give the clear advantage to virginity, sometimes more emphatically than Paul himself.

Tertullian, for instance, links the notion of sanctification closely with that of sexual abstinence.[78] Origen, for his part, recommends periodic continence to married people as a mitigated form of virginity.[79-81] Ambrose attempts to convince the virgins of his day that the blessings of marriage, even in human terms, are not unmixed: Children mean added bother and work for mother; her sexual urges are a drag upon her; childbearing ages her; preoccupation with stylishness distracts her from important matters. From all these burdens, however, a virgin is freed so that she may more easily cultivate Christian virtues.[82, 83] "The bonds of marriage are blessed," he writes, "but they are bonds."[84-88]

Multiplication of Taboos

It is impossible for a contemporary Christian to assess ascetical writing on the meaning and purposes of virginity without some consideration of the social taboos which ancient times placed upon consecrated virgins. For as the patristic age advanced, those taboos became increasingly elaborate and lent historical color to Christian understanding of the very meaning and purpose of virginity. One of the earliest tracts on virginity is Tertullian's *De Virginibus Velandis (On the Need for Virgins to Wear Veils),* a treatise on proper attire for virgins in public, written in the year 206 A.D. The reason why virgins should wear veils, Tertullian argues, is an honest fear of yielding to their erotic desires. Besides being a "helmet" in public against temptations to lust, their veils will protect them against scandals and the suspicions, whispers, and envy of others.[89]

Tertullian's writings on virginity are also interesting in that they inaugurate a tendency which will become more and more common in patristic literature, namely, the tendency to rationalize the taboos placed on virgins by appealing, sometimes quite rhetorically, to biblical notions which will give such restraints the appearance of being divinely sanctioned. He justifies the veiling of virgins, for example, by insisting that virgins are, after all, the brides of Christ and that they have, therefore, not only the right but also the obligation to veil themselves in public.[90] One of the inevitable results of such pious rationalizations was, of course, the gradual identification in the Christian imagination of the very ideal of virginity with the concrete social restrictions imposed upon virgins in the course of time.

Moreover, as time advances, each of the Fathers seems concerned to add some new item to the list of things a consecrated virgin cannot do. Cyprian, for instance, appeals to his fear of human frailty in sexual matters in order to discourage anything like fashionable dress among consecrated virgins: "But if you attract attention publicly with your fancy hair-do and solicit the glances of young men, and draw the sighs of adolescents in your wake, and feed their lusty desires, and ignite [in them] the sparks of hope so that you lead others to perdition without yourself perishing, if, I say, you prove to be a sword and poison to those who gaze upon you, you cannot be excused simply because you are chaste and modest in your heart."[91,92]

Athanasius is even more severe. He warns consecrated virgins that worldly ways leave them as tainted in body and soul as intercourse would leave them physically defiled.[93] To dress beyond one's years, to eschew makeup, to remain veiled in the presence of men—all such practices, he insists, signify holiness. Athanasius also adds to the growing list of restrictions a practical piece of advice. "Don't take a bath, if you are healthy, without serious necessity," he counsels, "and don't completely immerse your body in water, because you are sacred to the Lord." In view of the fact that Athanasius also forbids virgins the use of perfumes and precious ointments, one is inclined to draw the facetious conclusion that even if veils, matronly dress, and the absence of makeup failed to fend off prospective suitors, the odor of sanctity which must certainly have preceded those who followed his suggestions on bathing would have provided powerful discouragement to any prospective Don Juans.[94-97]

One cannot, of course, reduce the Fathers' understanding of the meaning of virginity exclusively to their elaboration of what must seem to contemporary readers bizarre and dated social taboos with which to buttress virginal virtue. Indeed the duties they seem to associate by preference with virginity are fasting, prayer, and almsgiving.[98] They regard virginal consecration to Christ as involving dedication to study, especially to the study of the truths of revelation, to the cultivation of all the virtues, and to inner recollection and tranquility.[99] Moreover, by associating virginity with almsgiving and concern for the poor, they also manifest an awareness that the virginal life has an actively ecclesial dimension beyond the mere edification afforded the community by people who have eschewed the comforts of marriage and of gracious living in order to prepare their hearts to meet the divine bridegroom joyfully at the moment of death. [100-105] But when all is said and done, one cannot avoid the feeling that during the patristic age becoming a eunuch for the sake of the kingdom had somehow been transformed from the biblical ideal of a life of prayer and apostolic involvement to the public display of the number of social and emotional inhibitions one could endure.

Discipline of the Church

The earliest pronouncements of Church authorities on virginity in the post-apostolic age were mostly of a disciplinary nature and are of limited dogmatic significance.[106-109]

Perhaps the first really significant dogmatic statement concerning the meaning of celibacy is found in Trent. As in the preceding pronouncements of the magisterium, the Tridentine Fathers were most concerned to reinstate correct discipline in the observance of canonical celibacy and virginity. Their decree on matrimony, for instance, approved in 1563 during the twenty-fourth session of the Council, was directed against "those raving and impious men of the world" who impugn the holy sacrament of matrimony and "under the pretext of the gospel introduce the freedom of the flesh." The bishops deny, among other things, that priests and religious who feel they cannot continue to live a life of celibacy or of virginity may simply ignore both their vow and existing Church legislation, in order to marry.[110]

More significantly, however, the Council Fathers also affirm in the tenth canon of the same decree that it is "better and more blessed" to prefer celibacy and virginity to marriage.[111-113] The canon should, of course, be read in the context of the reformers' attempt to repudiate canonical celibacy and virginity as another abuse of an all too decadent tradition. The canon in effect both rejects the reformers' position and reaffirms the teaching of Jesus in Mt 19:11, which counsels virginity to those who can accept it, as well as Pauline teaching to the same effect in 1Co 7:25ff, 38, 40. The canon fails, however, to make clear under precisely what aspect or aspects celibacy and virginity might be considered "better and more blessed" than marriage, although the first canon of the same decree, which defines that marriage is indeed a sacrament instituted by Christ, makes it clear that that aspect is certainly *not* sacramentality. The tenth canon of the decree on matrimony must also be balanced by the magisterium's prior and repeated reaffirmation of the goodness and holiness of Christian marriage itself.[114,115]

In 1954, Pius XII in his encyclical *Sacra virginitas* reacted strongly to the suggestion that marriage is "more perfect" than virginity. First of all, he condemns as "false and harmful" the notion that the *ex opere operato* grace of marriage renders its use so holy that certain souls can become more efficaciously united to God in the act of intercourse than they could by embracing virginity. His real objection, however, is that as a theory of sacramental grace the suggestion betrays a misleading preoccupation with intercourse itself by describing the teleology of sacramental grace as though its purpose were to make the use of marriage "of itself" a more apt instrument for uniting the married couple to God than virginity or celibacy. In point of fact, Pius insists, the grace of the sacrament seeks only to help the couple perform the duties of married life holily and to confirm them in their love for one another.[116] Pius also denies that the mutual help of the spouses is a "more perfect" way of achieving sanctity than the solitude of heart proper to the life of a celibate religious, since the virgin and the celibate both receive from the Giver of all gifts "something spiritual" which surpasses any help married people may owe one another.[117]

Teaching of Vatican II

The frankly pastoral mood which characterizes the teachings of Vatican II concerning celibacy and virginity is a refreshing departure from the disciplinary and dogmatic tone of the earlier decrees of the magisterium on the subject. The Council Fathers praise virginity and celibacy as facilitating total self-consecration to God. "This total continence," the bishops write, "embraced on behalf of the kingdom of heaven has always been held in particular honor by the Church as being a sign of charity and stimulus toward it, as well as a unique fountain of spiritual fertility in the world."[118]

In their decree on priestly formation, the bishops are careful to link the celibate option with apostolic service of others in the name of Christ. They reaffirm the basic values inherent in celibacy and decree that seminarians should be trained to recognize those values.[119,120]

The bishops reaffirm unequivocally the possibility of living a celibate life in the twentieth century, in spite of some contemporary claims to the contrary.[121] At the same time, they recognize that the successful living of such a life in the image of Christ does not come automatically. And they show concern that the training given to priests and religious should show them how to integrate a life of virginity and of celibacy with a life of fruitful apostolic service. They also demand that candidates to the religious life be carefully screened on the basis of their psychological and emotional maturity and that they be tested in their ability to lead a virginal life before being admitted to vows. The bishops also manifest an understandable concern that celibate living should contribute to the enrichment and not to the impoverishment of the celibate's own personality.[122]

Pope Paul on Celibacy

In his encyclical on priestly celibacy, Pope Paul presents lucidly some of the most frequent objections raised against continuing obligatory celibacy for diocesan priests in the Occidental Church. Briefly summarized, they are: the fact that Jesus did not demand celibacy of his own apostles; the fact that in the early Church clerical celibacy was not obligatory; the fact that a vocation to celibacy and a vocation to the priesthood are not identical vocations; the possibility of remedying the shortage of priests in many places were celibacy abandoned; the possibility that the right to marry would prevent many priestly defections; the fact that married priests could witness more fully to the sanctity of the married state; the charge that celibacy is in fact detrimental to the development of a mature and well-balanced human personality; the charge that in practice present Church discipline does not allow seminarians the amount of freedom they should have to make a personal choice of a celibate life.[123]

Instead of replying to this rather imposing array of arguments point by point, the encyclical is content to reaffirm some of the basic values underlying a celibate option and in so doing discusses several notions which are pertinent to the question of the meaning and purpose of a celibate life. In discussing the Christological aspects of celibacy, the encyclical points out that marriage was part and parcel of the first creation, and that its divine institution is described in the second chapter of Genesis. But, the text goes on to observe, the new creation in Christ has not only raised marriage to the sacramental status of being a "mysterious symbol" of Christ's union with the Church, but has also offered the ideal of celibacy as a means of adhering "wholly and directly to the Lord." Celibacy thus manifests "in a clearer and more complete way the profoundly transforming reality of the New Testament."[124-129]

The Manual Tradition

Manual asceticism frequently opposes the vow of chastity to the second great concupiscence, the concupiscence of the flesh. We are warned that the vow does not, of course, put an end to concupiscence although occasionally men and women of singular virtue have been gifted with total freedom from any inordinate movement of the flesh. But for most mortals, the sting of man's disordered lust for pleasure remains lifelong, with the result that one vowed to chastity must be constantly on his guard to check his sense appetites, to avoid all forms of idleness, to stir the fires of the love of God in his heart, to avoid the sources of temptation, and to live a life of mortification and strict self-control.

At the same time manual asceticism assures one that however difficult the celibate life may at times be, it is not without its compensations. One vowed to chastity is freed from all the troubles and distractions of raising a family, freed too from the need to be concerned about pleasing one's spouse, freed finally to seek to do what is pleasing to God alone.

The purpose of the virtue of chastity which corresponds to the vow is, we are told, to check what is inordinate in voluptuous pleasure. It is, therefore, called the "angelic" virtue, because angels (at least certain patristic and medieval angels and selected biblical ones) have no bodies and live unsullied by carnal lust. It is, too, a frail virtue, since as far as chastity is concerned, the least fall leaves one wholly tarnished and impure. It is an austere virtue since our fallen nature is constantly inclined to take excessive pleasure in sensible delights, whether of the internal or external senses, and is constantly buffeted by our unruly passions.

In treating the second vow, manual asceticism distinguishes different degrees in which the virtue of chastity may be possessed. At its most fundamental level, it keeps one from consenting to thoughts, fancies, feelings, or actions contrary to the virtue. In its second degree, it strengthens one to oppose such movements of the flesh vigorously and energetically. At its third level, it enables one to treat matters pertaining to purity as calmly as one would treat any other matter.

Manual asceticism warns us, moreover, that there are two kinds of chastity: conjugal chastity and pre-marital chastity or continence. The former virtue, we are told, ensures the mutual fidelity and devotion of spouses in their marital relations by helping both to free those relations from carnal lust and to preserve in the use of sex a pure intention about seeking posterity as the ultimate purpose of intercourse. The virtue also endows them with fidelity and candor in the fulfillment of their marital obligations, and with moderation in their pursuit of sexual pleasure.

The continence demanded of the unmarried is, we are warned, absolute abstention from all thoughts, desires, and actions that prepare the way for the marriage act. Though difficult for the old Adam, such self-restraint is rendered easier by cultivating fear of one's own carnal weakness, by trust in the grace of God, by avoiding all occasions of sin, by curbing one's attraction to the opposite sex and to young children, by avoiding fashionable dress, by frankness with one's confessor, and by constant mortification. This last aid to chastity is, we are told, particularly efficacious and includes guarding one's eyes from suggestive and distracting sights, keeping one's conversation pure, special avoidance of the pleasures of touch, firm control of one's imagination; the avoidance of day-dreaming, control of the affections of one's heart, and watchfulness over the progress of one's friendships even with persons of holy character. Other useful aids to continence include the avoidance of idleness, attention to the duties of one's state, devotion to study, prayer, and a cultivated love for Jesus and his Mother.

By the vow of chastity, a religious is obliged to abstain from every sin against the virtue of purity, even internal, and to renounce any use of sex that would be lawful in valid marriage. Solemn vows render marriage contracted while still under vow invalid as well as illicit. Solemn profession dissolves an unconsummated marriage.

In treating the second vow, manual asceticism insists, therefore, primarily upon the values of self-control and self-mistrust in matters of chastity. Needless to say, granted the partly instinctive and subconscious nature of the sex drive, such an insistence has a certain place and value; but as a complete explanation of the meaning and purpose of the second vow it is static, negative, emotionally repressive, and theologically inadequate.

Problems and Perplexities

Its inadequacy is, moreover, reflected in the current malaise which American religious tend to display when they are asked to explain the meaning and purpose of the vow of chastity. The problem is not ignorance of the manual explanation; the problem is rather that somehow the traditional answers do not seem to make as much sense as presumably they once did. Contemporary religious know, for instance, that the Fathers of the Church were lyrical in their praises of the contemplative tranquility which attends a celibate existence. But being somewhat less inclined than some of the Fathers to seek God by way of contemplative transcendence, many American religious are inclined to wonder whether certain kinds of tranquility might not in fact be humanly tranquilizing. Might not the cultivation of spiritual tranquility, they ask themselves, actually be just an ascetical euphemism for avoiding all inconvenient or costly human involvements with other people? An examination of the conduct of some religious would seem to lend support to such a hypothesis. At the same time reflective religious can scarcely avoid wondering whether such an ascetical ideal can ultimately be reconciled with Christian love. Today religious know that a celibate life is supposed to be more apostolically efficient than married life; but when they measure the actual effectiveness of some religious with that of committed lay apostles, they somehow find an argument for celibacy based on mere apostolic efficiency less than convincing. In a word, contemporary American religious know perfectly well the do's and don't's of pre-marital chastity associated with a traditional explanation of the second vow; but what they are looking for and often do not find is a conceptually adequate explanation of why one could ever opt for pre-marital chastity when marital chastity is always a possibility.

American religious are also inclined to show occasional uneasiness about the possible subconscious motivations which may lie at the basis of a celibate option. Part of such uneasiness, of course, derives from the fact that Americans are all too inclined to replace the spiritual self-dissection of their Puritan forebears with a popularized and often ill-informed species of self-psychoanalysis. Studies of the religious life like that of Fr. Joseph Fichter, together with the barrage of psychological tests currently required of candidates in many orders and congregations, give us good reason to believe that those who enter religious life are as a group in sound mental health.[130] But we need more than mere factual assurance. One might, for instance, ask with all legitimacy: Is there anything in a manual explanation of the living of the second vow which clearly distinguishes it from the neurotic conduct of those who are psychologically incapable of loving? Unfortunately one must confess that a manual asceticism of the second vow offers few characteristics which would justify a positive answer to such a question.

Doubts and perplexities such as these have also given rise to a growing feeling among American religious that, granted the time and culture in which they live, they are unrealistically over-protected from "sex," especially during their formative years; that they are too often denied ordinary and legitimate social contacts with members of the opposite sex, contacts which are ultimately necessary for their sound emotional development; that they are needlessly forbidden many legitimate expressions of normal human affection.[131] Once again one must concede that there is little in the manual explanation of the second vow that might serve as a positive guideline in reaching a workable resolution of such perplexities.

The problems surrounding the second vow are, therefore, not merely psychological. If, for instance, one accepts the manual description of chastity as, in general, the virtuous effort to control what is inordinate in one's desire for voluptuous pleasure, and, in the case of unmarried people, as absolute abstinence for the use of sex and from direct stimulation of venereal pleasure, one is hard put to justify speculatively the more positive characteristics ascribed by the magisterium to a life of voluntary celibacy. How, for example, does the mere avoidance of venereal pleasure bear fruit in the apostolic service of the Christian community? How does it stimulate pastoral charity? In what possible sense is complete abstention from sexual intercourse a meaningful symbol of the union of Christ and his Church? How is it an anticipation of the fulfillment of the kingdom? How, in priests, is it alone a sign of a genuine fatherhood? In comparing the documents of the magisterium with the manual explanation of chastity, one cannot avoid the feeling that however ascetically important the prudent abstention from dangerous sexual stimuli might be, some rather crucial positive elements have been omitted from the latter's account of the meaning of religious chastity.

Recent Speculation

Moreover, as in the case of poverty, as soon as we attempt to understand the meaning of the second vow, we are driven to investigate its purpose. Fortunately, contemporary theology has provided us with a number of interesting suggestions to illumine the problem. Following the lead of thinkers like Fr. Rahner, contemporary theologians insist that the celibate witnesses in a special way to the eschatological dimensions of Christian belief. As in the case of Mary, whose virginity was a manifestation in her flesh of the transcendent origin of God's Son, so those vowed to a celibate life witness, we are told, to their belief in the transcendent character of God's grace. That is to say, by their renunciation of the blessings of marriage in confident expectation of the reward that will be theirs on the last day, religious manifest their hope for a fulfillment which transcends the present order of things. In Fr. Örsy's words, the "center of gravity" of a celibate's life has shifted to the world to come.[132]

Other contemporary theologians regard a life of celibacy as an expression of special love for the person of Christ, one which assumes absolute primacy over any other love. Fr. Häring, for example, in a recent article locates the essence of celibacy in "an ardent overflowing love for Christ."[133] Fr. Örsy suggests that the celibate by his love for Christ ceases to "want to share his mind, his heart, his body with another human person, because human nature is too limited for two overwhelming relationships." Even though the celibate's charity "will overflow to everyone," it will never be "exclusively concentrated on anyone."[134] Fr. Martelet has suggested that this personal and exclusive love of Christ is an essential factor in the eschatological witness of celibate living.[135]

Fr. Örsy also speaks of the celibate life as sharing in the "companionship of God" and as "the best disposition to hear God's words of silence." He insists that God's companionship is "spiritual" and is manifest in those dimensions of a religious's life in which "the Holy Spirit lifts the whole man into another spiritual world where the grace of God enriches even the body," without, however, satisfying bodily desires, as, for instance, in the spiritual support a religious receives in order to practice a penitential fast.[136]

In his book on priestly celibacy, Schillebeeckx insists more on the apostolic dimensions of the celibate life. He sees religious celibacy as the sacralization of "secular celibacy." Secular celibacy he defines as the pursuit of secular goals with a degree of concentration which precludes assuming the responsibilities of married life.[137] Religious celibacy differs from secular celibacy in that the goals it pursues are explicitly religious. Like secular celibacy, however, religious celibacy calls dramatic attention to the purposes it seeks to accomplish. Hence, the sacralization of celibacy bears dramatic witness to the fact that the kingdom of God comes into being through the ecstatic gestures of those who serve it. There is, to be sure, a certain artificiality in seeking the justification of religious celibacy in the sacralization of an almost non-existent secular phenomenon; but Schillebeeckx insists, too, on the fact that celibacy is a more effective world-transcending sign of the kingdom than marriage, which commits one to life in the world and for the world.[138] Schillebeeckx concedes, however, that both marriage and celibacy are for the sake of the kingdom.

More Perplexities

There is much that is of positive value in all of these reflections and insights. Still, the light they shed on the second vow does not completely dissipate every conceptual difficulty. One can legitimately wonder, for instance, whether the celibate has really cornered the market on the transcendent aspects of belief and Christian witness to the extent that contemporary theology seems to suggest he has. If, for instance, one seeks to correlate an existential witness to one's belief in the transcendent origin of divine grace with the extent to which one is willing to renounce for religious motives some of the experienced values of this life, the renunciatory demands present in a monogamous, indissoluble marriage often provide a very striking witness to a belief in the divine transcendence, especially in those instances when the reciprocity of love ideally present in marriage is lacking or defective.

Indeed, one cannot help but suspect that part of current theological insistence on the witness to transcendence that is supposed to characterize in a special manner a celibate option stems from an ascetical tendency as old as the patristic age to romanticize the bliss of married existence in order to dramatize rhetorically the renunciation present in celibacy. It is true, of course, that even the Fathers recognized that in choosing a single life, the celibate successfully avoided many of the real headaches of married existence as well. Still, one cannot help but wonder if by a peculiar reverse logic contemporary theological idealizations of the joys of marriage in the manner of the Fathers, even when initially conceived as a rhetorical eulogy to the celibate's renunciatory asceticism, may not be partially responsible for some of the more recent defections from the religious life and the priesthood. One must be deeply stoic in bent to appreciate the advantages of renouncing something idyllically beautiful because it is idyllically beautiful.

More directly to the point, however, is what seems to be an element of the arbitrary in the efforts of some theologians to contrast the mission of the celibate religious and the mission of the married layman by appealing to the fact that the latter lives "in the world" and "for the world" while the former does not. For if, on the one hand, the "world" means the human community, then clearly even though one's most immediate concern is the formation of an authentically Christian community of the sort that we currently call "religious," such a community is not only itself composed of human beings with human needs but can in fact exist in no other place than "in the world," i.e., as an integral, contributing part of the larger human community, if, that is, such a community is to have a genuinely Christian *raison d'être*. Similarly, any community that actively and publicly professes the ideals of gratuitous sharing cannot avoid living in the most fundamental sense "for the world," by seeking to use the material goods at its disposal for the upbuilding of a human community of mutual love and concern in the name of Christ. And if, on the other hand, "the world" means human selfishness, egotism, sin, unbelief, and the oppression of one's fellow man, then the obligation to shun "the world" is in fact incumbent on celibate and non-celibate alike. It would seem, therefore, that if celibates have no corner on "transcendence" and on "worldly" detachment in their existential witness of faith, married people have no corner on "immanence" or on "worldly" involvement in theirs.

Needless to say, such a conclusion should come as no great shock, since every Christian vocation, if it is to be authentically Christian, must seek to keep the immanent and the transcendent aspects of religious living in a state of vital balance. We may conclude, therefore, that any effort to characterize either the lived witness of religious exclusively as a witness to the transcendence of grace or the witness of laymen exclusively as a witness to the immanence of divine grace is arbitrary and inadequate. That is to say, the "center of gravity" of a religious's life is no more in the next world than is the layman's. The "center of gravity" of the layman's life is no more in this world than is the religious's. For both, as Christians, must be in the world but not of it. Both as Christians must live in such a way that it is clear that their real treasure lies in heaven. In point of fact, to place the center of gravity of any man's life either in this world or in the next is to run the risk of supposing that the two worlds have not been indissolubly united in the Christ event.

Similarly, if one argues that the eschatological character of the love of Christ is more clearly manifest in a celibate option than in marriage because the celibate's love of Christ has no immediate human object to come between it and the person of Christ, one comes dangerously close to dissociating radically the transcendent love of a risen Christ from the immanent love of one's fellow human beings—a hazardous theological option at best for the disciple of one who taught: "Whatever you do to one of these the least of my brethren, you do to me."

Serious objections can also be raised against any attempt to describe the celibate's love of Christ in terms of the exclusivity which characterizes conjugal love. If, as has been suggested, the celibate truly is one who claims to love Christ so much that he has no really deep love left for his fellow human beings, then how is the celibate to answer the inspired challenge of the first letter of John: "Anyone who says, 'I love God,' and hates his brother is a liar, since a man who does not love the brother that he can see cannot love God, whom he has never seen"? Furthermore, if one chooses to describe the celibate's love of Christ in such exclusive, quasi-conjugal terms, then how is one to justify conceptually and logically the further affirmation, unavoidable in any Christian understanding of the love of God, that the celibate's exclusive and all-absorbing love of the person of Christ must "overflow" into acts of love for other people? That is to say, to be authentically Christian, must one not, from the very first, regard the love of other people as integral to the love of Christ and, hence, as integral to celibacy itself?

But there are still other problems which remain, Patristic rhetoric, for instance, pictures the celibate as renouncing the human companionship of a spouse for the "spiritual" companionship of God. And the notion persists in some of the contemporary theology of the second vow. Still, we should not allow our factual theological claims to fall victim to our ascetical metaphors. The fact of the matter is that many celibates who seek to "listen to God's words in silence" find him a remarkably poor conversationalist, while married people can be spiritually gifted with real depth of understanding. Moreover, is God's "spiritual companionship" which strengthens a religious in soul and body to undertake some penitential act like fasting radically different from the divine "spiritual companionship" which strengthens a layman to care in faith and love for a retarded child or even to perform many of the ordinary thankless tasks involved in raising an infant? In other words, does it not seem as presumptuous for the celibate to lay special claim to a lion's share in divine companionship as it is for him to lay claim to a deeper love of Christ than is possible for married people?

Toward a Redefinition of Purpose

The problem of the purpose of the second vow of religion is closely tied up with the problem of the purpose of Christian marriage. Manual asceticism has been quite correct in presenting the negative aspects of the vow as involving a renunciation of married life. But in failing to provide an adequate account of the vow's positive purpose, manual asceticism has too often left religious without motives adequate to justify the very renunciation demanded by the vow.

A way out of this impasse lies perhaps in the notion that both Christian marriage and Christian celibacy are signs of the new covenant. Marriage is, of course, a sacramental sign of the covenant. The commitment to celibacy, on the other hand, is not a sacramental sign; but it is an existential, ecclesial sign of the covenant and presupposes a sacramental context to give it meaning. That is to say, celibacy is, as the magisterium assures us, a fulfillment of the basic faith commitment which is present in baptism itself and is by that very fact a sign of the new covenant.

Theological explanations of the second vow of religion have, as we have seen, tended to emphasize the symbolic significance of its negative renunciatory aspects. One may, however, legitimately wonder whether there is not some more positive, active, dynamic dimension to the celibate's existential and ecclesial witness. It is clear, for instance, that if celibacy is truly a sign of the covenant, the celibate's renunciation of marriage cannot be conceived as a renunciation of every manifestation of human love. For if the new covenant is itself the revelatory embodiment of divine love for men in the human love of God's glorified Son and in the response of love of those who believe in him, then it is difficult to see how celibacy could ever be an existential sign of that covenant unless it were also recognizable as a graced response of human love to God's revelatory intervention in human affairs. At the same time, in a Christian context, it is impossible to dissociate the love of God from the love of one's fellow human beings. If, then, both marriage and celibacy are to be lived signs of the new covenant, they must embody, each in its own way, some dimension of the kind of love for others which is demanded by the revelatory incarnation of God's love for men.

Now, the love for one's fellow man demanded by the Christian sacraments of initiation is unrestricted in its scope, in its conditions, and in its consequences. It is unrestricted in its scope in the sense that it excludes no man from its compass. It is unrestricted in its conditions in that it does not demand as a precondition to the offer and maintenance of love that men actually be worthy of love before it is offered them or respond to it once the offer is made. It is unrestricted in its consequences in the sense that it is willing to risk everything in Christ's name for the sake of the beloved in imitation of him who said: "Greater love than this no man has, that he lay down his life for his friends." If, then, we are to understand the meaning of the second vow of religion, we must see it as the extension and fulfillment of this fundamental love-commitment demanded by the Christian sacraments of initiation.

Marriage, on the other hand, is, as a sacrament, a radical particularization of a Christian's initial baptismal commitment to love others in the name and image of Christ. Like the baptismal commitment to love it is unrestricted in its conditions and in its consequences; and hence it is by its irrevocability indissoluble by the contracting partners themselves. But the very nature of the marriage contract demands that the love-commitment it embodies be more restricted in its scope than the love-commitment embodied in the Christian sacraments of initiation. That is to say, as baptized and confirmed Christians, married people are committed to love all men in Christ's name. As married, they are only committed to love one another and by implication their children with the selfless and atoning love of Christ. Hence, the love-commitment embodied in marriage is restricted in its scope, though it remains unrestricted in its conditions and in its consequences.

Signs of the Covenant

We should also note that both the second vow of religion and the marriage contract are signs of the covenant because they are public ecclesial acts. By an ecclesial sign of the covenant we mean an action which is formally and publicly recognized by the believing community both as an appropriate response to the covenant and as demanding the covenant as the condition for its possibility. Needless to say, marriage is an ecclesial sign of the covenant because it is a sacramental sign. That is to say, the public commitment of each spouse to love one another in Christ's name and image with a love that is unrestricted in its conditions and consequences signifies and mediates to each of them Christ's own unrestricted covenant commitment of love to them in his Father's name. It also transforms the married couple's fidelity to their love commitment into a lived ecclesial sign of the new covenant which is characterized specifically by its particularity and reciprocity.

Though expressed in a public vow, the love-commitment embodied in celibacy is not sacramental. To begin with, though the vow is publicly accepted and officially approved by the community, the commitment it embodies is essentially the loving act of a single person. By contrast, seen from the viewpoint of the structure of the human act involved, it takes two to make a sacrament: a minister who renews with divine authority the Father's love-commitment made to men in Christ and a recipient who accepts that commitment in love and faith. Similarly, a sacrament always seeks to mediate Christ's love to a specific individual; but, as we have seen, the love-commitment embodied in the second vow of religion is unrestricted not only in its conditions and consequences but in its scope. Hence, paradoxically from the viewpoint of the structure of the public act involved, the particularization of the scope of the love-commitment present in the marriage contract is an unavoidable pre-condition for its sacramentality. Similarly, precisely because the scope of its love remains unrestricted the second vow of religion can never be a sacrament in the full sense of the term.

But because it is a public act whose faith dimension is acknowledged and sanctioned by the believing Christian community as an appropriate response to the covenant, the love-commitment embodied in it is, as in the case of marriage, not merely a personal but a public, and a quasi-sacramental, ecclesial sign of the covenant. But whereas the love-commitment embodied in the marriage contract is a sign of the covenant in the particularity of its scope and in its reciprocity, the love-commitment embodied in the second vow of religion is a sign of the covenant in the unrestricted character of its scope and in its gratuity. That is to say, in the marriage contract two individual Christians bind themselves by a mutual public agreement to love one another in the name and image of Christ. Their love-commitment is reciprocal. In the second vow of religion, however, the love-commitment is the act of a single person and is made without any contractual assurance of a response. In other words, the gratuity of the love-commitment of the second vow is a function both of its non-sacramentality and of its unrestricted scope and consists in the fact that it embodies an offer of love which is simply there, for any man to accept or to abuse as he wills.

We may conclude, therefore, that the two love-commitments embodied in the vows of marriage and in the vows of religion resemble one another in at least two important ways. Both are unrestricted in their conditions and in their consequences. Both seek to evoke a response of love which resembles the love-commitment offered. In the case of marriage vows, the response is one of conjugal Christian love. In the case of the second vow, the response is one of the kind of wholly unrestricted and gratuitous love demanded by Christian baptismal consecration. The former is essentially ordered to the building and nurturing of a particular Christian family. The latter is essentially ordered to evoking from men the kind of love which, by the unrestricted character of its scope, grounds and nurtures that kingdom of love which is the universal Church of Christ. That is to say, the celibate renounces marriage because his baptismal love-commitment inspires him to the task of seeking to evoke from men a love which is itself unrestricted in its scope as well as in its conditions and consequences by loving them with the same kind of unrestricted love, because one believes it to be demanded by the Christ event. Essentially, therefore, the celibate's renunciation of marriage expresses his refusal to limit the scope of his love in any way. It is, therefore, a positive, not a negative, commitment. It is not the refusal to love human beings so that one can love God more exclusively. It is a lived affirmation that belief in the God who revealed himself in Christ must be embodied in faith in a love that goes out to every human being without exception, whatever his condition or response.

There are, however, real dangers latent in each of these love-commitments, precisely because each of them gives special emphasis to different aspects of Christian love and hence is open to real exaggeration. The particularity and restricted scope of the love-commitment embodied in the vows of marriage can blunt one's sense of the truly universal love demanded by membership in the kingdom, while the unrestricted scope of the love-commitment embodied in the second vow of religion can deaden one to the fact that human and, therefore, Christian love must terminate, not at an abstraction or at a collectivity, but at concrete individuals to whom one must truly and selflessly give oneself. In other words, while the married person runs the risk of restricting his love to his family circle to the neglect of the greater needs of the Church and of humanity, the celibate runs the risk of never really committing himself in love to any concrete human being. Similarly, the reciprocity ideally present in marriage can lead one to make the beloved's response of love a pre-condition to the maintenance of one's love offer and in the process can deprive the love embodied in a Christian marriage of its essential unrestrictedness in both its conditions and consequences. The lack of contractual reciprocity in the second vow of religion can, on the other hand, lead religious to forget that their love-commitment must always seek to evoke a response of love from each person they love in the name of Christ and hence that a commitment of unrestricted love demands of them a willingness to accept love as well as to give it. These dangers, then, latent in the love-commitments of both married Christians and celibates lead one to the conclusion that the two commitments call out to one another for completion. That is to say, in order to live out the love-commitment embodied in their second vow, religious need, humanly speaking, to meditate the love of Christian married couples and to take it as a partial model of their own celibate love-commitment, while married couples need to meditate the love of celibates and religious as a partial model of their own love, if their relationships in marriage are to retain their integral Christian character.

We should, moreover, protest at this point a tendency not uncommon among many contemporary American Christians, religious included, namely, the tendency to discuss the mission of vowed and of married Christians by contrasting the lives of outstanding lay Christians with the lives of mediocre religious or vice versa. Needless to say, to do so is to substitute somewhat bigoted stereotypes for authentic theological categories. Admittedly, in attempting to establish a problematic for the latter section of the present chapter, we included a few such sophisms in the difficulties we presented as a "challenge" to the reader; but the time has come to call explicit attention to their sophistical intent and to seek to introduce some measure of clarity into the confusion they cause. For if one is to discuss the mission of vowed and of married Christians in terms of concrete examples, one should choose ideal instances of both vocations as the basis of one's discussion. One might, for instance, compare the Christian mission which inspired a Tom Dooley with that which inspired a Mother Cabrini. Such a discussion would, no doubt, be illuminating; and we shall have occasion to return to the issues it raises in the following chapter. Our present concern is, however, to identify the real issue under discussion as the quality of love manifest, on the one hand, in an ideal Christian marriage and, on the other hand, in the ideal living of the second vow of religion. Moreover, our intent in such insistence is to forestall any objections that might arise from the de facto failure of individual religious or of individual married Christians to live up to their public love-commitment in the Church. Their failure is actual and practical and must, of course, be met at that level; but our problem is essentially ideal and speculative.

For ultimately any discussion of the mission of either religious or married people in the Church must concern itself with the discernment of an ideal of conduct, an ideal which seeks to relate the mission and message of Christ to the concrete situation in which contemporary Christians find themselves. Moreover, if the ideal articulated is indeed worthy of pursuit, the failure of religious or of married laymen to understand or pursue it is not necessarily a reflection either on its intrinsic value or on its practicality. Mankind is notorious for failing to pursue worthwhile ideals, especially selfless ones.

A Brief Retrospect

Before proceeding further, however, it will perhaps be useful to summarize our argument up to this point. We have suggested, with the magisterium for our inspiration, that both marriage vows and the second vow of religion are signs of the new covenant because each embodies a love-commitment which emphasizes by resemblance different aspects of God's own love-commitment made to men in the life, death, and glorification of Jesus. Both are ecclesial signs of that covenant, in that they are social commitments publicly approved and sanctioned by the believing community as appropriate responses, if limited ones, in faith and love to the new covenant in Christ. The reciprocity and particularity of the love-commitment embodied in the marriage vows help to ground, but do not fully ground, the sacramentality which is integral to its symbolic likeness to the covenant. (Other factors integral to grounding their sacramentality would, of course, be, for instance, the fact that the love-commitment embodied in those vows is unrestricted in its conditions and consequences and the fact that it is made formally in the name of Christ.) Moreover, when the love-commitment made in marriage vows successfully informs the lived relationship of husband and wife in married life, then those vows, in virtue of their being an ecclesial sign of the covenant, lend to the lives of the Christian couple an ecclesial significance which transcends their individual human love for one another. That is to say, in virtue of the fact that the Christian marriage contract is an ecclesial (because sacramental) sign of the covenant, the lived fidelity of the Christian couple to which that contract pledges them is transformed into an existential quasi-sacramental sign of the purpose and goal of every Christian love-commitment, namely, the mediation of a human community whose mutually selfless love and concern foreshadow the ideal relation of Christ and his Church to which all Christians aspire and which will one day reach fulfillment in the final nuptials of the Lamb. In other words, the mutuality of the love-commitment embodied in marriage vows transforms Christian married love into what might be called a predominantly consummate sign of the covenant, i.e., a sign whose eschatological meaning derives from the human fulfillment to which the love-commitment embodied in the vows tends. But marriage is also recessively an inconsummate sign of the covenant, a sign of the longing of the human heart for a fulfillment in love which transcends the fulfillment possible in this life, precisely through every breach in the lived mutuality of the irrevocable love-commitment embodied in vows which are indissoluble by those who make them, whether that breach occurs between the spouses themselves or on the part of the children they engender, whose spontaneous narcissism leads them to accept far more love than they give in return. In other words, because the love-commitment embodied in marriage is unrestricted in its conditions and consequences, it is an atoning as well as a fulfilling love which freely takes upon itself the suffering which results from the lovelessness of the beloved.

The Problem of Ecclesial Modality

By contrast, the vow of celibacy is predominantly an inconsummate sign of the covenant and only recessively a consummate one. That is to say, not only does the absence of mutuality and the unrestricted scope of the love-commitment embodied in the vow of celibacy prevent it from being a sacrament in the full sense of the term; but it also commits the one so vowed to live a life which embodies the gratuity of Christian love more perfectly than its mutuality. In other words, the celibate commits himself to living a life which is devoted in a special way to evoking a love response from those who are most in need of love and hence are in fact least capable of responding in kind to love's offer. But it is important to note that celibacy is only factually, not teleologically, inconsummate. That is to say, the celibate is not a person whose driving purpose in life is the avoidance of every exchange of love. The true celibate is vowed to much more than being a bachelor or an old maid. As a celibate, he must truly and lovingly give himself to others with the explicit purpose and hope of evoking from them that response of love which is the fulfillment of his own self-gift. But the fact of the matter is that the celibate's love remains to a large extent inconsummate, certainly more than does the married man's or woman's, to the extent, that is, that he actually lives his celibacy and seeks out those who are most starved for love and hence least capable of responding to it in kind. At the same time, to the extent that the celibate's love is successful in evoking a response of love from the beloved, it, too, is a consummate ecclesial sign of the covenant, but only recessively so.

But even in those instances where lived celibacy is in fact predominantly consummate, i.e., even if the celibate always encounters (as unlikely as it may seem) a fulfilling response of love to his or her self-gift to others, the celibate life, viewed as an ecclesial sign of the covenant, would remain only recessively consummate. For the absence of mutuality in the initial love-commitment, i.e., in the vow itself, provides a different ecclesial context for interpreting the meaning even of the mutuality of the human love experienced in the course of celibate living. That is to say, the absence of mutuality in the celibate's initial ecclesial love-commitment manifests more clearly than in the case of marriage vows that, ideally at least, the celibate has not made the beloved's response to his love in any sense a pre-condition either to the offering of love in Christ's name or to the maintenance of that offer, whatever the beloved's response may be.

Needless to say, however, no celibate can renounce the need for love which lies deep in the heart of every man and woman. This fact, togther with the factually inconsummate character of the love-offer made in celibacy, grounds the celibate's need for a community in which he or she can in fact find the affection, support, and acceptance humanly necessary to sustain the kind of self-gift which a life of celibacy demands. But we note this conclusion here only in passing and will have opportunity to return to it in a later chapter. It follows from what has been said that when viewed as an ecclesial sign of the covenant, celibacy, because it is a predominantly inconsummate and recessively consummate sign of the covenant, embodies more perfectly both the unrestricted scope of Christian love and its gratuity. For on the one hand, a married Christian's love of his fellow man, when viewed as an ecclesial sign of the covenant, remains unrestricted in its scope in virtue of his baptismal, not of his marriage, commitment. On the other hand, indissoluble Christian marriage, embodies the gratuity of love, not through the living of the marriage vows, but through the breach of the love-commitment they embody, whereas celibacy, when viewed as an ecclesial sign of the covenant, expresses better than marriage the wholly unrestricted character of Christian love precisely by being lived. For celibacy, in the living of its love-commitment, tends of its nature to be factually inconsummate, and hence gratuitous. Lived celibacy is, moreover, guided by need rather than by romantic attraction, hence, the unrestricted character of its scope.

Marriage, on the other hand, when viewed as a predominantly consummate ecclesial sign of the covenant, precisely because it is both particular in its scope and mutual, embodies more perfectly than celibacy the purpose and the sacramental character of Christian love. For the purpose of every love-commitment is the mediation of personal communion through the evocation of a response of love. At the same time, married love, by its particularity manifests more clearly than celibacy that love is, as a Thomistic philosophy of love insists, realistic, i.e., that it reaches out to the beloved in all of the concrete "taleity" of his being. By contrast, the predominance of the unrestricted scope of the celibate's love-commitment renders its particularity recessive, even though the celibate's love, if it is to be true love, must also be realistic; just as the predominance of the gratuity of the celibate's love renders its mutuality recessive, even though mutuality remains its ultimate purpose.

It also follows from what has been said that in order to live a successful life of celibacy one must do more than preserve one's chastity intact. The successful celibate embodies in his life a particular quality of love. Hence, the ultimate proof of whether or not one does indeed possess a charism for celibate living is not the capacity to preserve physical chastity alone but also whether or not one can maintain a love-commitment signalized by its unrestricted scope and by its gratuity, in spite of the loneliness and absence of reciprocity of love which often attends a celibate life. A bitter old bachelor or a bitter old maid is not a successful celibate, however physically or spiritually chaste, however temperate or mortified he or she might be. Success in celibacy is success in embodying love, not through sexual intercourse, but through spending oneself and one's means to evoke a love-response from the lonely, the embittered, the loveless, and the oppressed, and from those better situated, a response as unrestricted in its scope as the celibate's own ecclesial commitment of love.

The Semantic Problem

We may conclude, therefore, that as in the case of the first vow of religion, the vow of "chastity" or of "celibacy" poses serious semantic problems. For both terms, "chastity" as well as "celibacy," are strongly associated with an explanation of the vow which is more preoccupied with temperance than it is with the embodiment of love. For the sake of clarity, then, we shall in the future cease to speak of the second vow of religion as a vow either of chastity (or, more improperly, of celibacy). Instead, we shall refer to it as a vow of unrestricted love, of a love, that is, which is unrestricted in its scope as well as in its conditions and consequences.

Facing the Issues

The foregoing explanation of the vow of unrestricted love helps to remove many of the difficulties which have surrounded the second vow of religion. It helps, for instance, to explain the malaise of many contemporary religious with the manual explanation of the vow. To restrict the meaning of the second vow to a public exercise of temperance, as manual asceticism tends to do, is to miss the point and the purpose of the vow. Religious do not take a vow of unrestricted love merely as a display of moral one-upmanship over Christians who are carnal and oversexed. They take the vow because they experience a value in trying to bear special public witness, with whatever measure of success they can with the help of God's grace achieve, to the wholly unrestricted scope and gratuity of Christian love.

By the same token, the purpose of the vow has nothing to do with a neurotic flight from love. The self-gift that is demanded by it is a human and total one. It is the gift of one's heart and hence includes the gift of one's affections as well.

It also follows from what has been said that social taboos restricting the activity of religious in order to protect them from exposure to ordinary sexual stimuli have little to do with the positive purpose of the second vow and may in many instances pose obsolete and unnecessary obstacles to the active living of the love-commitment which the vow embodies. We no longer live in the patristic age with its elaborate social buttresses, ludicrous to American eyes, to strengthen and preserve the purity of consecrated virgins. In point of fact, in an American context, such taboos, precisely because they are largely absent from our culture, often suggest the very opposite of what they originally intended. In the patristic age, the taboos placed on consecrated virgins symbolized the inner consecration of those holy women to God. But in an age and country in which women have achieved a much greater degree of social emancipation, the artificial preservation of archaic taboos suggests, despite the questionable attempt of spiritual writers to ground them in some kind of divine mandate, not an inner commitment to purity, but an absence of it. In our day, country, and age, ordinary men and women cannot help but wonder why, if religious are so inwardly committed to chastity, they need to be preserved from the least erotic stimulus. Is their virtue after all so weak as to be vanquished by "temptations against purity" that any other Christian man or woman has learned to cope with and conquer as an integral part of his everyday living?

It is also clear that if young religious are to live a life of genuine love of others in Christ's name, they need normal emotional development especially during their formative years. One cannot show genuine affection for others in Christ's name without experiencing what genuine human affection is. To deny religious normal social outlets for their affection, to deny them ordinary social contact with members of the opposite sex, particularly in their formative years, is not to facilitate their living of the positive meaning of the second vow but to render it more difficult. For unless the unrestricted scope of a religious's love is constantly and vitally informed by genuine warmth and affection, it runs the serious risk of degenerating into mere bachelorhood or spinsterhood.

At the same time, an understanding of the positive purpose of the second vow provides religious with a positive norm for regulating their social relations, especially with members of the opposite sex. As religious, they are vowed to a life which witnesses in a special way to the wholly unrestricted scope of Christian love. If they are to be faithful to that love-commitment, they must avoid the radical circumscription of their love and affections which inevitably attends genuine romantic involvement. They must, in other words, keep a prayerful watch over their dealings with other people, particularly with persons of the opposite sex, as a means of safeguarding the quality of love to which they are publicly committed.

The understanding of the positive purpose of the second vow which we have proposed also makes it clear that its intent is not primarily to stimulate one's solitary, vertical ascent to God. The fact that the love-commitment embodied in a vow of unrestricted love is essentially ecclesial in its orientation demands of the one who makes it a deep human involvement with other people, not a flight from them, an involvement which, if lived, often exceeds the sacrifices of a one-to-one relationship demanded by a marriage partnership. The inner tranquility which Christian prayer produces comes with a genuine love of and concern for the needs of others in Christ's name. True Christian tranquility of soul is, therefore, contentment in one's personal love-commitment whatever the sacrifices it may involve. It is not the tranquility of apathy. In a religious of love, the cult of inner contemplative tranquility cannot rest upon the attempt to close one's eyes to the needs of others or upon the flight from personal and social involvement. The person, then, who turns to the religious life exclusively for such questionable motives in order to find there tranquil liberation from the worries of ordinary human living has reason to question the integrity of any prayers that emerge from such an easily won tranquility, even should one be able to achieve it in fact.

When, moreover, the second vow of religion is seen in dynamic terms as a human love-commitment embodying a special quality of love, instead of in static, repressive terms as an exercise in pre-marital mortification and self-control, then some of the claims for a life of celibacy take on greater plausibility. It is clear, for instance, that ideally, the vow of unrestricted love is a special ecclesial symbol of the love of Christ for his Church because, as an ecclesial sign of the covenant, it embodies the gratuity and unrestricted scope of divine love more perfectly than does the marriage love-commitment. For the same reason, one can also understand the Tridentine claim that it is "better and more blessed" to choose celibacy than marriage. The claim has nothing to do with the personal sanctity of celibates in comparison with married people but with the ideal ecclesial significance of a vow of unrestricted love when compared with the ideal ecclesial significance of marriage vows. Nor does the claim prevent marriage from providing ideally a clearer ecclesial witness to the mutuality, the sacramentality, and the particularity of Christian love than does the second vow of religion.

Moreover, the concrete living of a vow of unrestricted love becomes existentially a symbol of the final union of Christ and his Church precisely through the vowed Christian's active and loving service of others in Christ's name. It is a means of "adhering directly to the Lord" in the precise sense that in the love of Christ, understood in a genuinely spiritual rather than in an exclusive, quasi-marital, sense, one seeks to be genuinely committed without restriction or reservation to whomever one meets or has occasion to deal with in Christ's name. For as we have seen, even though the vowed Christian's commitment to Christ is total, nevertheless, integral to a commitment to the risen Christ is commitment in faith to one's fellow man in his name. Moreover, even though when viewed as the ecclesial sign of Christ's covenant, a vow of unrestricted love is only recessively consummate, in the sense explained above, nevertheless, to the extent that it is indeed consummate, it anticipates the fulfillment of the kingdom, not only negatively, i.e., in the renunciation which it demands and which will be rewarded on the last day, but positively as well, in the response and reciprocity of love which the gratuitous self-offering of the vowed Christian succeeds in evoking from those he seeks in love to serve. When viewed as a positive, dynamic love-commitment, unrestricted in its scope, the second vow of religion does indeed, as Pope Paul has suggested, open up the vowed Christian to the limitless possibilities of loving and should ideally broaden his sense of Christian responsibility. Similarly, when such a love-commitment is lived, it is truly a sign of a mature personality. In priests, it can indeed become a kind of spiritual fatherhood and should also stimulate pastoral zeal and lead to active dedication to the new and absorbing realities of the kingdom. To the extent that it involves one intimately with the problems and sorrows of the suffering and the oppressed, it can indeed give one a deeper knowledge of the human heart than a one-to-one marriage relationship. Finally, the special spiritual help claimed for one vowed to a life of unrestricted love need not be interpreted in terms of some quasi-mystical grace, mysteriously imparted to an isolated individual independently of his active involvement with the service of others in Christ's name. The special spiritual aid given to those vowed to a life of unrestricted love would seem, at least in the first instance, to be their own growth through actual involvement with other human beings in the name of their risen Lord, in a love which is not only gratuitously offered and sustained but which is also unrestricted in its scope. But while it is easy to see how the active living of a gratuitous commitment to unrestricted love involves, ideally at least, all of these characteristics, it is difficult, if not impossible, to understand in the terms of manual asceticism's view of the second vow, why the mere renunciation of marriage and the cultivation of the moral do's and don't's of pre-marital chastity need involve any of them.

The interpretation of the meaning of the second vow of religion as a vow of gratuitous and unrestricted love also enables one to evaluate some of the patristic reflections on the meaning of virginity. It alerts one, for one thing, to a certain anti-corporeal trend in patristic thought. The love-commitment made in a vow of unrestricted love is not "angelic" in the sense of being incorporeal or disembodied. Indeed, this love-commitment demands active embodiment, even though the unrestricted quality of the love involved precludes its becoming embodied in an exclusive romantic love, leading to sexual union. Instead, its embodiment must take the form of a life of gratuitous sharing—the free, loving, and affectionate gift to others in Christ's name of one's possessions, talents, and very self in the hope of eliciting from them a response of love that is equally gratuitous and unrestricted in its scope. Such a love is "angelic" in the biblical sense of the term. That is to say, it imitates the zealous consecration of God's messengers to the task of cooperating in the accomplishment of his eschatological kingdom on earth through the formation of a human community of mutual and gratuitous love in Christ's name. Thus, just as the first vow of religion demands the second in order to prevent gratuitous sharing from degenerating into a purely formal, external exercise, devoid of love, so the second vow of religion demands the first, if its love-commitment is not to degenerate into the merest self-deception. For unless a vowed Christian's promise to God of gratuitous and unrestricted love finds subsequent embodiment in a life of gratuitous and unrestricted sharing with others in Christ's name, that religious is deluding himself if he thinks he is practicing the virtues truly demanded by the second vow, even though he or she be in fact physically and mentally chaste as the archangel Gabriel.

The claim of some of the Fathers that only virgins belong

completely to God is also revealed to be an exaggerated one. Like the vow of unrestricted love, the irrevocable love-commitment made in marriage, unrestricted as it is in its conditions and consequences, demands and presupposes (not excludes) the complete offering of oneself in trust and confidence to Christ. By the same token, the second vow of religion is not the expression of a love for God which excludes the love of other people. On the contrary, analogously to marriage vows, it demands and presupposes a total dedication to other human beings in the name of Christ. The two love-commitments differ only in the ecclesial mode and scope of their love and self-dedication.

Moreover, it is quite clear that a vow of unrestricted love does not, in spite of the implications of some patristic texts, consecrate a religious to the pursuit of emotional apathy. The vowed Christian must in virtue of the love-commitment demanded by his second vow become humanly involved with the people he is trying to help in Christ's name; and human involvement is impossible without some element of affectivity. The vowed Christian must, however, be careful to avoid that species of affective involvement which would limit the scope and the gratuity of his love-commitment. The avoidance, however, is not a flight from love, but the effort to preserve a certain quality of love.

It is also clear that the "separation from the world" demanded of religious by a vow of unrestricted love should not be interpreted in crude terms of physical separation, nor does it consist in the careful observance of special social taboos for unmarried girls. On the contrary, the vow presupposes an active social commitment to others in Christ's name. (Even in the patristic age, virgins were signalized for their willingness to "give alms.") Moreover, in contemporary American society, we would suggest, the concrete living of the second vow demands that vowed Christians of both sexes, who are devoted to an active apostolate, should, while avoiding any conduct likely to lead to romantic involvement, be allowed in other matters to deal with their peers of both sexes on the same social basis as other unwed Christians. That is to say, in a contemporary American context, the active religious should remain "separated" from a selfish and sinful world not externally by social taboos, but prayerfully and existentially by the quality of his love for others and of his active involvement in the world.

Two Objections

Two final difficulties remain to be resolved. The first arises from the very explanation of the second vow of religion proposed in this chapter. For on the one hand, we have insisted that love is essentially realistic, that it seeks the beloved in all of his or her concrete particularity. At the same time we have also insisted that the love-commitment of the second vow is unrestricted, and hence universal, in its scope. On the face of it, therefore, the love demanded by the second vow of religion would seem to involve a contradiction, since it demands an object which is simultaneously universal and particular in its scope. To put the problem a bit differently, if actual love is essentially particular in the realism of its object, universal love would seem to be impossible of embodiment, an unbelievable ideal used to rationalize one's failure to love anyone truly and realistically.

The objection is a good one, since it forces us to concretize what precisely one means by unrestricted love. As we have already indicated, unrestricted love cannot terminate either at an abstraction or at a collectivity, not if it is to be truly love. In other words, the embodiment of the love-commitment made in the second vow of religion does indeed involve its particularization and, hence, in some sense, its restriction to one concrete individual rather than another. What distinguishes the vow of unrestricted love from marriage vows, however, is the fact that the ground of that particularization is not human romantic and erotic attraction, but the needs of the people with whom one lives and deals. The love-commitment in the second vow is primarily need-oriented, and secondarily individual-oriented. As a result, the individual object of love must shift as needs are satisfied and as situations change. In other words, to say that the love-commitment made in the second vow is "unrestricted in its scope" means that by it one is committed in every new situation to re-evaluate the hierarchy of one's human involvements and to seek out as the object of one's love whoever is in greatest need of it. Its scope is, therefore, not unrestricted in any merely collective or abstractly universal sense. Its scope is unrestricted in that the primary object of love cannot be determined a priori but only concretely and situationally. In this sense, the love-offer embodied in the second vow of religion does indeed differ qualitatively from the commitment made in married love; for by the latter commitment, one promises that one's spouse will remain the first and lifelong object of one's love even though one will almost certainly encounter during the course of one's life others whose needs will in fact be greater. Hence, one does in fact embody concretely the unrestricted scope of the love demanded by the second vow to the extent that one makes the greater need of the beloved the ground for the selection of the person to whom one especially offers love. In other words, unrestricted love is simply love which is "open-ended" in its object and situational in the selection of that object. It is need-oriented rather than individual-oriented love; but because within each situation it is concrete and particular, it is indeed genuine love.

The second objection is related indirectly to the preceding one. For it is quite clear that there can be and no doubt are married Christians whose deep religious faith leads them to practice the kind of unrestricted love of others in Christ's name which is supposed to characterize the second vow of religion. By their baptism and confirmation, they are, moreover, ecclesially committed to such love of others in the name of Christ. In addition, the mutual support in love and faith given one another by Christian married couples should ideally at least strengthen both partners in their practice of a more unrestricted extra-familial love. In other words, it is quite clear that religious have not cornered the market on unrestricted love any more than they have cornered the market on holiness and divine companionship. Is not, then, a vow of unrestricted love ecclesially redundant? What does such a vow add that is not already contained in one's initial baptismal commitment? Or to put the same question a bit differently, what is it that would ultimately justify one's assuming burdens and obligations of a vow of unrestricted love in addition to one's baptismal promises? Surely not just efficiency in one's apostolic work. The apostolic efficiency of many married laymen and the apostolic inefficiency of many religious deprive such a merely factual explanation of any real plausibility. How, then, are we to justify taking a special vow of unrestricted love?

The objection is also a useful one because it shifts our attention from the ideal of unrestricted love considered as an ideal to the vow of unrestricted love considered precisely as a vow. Moreover, there is good reason to suspect that one source of current difficulties with the second vow of religion considered as a vow is the fact that contemporary American Catholics, for a number of historical reasons not too difficult to discern, have lost and need to rediscover that ecclesial sense—that sense of the Christian community as a community whose organic structure has prophetic significance for the rest of human society—which gives justification to the vows of religion considered precisely as vows. The problem, needless to say, is not whether this or that individual should pronounce a vow of unrestricted love, but why the very possibility of making such a vow should exist in a community in which everyone is already pledged to a life of love which is unrestricted in its scope, conditions, and consequences.

One way of resolving the difficulty lies in the attempt to balance the following related and now familiar facts: (1) marriage, by reason of its sacramentality, is a public, ecclesial sign of the covenant. Through the quality of the love-commitment it embodies it represents primarily the reciprocity and particularity of God's own love-commitment made to men in the new covenant in Christ; (2) the sacramental particularization in marriage of one's baptismal love-commitment not only presupposes that the married partners have been baptized, but it is also a legitimate way of perfecting and bringing to fulfillment one's baptismal commitment to love others in Christ's image. At the same time, it draws prophetic attention in a public and ecclesial way to certain aspects of the Christian love-commitment more strikingly than to others; (3) the Christian community as a community, and not merely as individuals, has the obligation of bearing public witness to every aspect of divine and Christian love; (4) the fact, therefore, that the community of the baptized who have publicly and sacramentally accepted this very obligation as a community, sanctions and blesses a post-baptismal act which is an ecclesial sign of the covenant, viz., the exchange of vows which by the very structure of the act witness primarily to the particularity and reciprocity of divine love through the radical restriction of the scope of one's baptismal love-commitment, makes it, at the very least, highly fitting that the same community in virtue of its obligations as a community to witness publicly to every aspect of the divine love embodied in the new covenant encourage and sanction another kind of public act, viz., the taking of a public vow of unrestricted love, which will serve as a clear, prophetic, ecclesial countersign of the fact that the limited witness to divine love embodied in marriage vows is indeed limited, a countersign whose purpose is to make clear that the meaning and scope both of the divine love for men and of the Christian's baptismal love-commitment to others in Christ's name is not exhausted by the reciprocity and particularity of love to which marriage ideally witnesses. On the contrary, both divine love and Christian love are also unrestricted in their scope and gratuitous.

In other words, the public ecclesial witness given by married people in virtue of their public, prophetically significant vows to witness in a special way to the reciprocity and particularity of divine love needs to be counterbalanced at an ecclesial level by a public witness, sanctioned by the same community that recognizes the sacramentality of marriage vows, to the gratuity and unrestricted scope of that same love, if the total, public, prophetic witness of the community as a community is to be ecclesially and "sacramentally" integral, i.e., is to be a public, communal witness to every dimension of the divine love revealed in Christ. It follows, therefore, that individual acts of gratuitous and universal extra-familial love performed by married Christians are individual acts of piety, nothing more. But the same acts performed by a Christian publicly vowed to unrestricted love are, precisely in virtue of his vow which carries with it the public sanction and blessing of the community, no longer merely acts of individual piety but a public affirmation about the scope and gratuity of divine love made by a vowed Christian in the name of that community which wishes to dramatize prophetically that even though it recognizes that Christian marriage gives special emphasis to certain aspects of one's baptismal love-commitment, nevertheless the scope and gratuity of divine love exceeds the witness that is possible to Christian married couples *in virtue of their marriage vows.* In other words, the vow of unrestricted love gives to the practice of unrestricted love an ecclesial value and significance which is not present in spontaneous individual acts of unrestricted love and which is needed if the Christian community's existential, ecclesial, public witness as a community to the full scope of its common baptismal commitment to Christian love is to remain genuinely integral.

Needless to say, the option to spend one's life as a public and positive countersign to the valid, though necessarily limited, ecclesial witness to divine love undertaken by married Christians as married is a free one and cannot be demanded as a strict obligation of anyone. But if the above analysis is in fact correct, those drawn by the Spirit to pronounce such a public vow of unrestricted love should be Christians who are moved by a strong ecclesial sense of the importance to the prophetic integrity of the existential, collective, public witness of the Christian community as a community in every age of its existence to its enduring belief as a community of living faith in the gratuity and unrestricted scope of divine love.

But the vow of unrestricted love is not only important as a public, prophetic, ecclesial sign that Christian love is not exhausted by the quality of love embodied in marriage vows. It is important for more immediately pragmatic and practical reasons as well. For as we saw in our reflections on the preceding objection, marriage vows establish a hierarchy of loving which is relatively independent of the situation in which one finds oneself. Though married Christians must, of course, avoid positive sin in dealing with their neighbor, they are in fact committed to spend their thought and energy first of all and primarily on finding ways to embody their marital love for one another and for their family. Only when those needs are truly satisfied is the married Christian free to consider the needs of others less well circumstanced than they. Hence, even though it is not impossible for individual married lay people to give outstanding personal witness to their individual commitment to a love which is unrestricted in its scope and gratuitous, married Christians who take their marriage obligations seriously most often find their time primarily occupied in witnessing within the family to the reciprocity and particularity of the love demanded by their marriage vows. If then the needs of those who are humanly and culturally most deprived of love are to be met, it is practically speaking of considerable importance that a significant number of Christians devote their time and energies to meeting those needs before any others by living a life of love which is primarily and situationally need-oriented rather than individual-oriented. In other words, religious take their second vow not specifically to achieve greater practical efficiency in their work. To suppose so is, as we shall see later, to confuse a "job" with a "vocation." Work efficiency is dependent on personal endowments, limiting circumstances, and any number of other variables. What the religious seeks by his or her second vow is greater efficiency in loving, the freedom to seek out in every situation the greatest need for love and to spend oneself to the best of one's ability trying to meet that end.

One word of caution is in place before ending this rather lengthy discussion. Even though manual asceticism in its explanation of the vow of unrestricted love is deficient in providing a positive explanation of the purpose of the vow and is often couched in somewhat exaggerated language, its attempt to alert the vowed Christian to the possible psychological and moral consequences of excessive exposure to erotic stimuli is not without its point. Vowed Christians will not lose the sexual and romantic vulnerability of every child of Adam just because they may have achieved a measure of social emancipation from the patristic taboos placed upon consecrated virgins. Nor should they delude themselves about the difficulty of maintaining a commitment to a life of unrestricted love without the cultivation of emotional self-control or without the exercise of a reasonable vigilance over their exposure to persons and situations which are likely to lead to romantic involvement.

Our examination of the last two objections to the explanation of the vow of unrestricted love here offered has led us to an initial consciousness of the quasi-sacramental ecclesial dimension of religious living. An examination of the third vow of religion should, however, expand and explicitate that initial consciousness. We refer, of course, to the vow of service.

Notes

1. Ws 13:10–14:31.
2. Jdt 16:14;Ws 7:27–30.
3. Ps 104:30;Ez 37:1–14.
4. Ps 127:3;128:2–3.
5. Ps 109:8–11.
6. Jb 18:18–19.
7. Jdg 11:37.
8. Gn 11:30;16:1;25:21.
9. Jr 16:3.
10. Lv 21:7,13–15.
11. Jdt 16:22;8:4–6.
12. Lk 2:36–37.
13. Ho 1.
14. Dt 4:33.
15. Is 1:21.
16. Ez 16:7–16, *passim.*
17. Ez 23:47.
18. Is 54:4–5.
19. Jr 31:2–3.
20. Ez 16:55–56;Jr 2:2–3.
21. Ez 16:59–60;Is 54:6–10.
22. Is 61:10.
23. 1Co 7:25.
24. Mt 19:1–12;Mk 10:1–12.
25. Mt 19:10–12.
26. Lk 20:34–38.
27. Jn 15:13.
28. Jn 14:19.
29. Mt. 26:26–29;Mk 14:22–25;Lk 22:19–20;1Co 11:23–25.
30. Mt 25:1–13.
31. Jn 2:12.
32. Jn 3:29.
33. 2Co 11:2–3.
34. Rv 9:7–9.
35. Mt 1:23.
36. Lk 1:27,35.
37. Ep 5:25.
38. 1Co 7:29–32.
39. 1Co 7:33–35.
40. 1Co 7:5; 39–40.
41. 1Co 7:1–9.
42. 1Tm 5:5, 11.
43. 1Co 7:1–9.
44. 1Tm 5:5.
45. 1Tm 5:11–16.
46. 1Tm 5:16.
47. ML 2,915A.
48. ML 1,1316A.
49. MG 26,1173C.
50. ML 2,280C.
51. ML 1,128A;MG 52,563.
52. ML 4,461A.
53. MG 36,296C.
54. MG 47, 525; 48, 540.
55. ML 22,395.
56. ML 16,202D.
57. MG 36,576C.
58. ML 23,246C.
59. ML 16,191C;cf.ML 16,325A;23,255A;22,422.
60. ML 16,208C.
61. ML 22,871.
62. MG 28,253C,257B.
63. MG 36,296A.
64. ML 4,443A;4,461A;MG 28,253C;28,269D,276C,280A;30,725C;48,584; ML 16,278B,286C,291C,299C;MG 28,269C,276C,280A,302, 725C; 48, 584.
65. ML 22,404.
66. MG 12,529D.
67. MG 12,761B.
68. ML 4,443A.
69. ML 4,446A.
70. MG 30,672B.
71. MG 30,725C.
72. ML 32,808.
73. MG 11,1489D.
74. MG 25,640A.
75. MG 47,376;ML 16,205A.
76. ML 16,272D.

77. ML 16,273A.
78. ML 2,915A.
79. MG 14,1205A.
80. MG 31,625D.
81. MG 48,580.
82. MG 47,376.
83. ML 16,195D,197A.
84. ML 16,273A.
85. ML 23,227C.
86. ML 22,406.
87. ML 40,402.
88. ML 40, 433.
89. ML 2,910A.
90. ML 1,1188B.
91. ML 4,448A.
92. ML 4,451B,454A,457A,45AA.
93. MG 28,253C.
94. MG 28,264B.
95. MG 36,296C.
96. MG 37,1049A.
97. MG 32,289C.
98. MG 28,257B,264D,269D,276C; 47, 525;48,584;ML 16,225B,332C;22, 403.
99. ML 2,915A;16,200A;ML 16,222C, 278B;22,1056.
100. MG 28,257B,280A;46,348B;48, 580;50,745;ML 16,332C.
101. ML 16,278B.
102. ML 16,291C,299C.
103. ML 22,1113.
104. ML 22,871.
105. ML 22,1113.
106. DS 118–119.
107. DS 185.
108. DS 321–322.
109. DS 711.
110. DS 1809.
111. DS 1810.
112. DS 461–462.
113. DS 718.
114. DS 1012.
115. DS 1327.
116. DS 3911.
117. DS 3912.
118. *Dogmatic Constitution on the Church*, 42.
119. *Decree on Priestly Formation*, 10.
120. *Decree on the Ministry and Life of Priests*, 16.
121. *Ibid.*
122. *Decree on Priestly Formation*, 10; *Decree on the Appropriate Renewal of Religious Life*, 12.
123. *Sacerdotalis Caelibatus*, 5–11.
124. *Ibid.*, 19–20.
125. *Ibid.*, 22–24.
126. *Ibid.*, 26–32.
127. *Ibid.*, 33–34.
128. *Ibid.*, 56.
129. *Ibid.*, 57.
130. J. Fichter, S.J., *Religion as an Occupation* (South Bend, Ind.: U. of Notre Dame Press, 1966), pp. 34ff.
131. McNaspy, *op. cit.*, pp. 65–72
132. Örsy, *op. cit.*, p. 89.
133. Bernard Haring, C.S.S.R., "Love and Celibacy," in *Contemporary Spirituality* (New York: Macmillan, 1968), p. 81.
134. Örsy, *op. cit.*, p. 26; Gustave Martelet, S.J., "The Church's Holiness and Religious Life," in *Contemporary Spirituality*, p. 103.
135. Martlet, *op. cit.*, pp. 104–106.
136. Örsy, *op. cit.*, p. 88.
137. E. Schillebeeckx, O.P., *Celibacy* (New York: Sheed & Ward, 1968), pp. 82–85.
138. *Ibid.*, pp. 95; 105–109.

IV

Service

The people of Israel looked back upon their exodus from Egypt as a passage from slavery to the free service of the living God. By the Sinai covenant they freely bound themselves to worship Yahweh alone and to observe all of his commands; and they received in return Yahweh's assurance of the special blessings reserved for his faithful servants. The religious history of God's people can almost be summarized as their gradual collective realization of the full implications of the task of service to which they had committed themselves.[1-6]

Complexities of Divine Service

It might be well however, to recall at the beginning of these schematic reflections that our problem is not a simple one. Of all the concepts used in the Old Testament, that of "service" is one of the richest in connotation and, therefore, one most open to impoverishment by explicitation. Still, the attempt to explicitate such a notion is, in most cases, the only means available to us for comprehending at least some of its more important implications.

To begin with, then, the worship of service has as its purpose to school men in the rigorous discipline of faith, to teach them to place their whole confidence, without restriction or pre-condition, in the fidelity of the God who saves. Thus, Abraham, whose faith and obedience mediates God's first alliance with his people, merits the name of "servant of Yahweh." The same title is applied repeatedly to Moses, whose heroic faith mediates the Sinai covenant itself and whose belief in the Lord's saving power transforms him into the successful liberator of his people.[7] It is also one of David's titles, earned by his unselfish fidelity to the mission given him by the Lord of governing Israel with equity and of leading them to victory over their enemies.[8]

Clearly, then, in the context of Old Testament belief, faith learned through the service of God is not a passive or a static thing but on the contrary implies a confidence in God boundless enough to inspire great deeds in his name. To serve God is to be willing unhesitatingly to take any risk in order to bring about the accomplishment of the divine will on earth. For the willingness to do great things in the name of God is the real measure of one's faith in his saving power and of one's fidelity to his will.

As a result the true servant of God experiences the call to service as a mission proceeding from God himself. To serve is to be sent by God to accomplish some task of importance in the history of salvation.[9,10]

Moreover, because service proceeds from a divine commission, it also implies a real bond, a communion linking the living God and those who serve him one to the other.[11] As we saw, however, in the preceding chapter, the bond which links the living God to the people he has chosen is also a bond of love.[12] Moreover, as we have also seen, by the prescriptions of the covenant code, this same loving service of the living God had become linked inseparably to effective concern for the needs of one's fellow man.[13]

We may conclude, then, that the purpose of the service of God enjoined by the Sinai covenant was indeed a comprehensive one. The covenant sought to school man in the obedience of faith, to teach him to place his whole confidence in the Lord, and to dare great things in the name of his God. But to live constantly in such a worshipful spirit of inner abandonment is to live reconciled to God in a vital bond of mutual love which finds expression in one's personal fidelity to the task of accomplishing one's mission from God within the history of salvation in covenanted reconciliation with one's fellow man, according to the right order revealed by God in the prescriptions of the law. The purpose of the service of the living God was, then, nothing else than the establishment of God's justice upon earth through the right ordering of men's relations with God and with one another in society.

The Suffering Servant

But if we are to believe the message of the prophets, the people of God in their efforts to accomplish their mission of service were with predictable human fallibility by and large a failure.[14,15]

The punishment for this disobedience meted out by the terms of the covenant was the simple annihilation of the kingdoms of Israel and of Judah. But Israel's experience of political dissolution and exile also brought with it the realization of a new redemptive dimension to the meaning of the service of God. Written at the close of the Babylonian exile, the Book of Consolation of second Isaiah describes in a series of scattered songs or canticles the mysterious figure of the suffering servant of Yahweh. Scholars are divided in their opinions as to whether the songs should be treated as a literary unit, whether they refer to a real historical figure, and if so, whether they all refer to the same person. Whatever may be the solution to these exegetical puzzles, the songs provide a cumulative meditation on the meaning of service which reflects both the impact of the exile on Jewish religious experience as well as the messianic aspirations of the people of God at the approach of Cyrus, the conqueror of Babylon, whom they regarded as their divinely appointed liberator.

In point of fact, defeat and exile at the hands of Nebuchadnezzar, king of Babylon, had evoked a complex religious response from the devout Jew. He experienced a sense of the collective guilt of his people and a feeling of their abandonment by God, a sense of inner purification by passage through the fires of political disaster, together with mixed sentiments of grief and repentance toward God and of bitterness toward his conquerors. With the sudden approach of Cyrus and his armies, however, new hopes for national rebirth began to stir true believers once again and to motivate new longings for messianic deliverance and for a new reconciliation with God. Such a longing had indeed been kept alive even in exile by prophecies in the book of Jeremiah and by the writings of prophets in exile like Ezechiel.[16,17]

It is from this complex politico-religious experience that the figure of the suffering servant emerges in the pages of second Isaias, a messianic figure whose career is presented in terms which are colored both by the Jewish experience of national death and of possible rebirth and perhaps also by imagery adapted from the Babylonian cult of a dying and rising god.

In the first song the servant of Yahweh is described as the chosen one of God, set apart to establish a reign of universal justice upon earth.[18] He is also a compelling figure of quiet power and gentleness, one who "does not break the crushed reed nor quench the wavering flame."[19-20]

In the second song, the servant appears as another Jeremiah. Like the great prophet, the servant has been called from his mother's womb; his mission is to reunite the scattered tribes of Israel.[21-22] Like Jeremiah, the servant experiences opposition and personal frustration in the accomplishment of his mission, even though the faithful hand of God always sustains him in the face of every trial.[23] But the scope of the servant's mission exceeds that of any ordinary prophet: he is God's appointed instrument of a universal salvation.[24]

In the third song, the servant speaks in his own person; assuming the tone of a biblical wise man, he declares himself the docile pupil of the Lord, one who waits upon divine instruction daily in order to teach it to the oppressed.[25] But in the present song, the opposition to the servant hinted at before becomes both more explicit and more vehement. For despite the servant's docility to the divine word, he is greeted with insult, mockery, and derision.[26-29]

In the fourth and final song, the meaning and purpose of the suffering of God's servant is brought into sharper focus. Here the brutality of the servant's tormentors is presented vividly in terms of the enormity of his anguish and agony. Indeed, as a result of his suffering the servant is so disfigured that he can scarcely be recognized as human: He is pitiable, a shocking spectacle which evokes from men only astonishment and silence.[30] Though chosen by God and assured of prosperity and exaltation in the opening verses of the song, the servant has been transformed nonetheless into a thing of horror.[31] Though innocent of all fault, the servant is finally forcibly seized and unjustly condemned to death.[32]

Far from finding the tragedy of the servant pointless, however, the author of the song insists upon the divine purpose which motivates the servant's sufferings. For though the servant himself is innocent of all guilt and deserves no punishment for sins of his own, yet it is the plan of God that he accomplish the work of universal salvation appointed him by bearing in his own body the burden of the people's guilt. "And yet ours were the sufferings he bore, ours the sorrows he carried. But we, we thought of him as someone punished, struck by God, and brought low. Yet he was pierced through for our faults, crushed for our sins."[33]

In spite of everything, in spite even of the grave, the servant of Yahweh will yet be exalted if only he trusts in the very God who has burdened him in his innocence with the bitter task of atoning for the sins of men.[34]

The notion of service which emerges from these songs is an exceedingly complex one and results from the convergence of a number of distinct lines of Old Testament thought. The servant is a prophet, a wise man, a messianic king; but in each case the meaning of the service he renders is defined in terms of his fidelity in the face of innocent suffering. He "sets his face like flint" even to the point of submitting without protest to an unjust and degrading death. His ultimate triumph over the grave anticipates in some respects the third chapter of the book of Wisdom in which the death of the innocent poor man is described as "full of immortality" and his fidelity to God as an assurance of final victory beyond the grave.

What is, of course, especially striking in these songs is the association of innocent suffering with a specifically messianic figure. As a gentle messiah submitting mutely to insult and torture, the servant presents a startling contrast to the bone-crushing messianic king of some of the royal psalms.[35]

Taken, then, as a cumulative meditation on the meaning of service, the songs of the suffering servant add a new dimension to that meaning, a dimension which reflects a new consciousness of the reality and consequences of human sinfulness. For, just as suffering is the inevitable consequence of sin and of the abandonment of the service of true worship, so, too, reconciliation with God in a world still out of joint is seen as involving an inevitable passage through the purifying crucible of suffering. Granted, then, the existence of sin and its consequences, it follows that the suffering of the innocent can take on a positive meaning, namely, that of atonement. Granted, too, the fact of human sinfulness and need of reconciliation with God, such atonement is itself seen to be a supreme instance of the faithful service of God.

But if the suffering servant embodies an ultimate in the Old Testament ideal of service, he also raises some serious theological problems. For if the summit of service consists in atonement through innocent suffering for the sins of the guilty, what man can be regarded as truly qualified to perform such a service? As the gloomy prognostic of the psalmist puts it: "Yahweh is looking down from heaven at the sons of men, to see if a single one is wise, if a single one is seeking God. All have turned aside, all alike are tainted; there is not a single one."[36] If then the innocence of the messianic sufferer was to be the pre-condition for mankind's final reconciliation with God, the human race's chances of ever experiencing such an atonement must have seemed slim indeed.

The Service of Jesus

All four gospels place the baptism of Jesus at the beginning of his public career. As one would expect, the accounts of the three synoptics are similar in structure, although they differ in minor details, while the Johannine tradition shows certain characteristics peculiarly its own.

Matthew and Mark both record that Jesus came from Galilee to the Jordan where John was baptizing. Only Matthew introduces the protest of the Baptist and Jesus' reply that his baptism is indeed according to the divine plan of salvation. All three mention the fact that the theophany occurs after the baptism; all three mention explicitly the descent of the Spirit in the form of a dove. All three mention the voice from heaven; and all agree on the words spoken by the voice: "You are my Son, the Beloved; my favour rests on you."

St. John, however, puts the account of the baptism on the lips of John the Baptist himself, a fact which well accords with the role of witness assigned to the latter in the theology of the fourth gospel. Paralleling the synoptic accounts in part, the Baptist testifies that he saw the Spirit descend upon Jesus in the form of a dove, and he interprets this sign as proof that Jesus will one day baptize not merely with water but with the Holy Spirit. The Baptist makes no mention of the voice from Heaven, although he attests that he has learned from the vision of the dove that Jesus is "the chosen One of God."[37]

As a result of placing the account of the baptism in the mouth of a witness, however, the Johannine tradition is forced to diverge slightly from that of the synoptics in at least one respect; for in the fourth gospel, the Baptist, in order to function as a witness, is made to share at least in part Jesus' experience of the theophany. In the synoptics, however, the vision belongs to Jesus alone.

Scripture scholars have explained this divergence by appealing to the theological and polemical preoccupations of the fourth gospel; and, indeed, similar reasons may also have motivated Matthew's introduction of the Baptist's protest into his own account of the baptism. But if we accept the synoptic tradition as on the whole not only more primitive but also more historical in an abstract, "factual" sense, we may reasonably hypothesize that the theophany after the baptism was indeed reserved for Jesus alone.

Judged, moreover, as a human experience, the vision seems to have involved a profound and perhaps even emotionally shattering realization on Jesus' part of the consequences for his human life of the unique relationship of his incarnate person to the Father and to the Spirit, a revelation to him in his humanity of the concrete, human dimensions of his hypostatic involvement in the twofold reality of God and of human history. Moreover, it was this realization which apparently launched him formally upon the labors of his public ministry and ultimately on the road to Calvary.

The temptation to parallel this experience with the inaugural visions of the Old Testament prophets is an attractive one; but the attempt to do so labors under some serious difficulties.[38] To be sure, like the inaugural visions of the prophets, Jesus' experience at the Jordan is a theophany. Moreover, as in the case of the prophetic call, the vision inaugurates Jesus' public apostolate. But in the case of Jesus, his mission is specifically messianic, not merely prophetic. That is to say, Jesus is conscious of being sent to speak to men, not as one to whom the word of God is given from on high, but specifically as the incarnate Son of God, as divine Wisdom itself. Still because the theophany at the Jordan does inaugurate our Lord's public ministry, our understanding of the meaning and scope of his mission must depend radically upon our understanding of the meaning of the theophany itself. We may, then, limit our present inquiry to a single basic question: What does the theophany at the Jordan teach us about Jesus' own understanding of the meaning and purpose of the service of God?

In the synoptics, the most obvious key to understanding what Jesus grasped with his human mind and heart as he emerged from the waters of the Jordan is supplied for us in the words spoken to him by the Father. "This is my Son, the Beloved, my favour rests on him." Significantly, the words seem to refer to two passages from the servant songs of second Isaias. As we have already seen, the first song begins with the declaration, "Here is my servant, whom I uphold, my chosen one in whom my soul delights,"[39] while the second song presents God as addressing his servant with the promise: "You are my servant (Israel) in whom I shall be glorified."[40] The substitution of the word "son" for "servant" in the theophany at the Jordan also suggests a passage from the second psalm, a messianic hymn in which Yahweh promises his anointed king: "You are my son, today I have become your father,"[41] and continues: "Ask and I will give you the nations for your heritage, the ends of the earth for your domain. With iron sceptre you will break them, shatter them like a potter's ware."[42,43] Moreover, Scripture scholars find in the descent of the Spirit upon Jesus the suggestion of a passage from the book of Emmanuel in which Isaias looks forward to the coming of a virtuous king who will establish God's reign of universal justice.[44]

If these references to Old Testament prophecies are indeed implicit in the Father's declaration to his Son at the Jordan, we may legitimately suppose that the religious experience which Jesus underwent in his human nature as he emerged from the waters was indeed a complex one. It involved, in the first place, a vivid realization of his own divine sonship, although the account of the finding in the temple in the lucan infancy gospel provides some evidence that this aspect of the baptismal experience did not come to him as something completely new. Instead, what does seem to have been crucial about his human experience of divine filiation at the Jordan is the total context in which the experience occurred.

For what Jesus seems to have understood then with his human mind and heart was not only that he was Son but also that as Son he had been divinely commissioned by the Father with the messianic task of atoning for the sins of men, that as Son he had indeed been constituted the new David, the messiah promised by God through the prophets, the virtuous king whose mission it was to establish the Father's reign of universal peace upon the earth. But most decisive of all, he seems to have grasped clearly that as Son he must accomplish this messianic mission given him by the Father by living in the image of the suffering servant of second Isaias.

The Ideal of the Kingdom

Scripture scholars are divided in their opinions as to whether the synoptic accounts of Jesus' temptations are intended to form a single literary unit with his baptism at the Jordan. Luke for one separates the two incidents with a genealogy tracing Jesus' ancestory back to Adam. Whatever may be the literary connection of the two passages, however, the temptations seem to have occurred very early in the public ministry of Jesus, before he began the work of gathering disciples. Moreover, all three synoptics seem to attribute Jesus' desert sojourn directly to the impulse of the Spirit which descended upon him in the theophany at the Jordan. Hence, however one chooses to solve these strictly exigetical problems, raised by the texts, from the limited standpoint of our present reflections, the temptations in the desert can provide us with some useful additional insights into the sense of purpose which motivated Jesus as he launched the enterprise of service to which he had freely consecrated himself at the Jordan. In reflecting on the meaning of these temptations, we will, moreover, limit ourselves to the narrative order developed by Matthew.[45]

For the Jews, the wilderness was a lifeless place whose very barrenness marked it as a spot from which the living God, the source of all life and fertility, was singularly absent. To the Jewish mind, therefore, the desert was the natural haunt of all those forces opposed to God and to his salvific plan.[46] And like the sea, it came to be symbolic of the primal chaos from which God had by his creative word originally drawn the beauty and order of the universe.[47] By the same token, passage through the desert came to signify a period of testing and trial whose purpose was man's inner religious purification by his fidelity to God in the face of his temporary subjection to the forces of evil at work in the world. Hence, by a curious reverse logic, this same desert of chaos and sterility came to symbolize a place where man could rediscover the God who had called him into being and whose fidelity sustained him in his desert sojourn.

It is to this desert that Jesus is driven by the Spirit which descended upon him at his baptism—the desert of trial and testing, of wild beasts and demonic forces, in which God waited for those who could surmount the test. Jesus' conscious and deliberate purpose in making this initial descent into chaos at the outset of his messianic career is hinted at in the fact that he undertakes there a fast lasting forty days. Needless to say, the number forty is a highly suggestive figure in the Old Testament. For forty years the Jews had wandered through desert wastes in order to be purged of Egyptian idolatry before entering the Promised Land. For the people of God this had been their period of testing and trial and, unfortunately, of repeated infidelity to their covenant commitment. In the course of their desert wanderings they had murmured against the God who had chosen them in bondage, tested him, and even lapsed again into the worship of false gods. Now Jesus, under the impulse of his filial consecration as a messiah in the image of God's suffering servant, descends once again into the wilderness in order to relive the desert experience of God's people and, where they had failed, to emerge victorious over the powers of darkness. As king and messiah of the new Israel, he must confront the very temptations to which the people of God succumbed in their first desert wanderings; and in his own person he must conquer them.

If, then, the forty days indicates to us something about the inner sense of purpose which motivated Jesus' descent into the wilderness, his inner attitude of mind and heart as he begins this period of testing and conflict is expressed by the very fast he undertakes. Indeed, in a real sense the fast is his sole weapon against the forces of evil and of chaos he has come out to the desert to vanquish.

The purpose of fasting as we find it in the Old Testament is not "ascetical" in the sense of seeking to produce some inner religious experience of emotional exaltation; nor is its purpose primarily to cultivate the moral virtue of abstemiousness in food and drink. The devout Jew fasted primarily as an expression of his inner abandonment to God, especially in the face of some difficult enterprise.[48] The sole weapon, then, which Jesus chooses to employ in this initial messianic conflict with the prince of darkness is his complete abandonment to the Father who has sent him into the world as messiah and suffering servant.

It is no surprise, then, that the first temptation Jesus must face is against the whole sense and meaning of the fast. Taken in context, Jesus' first test is more than a temptation to give in to physical hunger. It is the temptation to prefer self-reliance to total abandonment to his Father in the accomplishment of his mission. It is also no surprise, then, that Jesus' response to the tempter, which is in fact a citation of the Deuteronomic code,[49] takes the form of a reaffirmation of his commitment to the whole meaning and purpose of the fast: "Man does not live on bread alone but on every word that comes from the mouth of God." What Jesus is in effect affirming by his victory over this first diabolic test is that the way of service on which he has entered is inseparable from the way of the innocent poor man, the way of humility and of absolute reliance upon God.

The second temptation is subtler and more insidious, and it builds on Jesus' response to the first. It takes the form of a temptation to test the actual fidelity of the God in whom Jesus has reaffirmed his trust. Matthew pictures Satan as taking Jesus to the temple parapet and taunting him with the words: "If you are the Son of God, throw yourself down; for the scripture says: He will put you in his angels' charge, and they will support you on their hands in case you hurt your foot against a stone." But Jesus remains unperturbed and counters with another citation of the Deuteronomic code: "You must not put the Lord your God to the test."[50]

To test God in the Old Testament means to make specific demands which God must fulfill as pre-conditions to man's willingness to place his whole confidence in God. It is, in effect, the selfish effort to make God conform to man's own finite preoccupations, the refusal to open oneself to the divinity in confidence and love. Ultimately it is simply a refusal to believe together with the blasphemous imputation of duplicity to God. Hence, for the covenanted Jew to test God ultimately amounts to reneging on his covenant commitment.

In his reply to the tempter, Jesus makes explicit reference to the incident at Massah recorded in both Exodus and Deuteronomy, when the Israelites had demanded of Moses that God give them water in the desert as a proof of his enduring fidelity to the Sinai covenant. In the blunt evaluation of the Book of Exodus, their grumbling was the expression of a deeper infidelity and amounted to the basic question: "Is Yahweh with us, or not?"[51]

In repudiating this second temptation, then, Jesus makes it clear that for one who embraces the service of God, there can be no reneging, no testing of God. For the true believer, the one indubitable fact is that God is faithful. Any man who would seek to test the fidelity of his God is, by his very desire to do so, himself the one who is proved unfaithful to his covenanted word.

The third temptation is the most direct of all: It is the temptation to abdicate utterly the way of service and to choose in its place the way of temporal power and dominion. "Next, taking him to a very high mountain, the devil showed him all the kingdoms of the world and their splendour. 'I will give you all these,' he said, 'if you fall at my feet and worship me.' " Jesus' reply is equally direct and unequivocal: "Be off, Satan! For Scripture says: *You must worship the Lord your God and serve him alone.*"

Thus, of the three temptations, the final one is perhaps the most crucial for a Christian understanding of the meaning of service. In it Jesus is presented with two clear options: either to continue upon the way of service which he has begun with a clear understanding of the risks and sufferings involved therein or to seek instead the way of political and temporal power. The two ways are incompatible: To choose one is to abdicate the other; and Jesus' resolution of the option is pointedly clear and unambiguous: He must abdicate the way of temporal power. For to do otherwise, to choose the path of power over the way of service would be nothing else than to place himself under the dominion of those very forces of evil and chaos which he had come out to the desert to conquer. What Jesus saw clearly in this final temptation, then, is that the renunciation of coercive power over men is inseparable from the sense of purpose which motivated him in his temporal mission as Son and messiah. That is to say, as the wisdom of God incarnate, he was aware that were he to yield to this final temptation and choose the path of power as a means of accomplishing his messianic mission, he would be effectively abdicating his very sonship, denying the divine reality he was conscious of being and in effect abandoning the salvific mission he had received from his heavenly Father. With this insight we are closer to understanding the ultimate sense of purpose which motivated Jesus in his mission of service; but we are still far from a final resolution of our problem.

Teaching of Jesus

We must, then, also turn to the gospel accounts of the actual teachings and ministry of Jesus, if we are to grasp the full meaning of the service he sought to embody in his public life.[52, 53, 54, 55]

One fact, for instance, is quite clear: Jesus did not understand the abdication of coercive power as implying his renunciation of all claim to authority. On the contrary, he presumes to teach men with real authority by explaining and even correcting the law and the prophets.[56] He claims authority from his Father to forgive sins and act as the eschatological judge of mankind; and he invokes his miraculous powers as proof of the fact.[57] He appeals to his divine sonship to justify his personal exemption from the temple tax;[58] and to the scandal of the Pharisees, he claims to be Lord even of the Sabbath, a prerogative reserved, like power over sin, to God alone.[59] By his miracles, he also seeks to vindicate his authority over the combined forces of evil in this world, over sickness, death, and the demonic powers which take possession of man.[60] Finally, he manifests authority even over the forces of nature themselves.[61]

Moreover, it is this very claim to possess real authority which indirectly brings him into repeated conflict with his own disciples. The gospel accounts of Jesus' public ministry seem to describe two distinct phases in his catechesis of the apostles. In the first phase, he gradually leads them to acknowledge his authority and to submit to it: his followers must confess him to be the messiah, the virtuous king whom the power of God has indeed sent into the world to liberate men from bondage and oppression. In the second phase, however, he struggles to teach them the further lesson that if he is to be true to his royal mission, the authority he wields must manifest itself exclusively in lowly works of service and of love. For the disciples with their dreams of the regal rewards of the kingdom, this latter lesson was a bitter pill to swallow. And the master was apparently forced to repeat it again and again in his instructions to them.[62]

One can, however, sympathize with the disciples' confusion; for what kind of authority is it which claims to rest on the abdication of coercive power? For Peter apparently the answer seemed clear enough: no kind of authority at all. But as a reward for his effort to enlighten the master on this particular point he was told that he had in effect aligned himself with the demonic powers that oppose God's salvific plan.[63] Moreover, on other occasions, the master is careful to rebuke every manifestation of political ambition on the part of his apostles.[64-66]

Moreover, the renunciation of material possessions together with the life of common sharing which he demanded of his closest followers was meant to be a concrete embodiment of the ideal of service to which he had consecrated his life, a visible expression of inner abandonment to the Father and of the abdication of coercive power over one's fellow men. Money is power; to choose the path of power is to become the slave of money. By contrast, the free service of God, the genuine inner abandonment to him which characterizes his true servants must find expression in the free and gratuitous sharing with others of the good things of this world. Though such sharing may render one physically vulnerable to the rich and powerful, yet it frees the heart of man from its egotism and opens it in an attitude of atonement and reconciliation both with God and with one's fellows.[67] At the same time the absence of anxiety which the master counsels to those who embrace the way of service through sharing must also be realistic: The true servant of God must face the fact that inner abandonment to the Father which finds expression in one's external renunciation of property and of coercive power over others involves real self-renunciation and real suffering: "If anyone wants to be a follower of mine, let him renounce himself and take up his cross and follow me."[68]

The notion of service which emerges from the teaching and public ministry of Jesus is, then, a polyvalent one. It is a service of atonement in which one's acknowledgement of Jesus as anointed by God with salvific powers of reconciling men to God and to one another and of his complete inner self-abandonment to the Father, motivates one's own external abdication of coercive power over others as well as one's free participation in a life of common sharing of the good things of this world not only in spite of the inconveniences which may result from such a course of action but precisely because one's ultimate hope of fulfillment rests in the fidelity of the saving God who has revealed himself to men in and through the mission of his Son.

The Final Lesson

But it was only in the passion and glorification of Jesus that the disciples finally grasped the full dimensions of the ideal of service to which they had committed themselves. Moreover, of all the evangelists, it is John perhaps who gives us some of our best insights into the passion as the master's final object lesson to his disciples in what it means to serve the living God.[69, 70] John begins his account of the Last Supper with the story of the washing of the feet. Jesus intends this act of self-humiliation to be his disciples' account of the Last Supper with the story of the final object lesson in the meaning of service before the events of the Passion itself. Moreover, what is crucial to our present problem is that for John the purpose of Jesus' mission of service on earth is manifested as the revelation of God's final and gratuitous offer of love to man; for John sees the washing of the feet both as the culmination of the life of service and of common sharing which Jesus had lived with his disciples and as the prelude to the supreme act of service he is about to perform on the cross. Thus, the washing of the feet not only manifests Jesus' absolute and unconditioned fidelity to his Father in spite of the death he is about to die upon the cross, but it also reveals the life of service and common sharing which the master had lived with his disciples as the revelatory incarnation of the same atoning love for sinful men which Jesus will bear them on the cross.[71]

Here, then, is the final key to the sense of purpose which motivated Jesus in the mission of service he had received from his Father on the banks of the Jordan. As son, he knew that he had been sent into the world to reveal God to men. But as Son, he was also profoundly aware that the Father who had sent him into the world is nothing else than a God of purest love who offers himself freely to all men and who demands of men that they love one another with the same constancy and gratuity as God himself. Moreover, as Son, he was also conscious that the messianic kingdom he had been sent to found must be compatible in its structure with the gratuitous love which motivated his mission. Hence, it *could not* be a kingdom based on the coercive power either of political might or of wealth. Instead, it must be a kingdom in which men use the material things of this world in order to express the gratuitous love they bear one another: a kingdom, therefore, of common sharing in which each man gives freely of what he has to whoever is in need and places himself at the disposal of others with the same simplicity and openhandedness as the Son of God himself.

At the same time, Jesus recognized that if service is the lived expression of gratuitous love and if love demands the abdication of power in order to become incarnate, then his mission of service also demanded that as the true servant of God he run the risk of being helpless in the face of those who repudiate his love. Before Pilate he would declare in all simplicity: "Mine is not a kingdom of this world; if my kingdom were of this world, my men would have fought to prevent my being surrendered to the Jews. But my kingdom is not of this kind."[72]

Hence, in a world still filled with human selfishness and egotism, to serve God in the image of Jesus is to be willing to place oneself in constant jeopardy in one's dealings with others, to be willing to love others even where the only response to love is rejection or indifference and, hence, to be open constantly to the moral certainty of suffering in the accomplishment of one's mission of atonement.

Moreover, as Son, Jesus also realized that fidelity in such a mission of love to men demands of the true servant of God inner conviction of God's own fidelity to him, an inner abandonment in confidence to the One who sustains his servant in his trials, a filial love of the Father so steadfast that it places no pre-conditions to one's response of love, refuses to test God, and looks unwaveringly to the Father instead of to oneself for final vindication. If, then, the temptations of Jesus in the desert give us some important insights into his understanding of the meaning of service, it is the love relation between Jesus and his Father which ultimately makes sense out of the temptations themselves.

Furthermore, as Son, Jesus also recognized that his fidelity in such a mission of love and service to men would itself be a supreme act of atonement for sin. In seeking atonement, however, his mission was in the first instance human at-one-ment, the reconciliation of men with God, with one another, and with themselves through their free acceptance of the universal and gratuitous love of God for them in Christ as the norm of their own human conduct.

But measured in human terms, the concrete results of Jesus' own apostolic effort were meagre indeed. And in the face of man's repudiation of this final offer of divine love, it is Jesus' own fidelity to his mission of revealing the Father's love, his fidelity in the face of suffering and repudiation, his fidelity even in the face of Calvary which itself becomes the initial, seminal atonement, the fundamental reconciliation of God and man in Christ crucified and risen which is the revelation of the Father's irrevocable and eternal will-to-be-reconciled with all men in the Son and through the Spirit.

Moreover, it is this persistent divine love for men in their sinfulness revealed in its full scope in the death and glorification of Jesus which is God's judgment upon the world. That is to say, God judges the world by the simple expedient of revealing himself in his incarnate Son as eternal and atoning love and by demanding that men take their stand in the face of that revelation.[73]

There are, however, still further important dimensions to the passion and glorification of Jesus which are relevant to our present enquiry into the purpose of service. For if Jesus' fidelity in his mission as suffering servant is the atonement and, together with the Father's response to that fidelity in the Easter event, the judgment as well, it is also the new covenant promised by the prophets and revealed at last to men in the person of the glorified Christ. Thus, in the institution of the Eucharist, Jesus is at pains to make clear to his apostles before the event itself the religious significance of the death he is about to die. In the words of institution he teaches them that the blood he is about to shed is not only the blood of atonement but the sacrificial blood of a new covenant, a new bond of life linking God and man.[74] In other words, he proclaims his own death as the supreme act of divine worship, the ultimate instance of man's faithful obedience to God, the archetype and fulfillment of the unquestioning homage of the innocent poor man to the God who made him, the re-consecration of humanity in its virginal integrity to the divine bridegroom, who in spite of every human infidelity is faithful in his love.

Henceforth, then, to worship God must mean to serve him in the image of Christ crucified, i.e., to accept Jesus' service of his Father as the paradigm of one's relations with one's fellow men and with God—as, therefore, the law of the new covenant revealed to men in Christ. In other words, for the believer, the fidelity of Jesus to his mission of service is the divine revelation of the meaning and purpose of a life of Christian faith. For in the Christian era, faith in the living God can only be one's personal, covenanted commitment to the same enterprise of universal and gratuitous service in which Christ himself lived and died. Thus, as the sacramental renewal of this new and everlasting covenant, the eucharist is the central act of Christian worship, the renewal of one's baptismal faith in Christ and rededication to the task of Christian service in all that the term implies.

Finally, Jesus' death and glorification resolves the question of the meaning and place of authority in his mission of service. For if the death of Jesus is his self-offering in loving service to his heavenly Father, his resurrection is the Father's acceptance of that worship of service and irrevocable covenanted endorsement of the redemptive mission which Jesus had inaugurated in the course of his temporal life and death. The resurrection is, therefore, nothing else than the Father's final revelation to men of Jesus as Lord, as the anointed of God, as the new David, the virtuous king with authority from God himself to restore right order to the world and give just judgment to men. Thus, in raising Jesus from the dead, the Father gives his final answer to the question which had troubled the apostles in their dealings with the master. What kind of authority is it that rests upon the abdication of power? The Father's answer in raising Jesus from the dead is deceptively simple: It is sacramental authority, authority to speak to men in the name of God, to confront them prophetically with the event of Christ, and to renew to them even in their sinfulness God's offer of gratuitous love in the name of the incarnate Son of God himself. In other words, it is authority to continue Jesus' own work of reconciling men with one another and with God, not as a mere humanitarian project, nor even as a profession of personal religious belief, but as a sign of the new covenant of atonement concluded between God and man in the flesh of the incarnate Son of God. It is, therefore, authority to prolong the judgment begun in Jesus' own revelation of divine love to men, authority to announce in his name the prophetic message of salvation, that God has spoken his final salvific Word in human history; and it is authority to demand that man acknowledge his need and obligation to respond to that word with acts that are worthy of its graciousness. It is, as the master had insisted again and again with his recalcitrant disciples, authority to serve men in the name of Jesus and in his image.[75]

It follows, therefore, that for a man to accept the apostolic message of salvation is for him to accept his share in the mission of service which Christ demands of his followers, to submit to the "obedience of faith" which is the hallmark of the true servant of God.[76] The Church of Christ is, therefore, a servant Church, dedicated as a community to continue the mission of service which Jesus inaugurated in his baptism at the Jordan.

The Community of Christian Service

One is not surprised, then, to discover that it was by reflection on the meaning of Christ's own mission of service that the infant Church gradually discovered in greater and greater depth its own sense of purpose and identity as a specifically Christian community. For if the exodus had been the passage of God's people from the slavery of bondage to the freely covenanted service of the living God, the first Christians found in their lived submission to the obedience of their baptismal faith in a servant Christ the experience of a spiritual exodus, their gradual personal liberation from the bonds of selfishness and egotism, from the meaningless burden of religious and legalistic formalism, and from the nationalistic particularism of Judaic belief.[77] They found, too, the hope of their final transformation into the likeness of the glory of God's only Son, and they recognized that the scope of this liberation was truly cosmic.[78,79]

In closing these preliminary reflections on the biblical meaning of service, we should, however, emphasize once again that if the Church of Jesus is a servant Church, the function of the apostles and of those who bear the responsibility of exercising sacramental authority within the community is to be the servants of God, "the least of all" as Jesus had instructed them. Theirs is a threefold service: They preside over the community's sacramental worship, they supervise the orderly distribution of goods to the poor of the community as well as other administrative tasks implied in the pastoral service of others, and they proclaim to a sinful humanity the meaning and the need of sacramental conversion to God.[80] Moreover, the ordination of deacons to supervise the details of common sharing is symptomatic of the inevitable need for greater specialization in this triple task of serving an expanding Christian community and hence for the enlistment of those who are not apostles to act as the latter's official representatives in the work of service.

For the present, it is sufficient to have considered in a schematic way the fundamental purpose of service as we find it outlined in the pages of Scripture. In the following chapters we shall, however, attempt to trace in more detail some of the things which holy writ tells us of the ecclesial dimensions of this same organically unified commitment to serve others lovingly in the name of Christ.

The Patristic Tradition

It seems clear, then, that for Jesus himself obedience to the Father had taken the concrete form of his unswerving fidelity to the mission of forgiveness and atonement whose apostolic implications became clearly manifest to him in the theophany at the Jordan. For the first Christians, obedience to God consisted in their lived prolongation of Jesus's own mission of atoning service to others in the name of God. For the apostles, obedience to God had taken the form of their docility to the Spirit of Christ who strengthened them to proclaim sacramentally and in the name of the risen Lord the reconciliation offered to men in and through him and to dedicate themselves totally to the service of the community he had founded.

Clement I, for instance, exhorts the Corinthian community to obey God rather than the "leaders and authors of detested ambition." Moreover, he defines Christian obedience as willingness to embrace the way of humble service that Christ had come to teach us. Negatively, therefore, obedience to God means the repudiation of every manifestation of arrogance, anger, injustice, iniquity, avarice, bickering, deceit, ill-will, complaint, calumny, recrimination against God, pride, vainglory, or inhospitality. To live so, he insists is to fight under the command of Christ in an orderly and obedient manner, each person performing his appointed mission of service to others in the name of God.[81, 82]

Toward the end of the fourth century, however, Christian ascetical reflection was engaged in the process of evaluating the pros and cons of its eremitical experiment and in evolving new and revolutionary forms for religious living. Under debate were the advantages of cenobitic over eremitical living. One of the chief motives behind the formation of the first cenobitic communities was the felt need to bring under some kind of rational discipline the ascetical excesses of some of the desert solitaries. This fact plus the closed and explicitly contemplative character of the cenobitic communities came to exercise considerable influence on the theology of religious obedience.[82a] Jerome, for instance, comments on the advantages of cenobitic life, in the following terms: "You may believe that whatever the person in charge orders is for your benefit; also, do not judge the opinions of those greater than yourself, as Moses says: *Listen, Israel, and be silent.*"[83]

Needless to say, such texts do not express the whole of patristic teaching on the meaning and purpose of religious obedience. Augustine, for example, speaks of superior-subject relations in accents that are more comprehensive and more recognizably Christian. In an interesting letter to a community of religious women, he exhorts them, superiors and subjects alike, to mutual service in the name of Christ. Subjects, he writes, should show concern to obey the superior, show her reverence, and correct any failures in their docility to her decisions. The superior, on the other hand, "should not believe herself blessed with the power of dominion but with a ministering love."[84]

Nevertheless, the gradual drift in Christian reflections on the meaning of obedience from the explicit ideal of selfless service to others in the image and name of Christ to the submission of one's will to the decisions of ecclesiastical authority is both re-enforced and complicated by other tendencies in patristic thought. Particularly worth noting is the tendency, stemming in part from the neo-Platonic tradition, to speak of the divine will as though it were a universal and eternally immutable rule (*ratio, logos*) to which our fallible human wills must be conformed in order to be rectified. In commenting on Ps 31, for example, Augustine observes, "But let your will be corrected according to God's will, do not let the divine will be twisted to your own. For your will is wicked; his is the rule. And the rule endures, so that whatever is wicked may be corrected according to the rule."[85] The theme is a frequent one in Augustine's meditations on the psalms: The divine will is the *ratio, logos,* according to which a man must measure his finite desires and aspirations. Though revealed in space and time, the divine measure of human goodness remains eternally immutable (*incommutabilis*); and in the face of it man has only one reasonable choice: to submit. "Do you wish to hold to his will?" he asks. "Correct your own."[86]

Especially in the post-Augustinian era, there is evidence in the writings of the Fathers of the interweaving of three key ascetical themes. First, as Augustine had suggested, obedience tends to be conceived less in terms of concrete service to others in the image of Christ and more abstractly as the abnegation of one's own personal desires in order to conform them to the immutable archetypal will of God.[87]

Second, submission to authority is conceived as the criterion for measuring such genuine self-abnegation. Cassian, for instance, cites with approval the wonderful simplicity of Abbot John who at the command of his superior obediently watered a dead stick for an entire year and with the same unquestioning submission to authority tried single-handedly to lift a stone which many strong men together could not have budged.[88,89]

Third, the fruit of such submissive self-abnegation is increasing contemplative openness to the divine transcendence. This theme is often only implicit; but Abbot Rufus in the *Sayings of the Fathers* gives it enthusiastic expression. "Oh, obedience," he exclaims, "who open the heavens and lift men from the earth! Oh, obedience, nurse of all the saints, whose milk they have sucked and grown to fulness. Oh, obedience, companion of the angels."[90]

Defense of Authority

Prior to Vatican II most of the statements of the magisterium concerned with obedience in religious matters sought primarily to vindicate the authority of the hierarchy in disputed areas of Church discipline. In 1312, for example, the Council of Vienna condemned as erroneous the antinomian teachings of certain Beghards and Beguines. This charismatic movement in the medieval church had as its chief concern the adaptation of religious life to the needs of the increasingly urbanized society of the high Middle Ages. Apparently, however, extremists in the order with certain enthusiastic and catharistic leanings had contended that those who reach the highest grade of perfection cease to be bound either by human obedience or by the precepts of the Church.[91] Needless to say, such opposition to ecclesiastical authority was not new and would reappear in various forms in the subsequent development of European Christianity.[92]

Perhaps the most significant of these pre-Vatican declarations on obedience can be found in the condemnation of Miguel de Molinos, a gentle Spanish theologian who ran afoul of the Holy Office by publishing in the wake of the Jansenist crisis a dogmatically questionable treatise on religious perfection called *A Spiritual Guide*. The book, which attempted to vindicate the superiority of the contemplative life over the active, was an immediate success and proved to be a significant factor in the development of the quietist movement. In 1685, for historical reasons difficult to discern, Molinos was suddenly arrested by the Holy Office and for two whole years subjected to intermittent cross-questioning on his teaching. In 1687 he retracted sixty-eight errors derived from his writings, among which were certain propositions concerning the obedience of religious.

The pertinent propositions close the list of retractions and seek to withdraw from the competence of ecclesiastical jurisdiction all inner movements of heart in the soul's contemplative quest for God. The net result of these assertions is that only God himself, by his inner illuminations, and one's personally chosen spiritual director are permitted authoritative access to a religious's spiritual development. In other words, by confining ecclesiastical authority exclusively to the external forum, the propositions seek to free a quietistically inclined religious to choose a spiritual director of similar spiritual bent and with him to pursue a quietistic ascent to God irrespective of Church discipline and practice. In an age of flourishing religious convulsionaries and enthusiasts, ecclesiastical authorities looked upon such proposals with understandable alarm and condemned them severally as scandalous, temerarious, tending to the relaxation of Christian discipline, subversive, and seditious.[93]

The Wisdom of Vatican II

When one turns from these earlier pronouncements on religious obedience to the documents of Vatican II, such anxious concern on the part of Church officials to keep a firm, if necessary, grasp upon the reins of authority is replaced by a much more genial and positive pastoral concern. Though the absence of serious crisis in the Church at the time of the Council accounts in part for the change in tone, it is still refreshing and welcome.

Though the Council documents are careful to spell out in some detail those areas in which religious are subject to the jurisdiction of the local ordinary[94] and insist upon the obedience which all Christians owe to legitimate authority,[95] there is equal insistence upon the fact that the governing power of bishops cannot be interpreted as power to impose arbitrary episcopal whims upon the community of the faithful, but is rather authority rooted in the bishop's sacramental consecration[96] to serve the people of God in the name of Christ and in his image.[97] Thus, the bishops remind themselves and all legitimate religious superiors of St. Paul's warning that it is not for them to presume to stifle the Spirit in his diverse manifestations within the community, but rather to test all gifts when they appear and to foster and encourage all in them that is found to be good.[98]

Religious, for their part, are reminded that their special charismatic vocation within the Church is not only "deeply rooted in their baptismal consecration," but that their vow of obedience dedicates them in a special way to the service both of God *and* of the living Christian community. Hence, their obedience must re-embody the self-surrender of Christ himself by combining a life of contemplation with one of apostolic love.[99,100]

Moreover, the Council Fathers note that just as official approval by the Church raises to the canonical state vowed religious dedication to the service of God, so, too, the circumstances surrounding religious profession are intended to manifest publicly the meaning of that state within the community at large. Thus, the liturgical setting in which men and women pronounce their vows of religious profession manifests that the state of life on which they are entering is one specially consecrated to God. Second, the public acceptance of religious vows by Church authorities indicates that the whole Christian community acting in and through its hierarchy not only accepts and blesses the consecration of these men and women to divine works of service and to the "upbuilding of Christ's body," but also blesses them in their charismatic endeavors, commends them to God, and accompanies their self-offering with the eucharistic sacrifice.[101,102]

At the same time, the decree is at pains to remind religious superiors that they are not free to exercise their authority arbitrarily, but must do so in a spirit of loving service of their brethren. They must have due regard for the personality of their subjects and take pains to be paternal in their government. But paternal government must not degenerate into paternalism; and superiors are instructed to make every effort to encourage their subjects positively, each to make his personal contribution to the welfare of the community. Subjects must also be allowed freedom in the reception of the sacrament of Penance and in the choice of a spiritual director. Similarly, though responsibility in the community for ultimate decisions is reserved for the superior, the latter must make every effort to encourage responsible obedience among his subjects. Finally, chapters and councils are reminded of their responsibility to represent every segment of the religious community, not just one or other dominant group or faction.[103]

The Manual Tradition

Manual asceticism in its account of the vow of obedience tends to oppose it to the third great concupiscence, pride of life. The latter is described as the vain, complacent, egotistical worship of oneself in such a way as to make a god of one's own personal independence through inordinate self-love. Pride of life bears fruit in a bevy of vices: vanity, boasting, ostentation, hypocrisy, presumption, dissimulation, and disobedience. For by refusal to submit to the divine will, the proud man seeks in fact to arrogate to himself the glory that is due to God alone, to treat himself as his own first beginning and last end, and through his arrogant love of honor to wield despotic power over other men. On the other hand, by humbly recognizing God's supreme right as creator and judge to complete submission from his creatures, the obedient man renders to the divine majesty homage that in justice belongs to it. Obedience, therefore, like the virtue of religion itself is a species of the cardinal moral virtue of justice.

Obedience is defined in the manual tradition as a supernatural moral virtue which inclines one to submit one's will to one's lawful superiors insofar as they are the representatives of God. For logically, willingness to obey God entails willingness to obey his legitimate representatives both in the natural and the supernatural order. The natural order includes the family, civil society, and professional society. In the family, God's representatives are one's parents; in civil society, one's lawful rulers; in professional society, one's employers. In the supernatural order, God's legitimate representatives are the hierarchy.

Manual asceticism also distinguishes degrees in the practice of obedience. One classic division follows roughly the faculties of the human soul; the result is three degrees of obedience: obedience of execution (i.e., doing externally what one is told to do), obedience of will (i.e., doing it willingly), and obedience of the understanding (i.e., bending the understanding by force of will to approve of the command of the superior in order that one might not only desire and do what the superior wants, but also desire and do it for the same reason as he commands it). Logically, then, "perfect" obedience, as one manual author explains it, consists in such habitual submission to the judgment of one's superior that one does what he is told to do immediately and spontaneously, without even considering the reasons for the command.

True religious obedience, we are also told, has three outstanding qualities. It is supernatural; it is universal; it is entire. It is supernatural in the sense that the subject's ultimate motive for submission to authority must be his belief that the superior speaks to him with the authority of Christ. Thoroughly supernatural obedience must transcend all merely human motivation, such as the human attractiveness of the superior or the spontaneous pleasure which one would derive from the task that one is commanded to perform. True religious obedience is universal in that it undertakes any and every command with simplicity, or as the same ascetical writer puts it, without reflecting as to whether the command be bad or good, provided that the one who orders it has the authority to do so and provided the command serves to unite one's mind to God. True religious obedience is entire; that is, it loves the command itself, without reservation as to whether the command be a pleasing one or not. Entire obedience is also persevering and cheerful.

In the manual explanation, the excellence of obedience consists in the fact that it unites us to God by uniting us to his will. Obedience, therefore, is the mother and guardian of all virtues, because it is one with supernatural charity (for love, after all, when all its accidentals are stripped away, consists essentially in the union of the faculty of the will with the will of God). Obedience, then, makes us practice all virtues because every virtue can be subsumed logically under either one of the divine precepts or counsels. It is a martyrdom and hence a beneficial refinement of our natural human love. It offers us perfect security in finding the will of God, since we need never decide ourselves what God's will for us might be but can always turn to our superior, should ecclesiastical legislation or the rule of one's order or congregation prove insufficient. Finally, obedience supernaturalizes the most commonplace occupations of our life—such as meals, recreation, and work—and gives us the comforting assurance that even the most praiseworthy action done in defiance of one's superiors is an act of disobedience and both unmeritorious and displeasing in the sight of God.

The vow of obedience, we are told in the manuals, binds a subject to submit his will to God by obeying the formal commands of his superior in matters which concern both the vows of religion and the constitutions of one's order or congregation.

The power of the superior to issue formal commands (i.e., to invoke the subject's vow) is limited by rule.

Despite the high degree of logical consistency in this account of religious obedience, it labors under some serious difficulties. For if pressed theoretically, it leads to an unavoidable speculative dilemma. And if taken too seriously in practice it can lead to the purest kind of pharisaism. Moreover, because its conception of obedience is fundamentally one of constant submission to a pre-established divinely sanctioned and immutable arrangement of things temporally embodied in the official decisions of one's lawful superiors and in the sanctioned laws and customs of one's community, it transforms religious obedience from a dynamic and compelling ideal to a static and routine conformity.

Speculative difficulties with this manual explanation arise from its apparent attempt to locate the ultimate ground of the subject's duty to obey exclusively in the authority of the one who commands. The perfection of obedience, we are told, consists in obeying blindly, without consideration as to whether or not the command be good or bad, but simply because God's representative has commanded one to act. On the other hand, if the ultimate ground of a subject's submission is simply the authority of the one who commands, then, logically every command issued by one in authority ought to be self-justifying, i.e., justified simply by the fact that it is authoritatively commanded, with the embarrassing result that the traditional explanation can begin to sound in the concrete circumstances to which it is applied either remarkably like Adolf Eichmann's trial defense or like the mindless conformity of the contemporary bureaucrat whose loyalty to the system which nurtures him blinds him to the human misery it frequently produces.

To forestall these objections, manual asceticism is usually quick to add some important qualifications to its original theory. Thus, we are told that even though the ultimate ground of obedience is the authority of the commanding superior, still, subjects are not obliged to obey when superiors command them to do something which is in fact sinful or contrary to the rule.

On the one hand, this qualification is an important speculative concession to human rationality. On the other hand, however, even to admit the possibility that under certain circumstances the command of one's superior bearing as it would the official sanction of his authority upon it, has in fact no real binding force is to admit that the ultimate ground of obedience in practical matters cannot be restricted to the mere possession of authority on the part of the one who commands, but must include as well the nature of the action which is commanded. In other words, not only is the superior's possession of authority one factor among others which a subject must take into account in attempting to form his conscience concerning his obligation in a concrete circumstance as to whether or not he should obey a given command; but it is also a factor whose importance can in certain circumstances be nullified by the actual nature of what is commanded.

The attempt to qualify the original manual explanation of obedience thus leads one into a serious speculative dilemma. For its defender must either abandon the qualification of his original position and revert to the untenable thesis that every command of every lawfully constituted superior is in fact self-justifying, or he must admit that the perfection of obedience does not consist in a blind submission to authority, i.e., in an obedience which refuses to consider whether the command given be good or bad. But if the first horn of the dilemma is morally indefensible, the latter admission calls into question the whole manual approach to the third vow. For that approach tends in effect so to absolutize religious authority as to ultimately deprive it of any real purpose for existing beyond the exacting of complete and absolute submission of mind and will from those over whom it is wielded.

The same difficulty attends any attempt to define the limits of a religious superior's authority in terms of divine and ecclesiastical law. For even if one should affirm divine law to be perfect and immutable, our human understanding of it even under grace is most certainly shot through with imperfection and mutability. Similarly, one can scarcely pretend that Church law and religious rules have been fashioned with such absolute perfection and equity that they will never be beyond reform, that they will never in fact sanction and protect human blunders made by those who are in authority, or even that there is adequate provision in existing Church law for the sort of due process that would automatically correct such blunders. At the same time, if such is the case, then the legal ecclesiastical limits placed upon a religious superior's exercise of authority, while also providing one useful guideline among others in determining the extent of a subject's obligation to obey, can never serve as a perfectly adequate norm of religious obedience.

There are other difficulties as well with the manual explanation of the third vow. If, for instance, one is to measure the supernatural character of obedience by the unpleasantness of the superior and the repulsive quality of what one is told to do, and if only supernatural obedience is truly meritorious, it would seem to follow that the ideal superior would be one who is universally despised and abominated by his subjects and who delights in frustrating them at every turn, in charity, of course, so that they can accumulate through their present suffering the maximum of heavenly bliss.

Worst of all, perhaps, the theory seems to equate Christian love with exact and meticulous fidelity to external rules and regulations. Divine charity, we are told, is to conform one's will to the will of God. Hence, the will of God consists in the Church's authoritatively sanctioned legal and bureaucratic structures plus the decisions of one's legally constituted superiors. Therefore, to love God is to be completely submissive to those in authority and meticulously obedient to every existing rule and regulation. The deductive logic is inescapable once a person grants the presuppositions. Unfortunately, however, a reading of the gospel begins to make one doubt the compatibility of such ascetical deductions with the explicit teachings of Christ. To one familiar with the teachings of Jesus as they are recorded in the Scriptures, it comes, for instance, as a curious surprise that one contemporary writer on the religious life characterizes the obedience of Jesus to his Father as his submission during his life to all those in authority as well as to the existing laws, institutions, and customs of the period. In point of fact, however, Jesus on many occasions defied the authoritative interpretation of religious practices like Sabbath observance and encouraged his disciples in their neglect of the minutiae of the law. He also joined his voice to the whole prophetic tradition by roundly and publicly denouncing the formalistic approach to religious obedience practiced and taught by many official leaders of the Jewish people. The love of God which he preached was most certainly not that of blind and unquestioning fidelity to law but that of vital concern for the needs of one's fellow man. Indeed, in his preaching he explicitly rejected the concept that the measure of one's love of God can ever be submission to a law which ignores the actual human needs of those it was originally created to serve.[104]

Problems and Perplexities

For quite some time, there have been signs of a growing dissatisfaction with the manual explanation of obedience. This felt dissatisfaction at a grass-roots level achieved varying degrees of articulate consciousness; but it eventually found eloquent verbal expression in the words of the late John Courtney Murray, who suggested that the danger latent in the vow of obedience as it is ordinarily understood is a certain irresponsibility and purposelessness, which in turn is the result of the abdication of what is at the very heart of being human, namely, the power of personal choice. For if a human being has no power to choose his own destiny in the concrete, no opportunity to marshal his individual energies in its pursuit, then he runs the serious risk of never being himself in his relations either with God or with his fellow human beings.[105]

In recent years, moreover, a variety of historical factors have combined to nourish discontent with a manual asceticism of the third vow. To begin with, the documents of Vatican II depart significantly from the manual concept of obedience. As we have seen, the bishops are frequently at pains to identify the use of authority in the Church with the Christian ideal of service rather than with the moral virtue of justice. Prior even to the Council, however, the biblical movement had already introduced contemporary Catholics to the basic notions implied, for instance, in a Pauline approach to law.[106] Since the Council, outstanding theologians like Fr. John McKenzie have attempted to probe the real meaning and use of authority in the Church and have called for the kind of spiritual leadership which will transform its use into a genuine embodiment of Christian love. Moreover, American Catholics being democratically inclined by their national tradition, have also long been haunted by the thought that in a number of its institutional structures the Roman Church seems indistinguishable either from the modern totalitarian state or from the most impersonal contemporary bureaucracy.

Moreover, in practice, American religious have found the manual explanation of obedience inadequate. In an age of growing specialization, personal competence, and expertise, it has been increasingly difficult to accept as concrete embodiments of the will of God the decisions of a superior who, often through no fault of his own, has had no special training in administration and who has all too frequently been too caught up in the mechanics of his office to acquire the knowledge both of his subjects and of the problems they face to provide the kind of leadership that subjects can humanly expect, let alone blindly obey.[107]

In his now celebrated essay on religious obedience, Karl Rahner has attempted to provide a context for the re-thinking at a theological level of the meaning of the vow. He has insisted that the superior-subject relation is essentially different from the parent-child relation, the latter being essentially an educational relationship aimed at developing a child's ultimate autonomy and freedom from authority. Thus, the subject in religion stands in a relation of constant dependence on the will of the superior, while the superior is not for all that some kind of olympian papa or mama free to act arbitrarily and to ignore the experience, intelligence, and expertise of his subjects.[108] He has insisted that the meaning of religious obedience must transcend mere conformity to the traffic regulations that are a necessary means of preserving order in any human effort at group living.[109] He suggests rather that religious obedience is "a permanent life form giving man a God-ward orientation" by manifesting ecclesially the peculiar essence of the Church, that is to say, by agreeing to live according to a constitution "which the church has acknowledged to be a true and practical expression of a divinely oriented existence," a religious publicly renounces the pursuit of worldly objectives for inner submission to God.[110]

Fr. McKenzie has insisted for his part that genuine religious obedience must, however, be distinguished from the mere bureaucratic conformity of the "organization man" who characteristically buys social and personal security through blind submission to existing social structures at the price of his own depersonalization and who surrenders his human capacity to make personal decisions for the sake of his advancement within the fixed organizational machinery which gives structure to his life.[111]

Fr. Örsy has defined religious obedience as "a personal call from God to a human person calling him to the service of God in a closer way; and in particular, to do the will of God as God manifests it to him in the Church, through his superiors."[112] Such obedience, he observes, is a sacrifice in a twofold sense: First, it produces a greater union of heart with God in love; second, it involves great suffering through the submission of one's will to God's human intermediaries.

These suggestions are certainly useful for understanding what religious obedience is not. They help us to see that it is not simply conformity to the traffic regulations of community living. It is not the bureaucratic conformity of the organization man. It is not blind submission to an olympian papa or mama. But one may question the total adequacy of the positive alternatives offered instead.

There are advantages in speaking of obedience as a "form-of-life" rather than as a virtue. The term is philosophically suggestive and, unlike the term "virtue," raises none of the theoretical spectres of faculty theory that haunt the reduction of Christian obedience to one of the Aristotelian moral virtues. On the other hand, if obedience as a life-form has as its purpose to give the life of a religious a God-ward orientation, one may wonder in what way the suggested explanation has advanced beyond the manual one, if that God-ward orientation consists in nothing else than submission to an officially sanctioned religious rule. To put the matter in its starkest terms, does one's life take on a God-ward orientation simply because the bureaucracy to which one conforms is ecclesiastical rather than secular? One senses immediately the inadequacy of the suggestion. By the same token, what good is it to call obedience "a personal call from God," if all that one is called to do is to submit one's mind and will to the rule of one's order?

On the other hand, there can be no question but that the vow of obedience demands some kind of subordination of the will of the subject to that of the superior. The problem, however, is, as the late Fr. Murray saw well, to conceive the teleological ground of that submission in such a way as to leave the subject in possession of that fundamental and inalienable human responsibility and dignity which are both absent from any relationship of mere conformity, however one may seek to change the verbal trappings which cloak it.

Toward a Redefinition of Purpose

The problem is a real one, but hopefully not insoluble. And this much at least seems initially clear. Religious obedience is an imitation of the human obedience of the incarnate Son of God. If, therefore, we can discern the key to his human obedience to the Father, we may be on the way toward solving the riddle of religious obedience.

The obedience of Jesus, we would respectfully suggest, did not consist primarily in his submission to the existing laws and regulations of his day, nor did it consist primarily in his blind submission to familial, civil, and ecclesiastical authority. It consisted primarily in his fidelity to the mission he had received from his

Father. If our earlier analysis of his baptism on the banks of the Jordan is correct, that sense of mission had a triple dimension. It involved first and fundamentally his consciousness of his own divine person; second, flowing from that personal consciousness, an awareness of his messianic mission; and third, his evaluation of the basis of that dual consciousness of those elements in the religious traditions of his people which were in fact compatible both with his divine sonship and with the messianic mission that flowed from it.

As God's incarnate Son, he was immediately and peculiarly conscious of what it means for human beings to live as God's children. As the messiah sent by God, he was conscious of being divinely commissioned to form a new Israel, a community of men and women who would be dedicated to the ideal of living in a manner worthy of God's children. Hence, his acceptance of the religious traditions of his people and his submission to their religious legislation was always contingent upon the extent to which that tradition and that legislation actually contributed to the formation of a community of "little ones," a community of men and women willing to attempt to love one another with the same selfless and atoning love as he had lived among them and the Father had shown toward men in his provident care of good and evil alike. The obedience of Jesus, therefore, was not primarily an exercise in the Aristotelian cardinal virtue of justice at all. It was from first to last an exercise in a loving and atoning service which remained critically conscious of any humanly contrived decision, custom, or law which did not further the formation of a community of mutual reconciliation and of atoning love.

The Christian Experience

Moreover, it is useful in this context to recall that even though Christianity is truly an experiential religion, it can never be a religion of one's purely subjective experience. That is, Christianity is experiential in the sense that it is a religion in which the mystery of God is mediated to human minds and hearts by the experience of historical persons, realities, and events, which partly manifest and partly conceal the divine presence. To the extent that they reveal the presence of God, Christianity does indeed involve what might be called an "experience of God" although that experience remains essentially a sacramental, and hence a mediated, one.

But Christianity can never be a religion of purely subjective experience in the sense that it regards only those realities which have been immediately and personally experienced as worthy of belief. On the contrary, it is a religion which constantly challenges every individual in the community, including those in authority, to transcend through belief what he or she has directly and immediately experienced whether that experience has been formulated in concepts or not. As Christians, we believe, for instance, that God himself was indeed present in the inspired rabbi whom men experienced factually as Jesus of Nazareth; we believe that the Spirit of God is present in Christians whose Christlikeness is often less than experientially evident. More important still, Christianity demands that we accept the human experience of Jesus himself, his self-consciousness of his own person and mission as the conscious historical norm of what it means for a human being to be a child of God. And since his experience of divine sonship was uniquely his—uniquely his because hypostatically his, uniquely his, therefore, in a qualitative mode which transcends the manner in which any man's experience can be said to be uniquely his own—not only is every Christian challenged by faith to accept that experience as normative for human living; but every follower of Christ is also challenged to recreate in his own sinful consciousness, an experience of divine sonship which approaches the human experience of God's incarnate Son as closely as is humanly possible under grace for sinful men. This he attempts to do through a reflection on the teachings of Christ and on the collective historical experience of those who believe in him, through his effort to probe and understand not only the sense of purpose which motivated Jesus' human experience but also that which motivates the meaning of the disciple's own salvifically ambiguous human experience. That is, the disciple of Jesus is committed by faith to seek to understand and to re-embody in his own life to the extent that this is possible for him under grace Jesus' own motivating vision of what it means to be sent into this world as a child of God. We may conclude, therefore, that to the extent that each Christian, living as a member of a community of sinful and yet repentant men and women who believe in Christ, and hence who share, at least in aspiration, his ideals and purpose, actually succeeds in understanding and in embodying that vision, insofar as he or she is an obedient Christian.

Moreover, since the vision of Christ was the vision of an ideal community of "little ones," which he as messiah and Son had been sent to found, that vision precisely because it transcends the finite experience of any one Christian or any historical community of Christians remains to challenge any concrete human attempt to give it conceptualization and historical embodiment, even though that attempt be made under grace and the inspiration of the Spirit of Christ.

For no historical attempt to embody the vision of Christ exhausts all of the historical possibilities of that vision; and no intelligent attempt to grasp it individually or collectively comprehends all of its possible implications. No attempt of sinful men to relate that vision to the concrete circumstances of human living, even if it be done under the aegis of ecclesiastical authority, can claim to have given final and hence absolute expression to it. Hence, we may conclude that in approaching the problem of religious obedience, one must avoid in practice falling into some of the blunders into which a nominalistic logic leads one in the speculative order. For the speculative nominalist is one who attempts to substitute a particular historical formulation of Christian belief for the Christ-event itself. There are many symptoms of this particular logical disease. Advanced cases fall into what might be called the error of "practical infallibility," which attempts to treat as absolute and ultimate pronouncements of the magisterium which make no claim whatever to absoluteness and ultimacy, and which attempts to give to such pronouncements the same kind of speculative handling that one would give a solemn dogmatic definition. Another symptom of a mind imbued with a nominalistic bias is its attempt to treat the mere repetition of a proposition of the ordinary magisterium as the grounds of its ultimate theological justification. Typically, too, the nominalistic mind appeals exclusively to the magisterial charism, or grace of office, from which every official pronouncement of the Church proceeds as sufficient grounds for one's intellectual assent to it, no matter what its intellectual content or grounding in tradition might be.

Needless to say, the ordinary magisterium of the Church demands a respectful hearing and cannot be simply ignored by devout Christians. One should attend to it with an initial presumption in its favor and with the expectation that what it says will in fact, when reflected on, prove perfectly acceptable and true. But one can never be certain a priori of the truth and acceptability of a statement of the ordinary magisterium independently of its rational justification or of its historical basis in revelation. What a nominalistic logic attempts to do, however, is to force one into a false choice between immediate blind acceptance of all official teachings of the magisterium and total repudiation of the Church's teaching authority. In those instances in which an unreflecting acquiescence in nominalistic logic leads to the affirmation of such a false and untenable ideal of the Christian community, it usually remains, at least in this country, only a crypto-heresy, not a full-blown one, for the simple reason that even though it is proposed as a doctrine of faith, often its proponents are too theologically unreflective to be reflexively conscious of the untenability of their own affirmations.

The Nominalistic Fallacy

Needless to say, one cannot do justice to the strength and the weakness of a nominalistic position in a few short sentences. But these brief remarks may help to illumine some of the more perplexing affirmations of a manual asceticism of obedience. For that asceticism simply transposes into the practical order many of the same misapprehensions which the nominalist affirms in the theoretical order. That is to say, it treats the ordinary, practical decisions of ecclesiastical authority as if they were self-justifying embodiments of the divine will, when in fact such decisions must be justified, not merely by the authority from which they proceed, but also by their relevance to the situation in which they are made and by their conformity both to the ideals of Christ and to the divinely determined function of authority within his community. That is, any concrete, practical, fallible decision of any legitimate religious superior must be judged on the one hand by its compatibility with an accurate understanding of the vision of the ideal Christian community that Jesus as God's incarnate Son consciously felt himself sent to found and on the other hand by its relevance to the concrete historical situation in which it seeks to realize such a community.

Moreover, there are indeed certain uses of religious authority which are endowed with an absolute character. The sacramental use of religious authority is, for instance, absolute because it mediates to an individual in an action whose meaning and purpose has been historically pre-determined by God's incarnate Son, God's own absolute, i.e., universal and irrevocable, commitment to men made in the person of Jesus, through the historical form which his life and death assumed on this earth and through the Father's ratification of the permanent and unique significance of that life and death in the Son's revelatory glorification. This sacramental authority of the Church is, moreover, radically eucharistic, the other sacraments being a mediation to individual men in important salvific situations of their lives of the divine commitment that is sacramentally re-presented most solemnly and explicitly in the eucharistic action.

Now, the absolute use of authority present in the sacraments, especially in the sacrament of the Eucharist, presupposes priestly ordination: that is to say, it presupposes that the action be administered by one who can speak to men, not merely as a concerned human being, not ever simply as a believer in the Christ event, but authoritatively in the name of Christ himself. For the prophetic mission of the priest as a member of the Christian community is to confront both the people of God and non-believers as well with the Christ--event precisely as an event transcending all that is merely human, by insisting that the salvific significance of the sacramental words he pronounces derives, not from his personal merits or intelligence or virtue, but from his sacramental mission to renew to men in the name of God's own Son the Father's absolute commitment of love revealed in Christ and to summon men prophetically to an appropriate response. This sacramental use of the authority of Christ, by the simple fact that it is consciously and flexibly performed by a validly ordained minister of Christ, may be meaningfully regarded as self-justifying, i.e., as a use of divine authority which as a result of the mere intent to use it embodies God's grace-giving salvific will toward men.

At the same time, it should be evident that no other use of authority in the Church enjoys the same kind of self-justifying character as the sacramental use of authority, for the simple reason that every other use of religious authority lacks the divinely predefined significance of a sacramental act and hence engages a greater degree of human fallibility in its successful performance. The basic error of a manual asceticism of obedience is that it seeks to equate the practical, prudential use of religious authority with its sacramental use. But for the same reason that it is important not to treat fallible, theoretical non-absolutes as though they were theoretical absolutes, it is equally important not to treat practical, prudential non-sacramental uses of religious authority as though they were sacramental, as though by the mere doing of them in Christ's name they bore the full sanction of divine authority upon their every aspect.

On the other hand, the possession of sacramental authority brings with it special responsibilities within the Christian community. The key word here is "responsibility." Thus, ordination to the eucharistic priesthood imposes the responsibility of leading the Christian community in its central act of worship, an act which alone fully embodies its ultimate *raison d'être* as a community. But precisely because the Eucharist is the public communal re-affirmation of a commitment to Christ in faith and love, whose practical implications extend into every aspect of human life, and because in assuming the responsibility for leading the Christian community in such an act the ordained eucharistic priest also assumes the public responsibility of seeing to it that the members of the worshipping community perform this act responsibly, the ordained eucharistic priest also bears the public responsibility of watching over the faith of his community and of leading them by personal example, by exhortation, and by the encouragement of community projects which express the believing community's common faith. For to the extent that the believing community's participation in the eucharistic action fails to be genuine re-affirmation of a common faith in Christ or fails to find practical expression both in individual and communal acts of faith and love, to that extent the eucharistic action itself is frustrated of the effect Christ intended it to produce when he instituted it and commissioned men to celebrate it in his name.

Purpose of the Third Vow

We may conclude, therefore, that in accepting the public responsibility of proclaiming at once kerygmatically and sacramentally (i.e., eucharistically, since the heart of the eucharistic act, the consecration and communion, of the eucharist are, taken together, kerygmatic as well as sacramental) the new covenant in Christ, the ordained eucharistic priest accepts too a permanent, public responsibility for exercising a leadership function within the worshipping community. Now, a religious may be described in the most general terms as a baptized Christian who, though not himself an ordained eucharistic priest, freely offers himself, his talents, and his superfluous possessions in a public and permanent fashion for the purpose of cooperating in the task of assisting the eucharistic priesthood in the fulfillment of its *diakonia,* of its public, ecclesial service, and who to that end promises solemnly and publicly to cooperate with other likeminded Christians, with the leaders and members of the eucharistic priesthood, and with those who speak in their name, in the common and *responsible* discharge of their mission of service to the worshipping community. But this promise of cooperation in a common enterprise of service, with the subordination of wills that its cooperative character necessarily implies, is not a simple blind act of submission to religious authority for its own sake. The submission is a means to an end, a means to assisting the eucharistic priesthood in the discharge of the responsibilities it has publicly and collectively assumed.

Testing the Definition

These reflections should help to illumine some of the definitions of obedience offered above. For instance, even prescinding from the multiple objections that could be brought against a "faculty theory" of obedience, if we define obedience as: "a supernatural moral virtue which leads one to submit one's will to lawful superiors to the extent that they are God's lawful representatives," then we must be careful not to equate the mere possession of office with the possession of a divine sanction upon one's every practical use of that office. In the fullest sense, possession of office in the Christian community means that one has officially and sacramentally assumed the public responsibility of seeing to it that one's every decision with regard to the community is in fact in conformity with the will of God as that will has been revealed in Christ and in the concrete situation facing the community. It does *not* mean that every official, public, practical action taken by a religious superior is automatically guaranteed by grace, charism, or what have you, to actually measure up to one's official responsibilities. In a word, one in office cannot be said to represent God in a way that demands complete submission of will on the part of his subjects unless his official decisions do in fact promote the concrete realization of the kind of community Jesus came to found. By the same token, for a subject to oppose respectfully but prophetically those of the superior's decisions which fail to do precisely that, is not to repudiate the superior's office but is for the subject to fulfill his own publicly assumed responsibility of helping the superior to conduct his office so that men can indeed recognize in his use of authority an embodiment of the will of God.

Similarly, if we define obedience as a life-form, which gives to the life of a religious a God-ward orientation through his agreement to live according to a constitution which the Church has acknowledged to be a true and practical expression of a divinely oriented existence, one should be careful not to regard the ecclesiastical sanction of a rule or constitution as placing it beyond the pale of historical change and adaptation to new circumstances. A *Lebensform* (life-style) which suited the ninth or even the nineteenth century may have ceased—even in many concrete details that were formally regarded as "essential" to its structure—to be a *Lebensform* fully adapted to the twentieth century. Church sanction upon a particular rule or religious form of life does not, therefore, fix it for all time as an immutable embodiment of the absolute will of God. Rather it gives public ecclesial approval to a specific historically conditioned formula for communal religious living whose particular historically limited preoccupations with this or that aspect of public Christian witness provide those who agree to live using that formula with one guide among others for the way in which they should order their lives in Christ. That is to say, it gives the members of a given institute a specific ascetical tradition to consult with genuine respect in their efforts to penetrate more deeply and to re-embody the ideal Christian community demanded by Christ and by the times in which they live. For no order or congregation can preserve its specific historical identity by clinging blindly to the forms of its past. If it clings to the past it must be because the past helps it to love living men and women and thus to provide genuine inspiration for the life of the Christian community as a whole. The members of an order must, therefore, study their own traditions as a means to understanding the specific purpose that historically called them into existence as a community in order that they can measure that original purpose against the existing needs of the Christian community and when necessary make the needed adaptations. It should, for instance, be quite clear that an order initially founded to redeem captives from the Turks has, when the Turkish threat subsides, to find some equivalent moral purpose for its existence as an order if that existence is to remain justified. And the same is true of every other order or congregation.

Finally, if one defines obedience as a call from God to do his will as it is manifested in the Church through one's superiors, one must be careful to understand that the superior can claim to manifest the will of God by his decisions only when he in fact asks his subjects to perform actions which, given the concrete circumstances in which the community finds itself, tend to the realization of the ideal community which Jesus came to found. Constant dialogue with one's subjects, an alertness to the factual variables in the community and among those it serves, a willingness to reverse specific decisions if they prove inadequate, a flexible approach to rules and regulations—qualities such as these are not the optional traits of a soft superior. They are not newfangled notions which have crept into the asceticism of the third vow. They are a very old Christian ideal, essential to the responsible conduct of any religious office. So essential indeed are they that their culpable absence in any superior is the mark of grave irresponsibility on his part. Moreover, the higher the office, the graver the irresponsibility and the guilt.

Might we not, then, describe the vow of obedience as a promise made to God in which a baptized Christian freely dedicates himself on a permanent and public basis to cooperate in a responsible manner with the members of the eucharistic priesthood in their effort to serve the Christian community by providing responsible leadership for that community in its worship of God and in its efforts to serve men in the image of Christ? That is to say, precisely because the ordained eucharistic priest enjoys a servant status involving permanent and public responsibilities which derive, not from his acceptance as a person by the community, nor from his personal worthiness, nor from the current sociological structure of society at large, but from his public acceptance of the responsibilities involved in priestly ordination, which in turn is itself so integral to the sacramental structure of a formally eucharistic community that that community would cease to exist as such without an ordained eucharist priesthood, therefore, the religious through his vow of obedience shares analogously in the public servant status of the eucharistic priesthood precisely because through the third vow he also shares a measure of the priest's cooperative responsibility for seeing to it that the eucharistic community truly strives to embody the ideal community envisioned by Christ. In other words, by the vow of obedience, one is not obliged to accept the Christian community or even one's own particular religious community blindly in the state of historical evolution or decadence in which one actually finds it. Nor is one obliged to look for the decisions of those in authority as ideal, i.e., as the embodiment of God's will, simply because they have actually been made. In associating oneself permanently and publicly with the servant status of the eucharistic priesthood, one declares one's concern in faith and love for the actual Christian community and for its leaders. But one's ulterior commitment in taking the vow is obedience to Christ's own ideal of that community, an ideal which transcends one's own limited vision and the limited vision of every other sinful individual in the Church, whether he is endowed with public responsibility or not, an ideal which must, therefore, be collectively discerned through reflection on revelation, tradition, and the factual situation of the actual Christian community as it concretely exists. Now, because the realization of that ideal is a cooperative venture, undertaken under responsible leadership, permanent and public association with the mission of service of responsible Church leaders does indeed involve a subordination of will in practical matters. But such practical subordination is justified only to the extent that it is a means and not an end in itself, a means, moreover, to embodying an ideal which cannot be rigidly limited to any single conceptualization of it or to any single historical decision or set of rules and laws which may seek to realize it.

Primacy of the Third Vow

We must, therefore, disagree with the suggestion that it is the second vow of religion which enjoys the primacy in religious consecration,[114] if by that one would wish to imply that it is this vow which constitutes the essence of one's commitment to God as a religious. One may take a private vow either of chastity or of poverty and still retain the ecclesial status of an ordinary layman. A religious, on the other hand, is precisely a layman who enjoys publicly a servant status within the community through his permanent, public association with the servant status of the eucharistic priesthood.

In other words, just as the main function of the vow of unrestricted love is to provide a context of interiority for the first vow of religion by reminding one of the inner love-commitment which must motivate external gratuitous sharing, so, too, the vow of obedience provides a public, ecclesial context for the living of the first two vows. It binds one to a life whose gratuitous sharing and unrestricted love is an extension of the public mission of leadership in service proper to the community's eucharistic priesthood. Therefore, in a less sacramental manner, but one nevertheless analogous to that of the ordained priest, the religious, by his vow of obedience, assumes a personal share in the eucharistic priesthood's public responsibility for exercising collective leadership in the service both of other members of the Christian community and of those outside the household of the faith. It is, to be sure, leadership in sharing gratuitously with others as an expression of one's unrestricted love. But precisely because the third vow of religion by encompassing the love-commitment contained in the first two endows them with special public ecclesiastical status and manifests the unified and integral character of the religious life, the third vow of religion, rather than the second, would seem to hold the primacy among the three vows.

The Semantic Problem

As in the case of the first two vows, however, serious semantic problems surround the traditional name given to the third vow. As a result of its de facto association with the manual tradition and its explanation of obedience, the term today summons up ascetical spectres of unreasoning and blind submission to authority, of a nominalistic legalism, of a rigid and rule-oriented pharisaism and of a platonized metaphysics of obedience in which every decision which bears the actual sanction of office is converted into a concrete embodiment of the divine ideal for man.

Rather than try to explain away these misleading connotations every time one uses the term "obedience," it seems in fact far simpler to re-name the vow. Calling it a vow of service has a number of advantages. It is active and purposeful in connotation, implying more than mere static submission to a predetermined norm. At the same time it connotes the proper subordination of will that must attend any cooperative effort to provide responsible leadership in service for the Christian community. It is rich in biblical connotations and implies the service of worship as well as practical public service. Finally, the name is a reminder of the servant status of anyone associated with the mission of the eucharistic, and hence servant, priesthood.

Several advantages accrue to this approach to obedience. For one thing, it makes it quite clear that recent demands by American religious for professional training in administration for religious superiors prior to their assumption of office, for superiors to establish an effective and on-going dialogue with their subjects, for superiors to respect and consult their subjects' areas of special competence, for superiors to encourage responsible initiative in their subjects, for the effective application of the principle of subsidiarity in religious government, are not alien to a life of religious obedience but integral to a truly Christian understanding of its purpose and nature.[115] For the failure of a religious superior to respect demands such as these, which flow from an understanding of the genuinely traditional meaning of Christian service, is in fact for him to act irresponsibly in the conduct of his office, and, in certain circumstances, perhaps even with culpably grave irresponsibility. When such irresponsibility occurs, then it is the mark of a truly obedient man, one pledged to obedience in the image of Christ, to do what is necessary in a spirit of love to see to it that such irresponsibility ceases. And this he must do, not in spite of his vow, but because of it, because by pronouncing a vow of service within the Christian community, he has publicly assumed the obligation of assisting Church leaders in the responsible conduct of their own office.

But needless to say, the effort to amend the possible irresponsibilities of Church leaders must itself be undertaken in a responsible manner, with a view to building up the community rather than to vindicating one's superior personal insight or personal moral integrity. These remarks are not, therefore, intended to give *carte blanche* to religious imbued with a permanent penchant for protest. Professional protesters who are militantly opposed to the institutional expressions of religion as such are too often inclined to speak in tones that are best dubiously recognizable as either responsible or loving.

The Biblical Ideal

At the same time, the preceding description of obedience seems much closer to a truly scriptural understanding of the meaning and purpose of the vow. We have already dwelt at some length on incompatibility with the New Testament ideal of service through atoning love, which is itself the flowering in the teachings of Christ of certain aspects of exilic and post-exilic Jewish thinking. What may be less obvious is its compatability with other aspects of the biblical notion of service.

The approach to the third vow presented here does indeed demand an obedience of faith. But it does not attempt to conceive of faith exclusively in the static terms of assent to a series of propositions. Faith is conceived here fundamentally as a commitment to a specific ideal historically embodied in the person of God's Son, an ideal which is mediated to us through propositions but which transcends any single formulation of it or any subsequent historical attempt to embody it. It is an ideal which demands that one place one's confidence in God; for, while it commits one to the enterprise of founding a specific kind of community, it precludes the use of power as a means to realizing that ideal. For it demands that a person be committed to other men with a love which forgives in advance every manifestation of hostility, malice, and indifference on their part. It demands, in other words, a love which leaves a man completely vulnerable in his dealings with others, yet completely willing to sustain a love-commitment to them come what may because his hope for the fulfillment of his love is rooted ultimately as Christ's was in his confidence in the Father's indefatigable love both for himself and for every man who exists.

In brief, the ideal Christian community is a community founded on the service of an atoning love; and the attempt to embody such a love in a loveless and alienated world still dedicated to the quest for power can indeed be an enterprise that challenges every aspect of one's person if it is taken seriously. In the case of religious especially, public association with the mission of the eucharistic priesthood demands that a person accept the public responsibility of helping to lead others in the enterprise of forming such a community by loving them in the name and image of Christ: personally, effectively, imaginatively, generously, gratuitously, without restriction or pre-condition, out of love for God, out of inner abandonment to God, out of a refusal to test God, as a member of the sacramental community, of the "little ones" his Son came to found, content to prophesy in his name without the protection of coercive power, content to accept the consequences of the repudiation and indifference of others. Can there really be any doubt that to assume a share in the public responsibility of attempting to lead the Christian community in its living of such a life is truly to dare great things in the name of God?

The Wisdom of the Fathers

The patristic theory of obedience which holds that submission to the decisions of one in religious authority is submission to the will of God can be accepted only with certain very important qualifications. For one thing, it should be made clear: first, that all things being equal, the will of an obedient subject can find conformity to God's will by conforming to the will of the superior only if the superior's command is itself conformed to God's will; and, second, that the conformity of the superior's command to God's will is not automatically guaranteed by the mere possession and exercise of office. Moreover, it should also be made clear that, although responsible submission to direction by others demands a certain self-abnegation, the main purpose of the vow of obedience is not to mortify one's prideful inclination to do what one wants by forcing oneself always to do what one's superior wants but to associate one with the enterprise of providing responsible public leadership in the service of atoning love within the Christian community of service. Since that leadership is collective, it entails necessarily the subordination of the subject's will to that of the superior. But the subordination is never an end in itself, nor is it simply a means to personal self-abnegation, even though if it is in fact to be a means to effective service of the community and to its effective public leadership, it will bring with it abnegation aplenty. Finally, it should be clear that although the vow of obedience does demand a contemplative openness to God, this openness should be conceived in active as well as in passive terms, as involving commitment to the realization of a common ideal in faith which any given decision of one's superiors on any single historical attempt to penetrate it or to embody it can never exhaust.

The explanation of the third vow offered here also helps to throw some light on statements of the magisterium concerning religious obedience. Not only does it insist on the necessity for official Church leadership, but it roots the responsibility for providing such leadership in the very sacramental structure of the Christian community. And while it does not exempt voices of prophetic dissent from being supervised by official Church leaders, it does insist on the need for those publicly and collectively responsible for Church leadership to remain sympathetically sensitive to legitimately dissatisfied elements within their midst.

At the same time, the explanation of the vow of service provided here is dramatically opposed to an individualistic piety of inner enlightenment. Both membership in a community of mutual and atoning service and a fortiori the acceptance of public responsibility for providing leadership in service for such a community commits one to a way of life that is constituted by dialogue, by shared responsibility, by an indefatigable concern to understand and to meet the actual needs of the community. Hence, any attempt to sunder the inner piety of the members of the community from the task of mutual service to which all of its members are commonly and sacramentally committed is indeed suspect.

Finally, the approach to obedience taken by the bishops at Vatican II is seen to be, not a departure from tradition, but a return to tradition that is more authentically Christian than a great deal of "traditional" ascetical writing. For the bishops have been at pains to remind us that the purpose of the third vow is in fact the more effective service of the members of the Christian community. The vow provides the one who takes it with greater security in finding God's will and imitating Christ, not in virtue of an automatic divine sanction that is supposedly attached to every authoritative decision of one's religious superiors, but by involving the subject in an effective and ongoing dialogue with Church leaders, with the community at large, and with others who like himself have by their vows assumed the public responsibility of providing the community with an example of leadership in service.

The Religious State

The explanation of the third vow offered here also helps to explain the sense in which religious can be considered to aspire to a "state of perfection." Even in a manual account of the religious life, religious were presented as Christians seeking perfection rather than as possessing it. Unfortunately, however, since "perfection" tended in that tradition to be equated with personal sanctity, the pursuit of holiness seemed to become the exclusive prerogative of religious. The repudiation of such a conclusion by the bishops at Vatican II raises the question: Is there any sense at all in speaking of the religious life as a life devoted in a special way to the "pursuit of perfection"? We would suggest that there is, but that the phrase refers not to the degree of personal sanctity of religious but to the specific ecclesial responsibilities that are theirs as a result of their active, public association with the sacramental mission of Church leaders, who by their ordination are commissioned by Christ to provide genuine leadership in atoning service within a servant community. Moreover, these responsibilities proper to religious derive from their threefold public commitment within the community: from their free dedication of their possessions and labor to the service of those in the community most in need; from their public commitment to a way of life that seeks to witness especially to the gratuity and unrestricted character of Christian love; and from their public association with the collective leadership function of the eucharistic priesthood. To live by such ideals is indeed to seek to be "perfect" like one's heavenly Father, whose love is truly gratuitous and universal and who sends his blessings upon good and evil alike.

It should, however, be quite clear that the ideals espoused by religious are continuous with the ideals espoused by every Christian. All Christians are committed to share gratuitously with others, to profess a love that is gratuitous and unrestricted in its scope, and to cooperate with Church leaders. What distinguishes a religious from a layman is the ecclesial modality of his commitment, with the public responsibilities of leadership in service that are thereby entailed. The layman's commitment is more individual and personal, in the sense that he remains ecclesially freer to join or to dissociate himself from any given group activity sponsored by the community, to choose as an individual those members and groups in the community with whom he desires to share his personal possessions. Moreover, if married, a layman is in virtue of his marriage vows publicly committed to living out his Christian ideals in the first instance within the context of individual-oriented rather than need-oriented love, with all that that implies. The religious, on the other hand, is in virtue of his public vows committed not only to living a life of need-oriented love but of doing so as one who has publicly and permanently consecrated his possessions and his labor to the support of the collective effort of the eucharistic priesthood to provide responsible leadership in service for the community of service to whom they have been sacramentally consecrated to minister. If, then, we choose to speak of religious life as aspiring to a "state of perfection," we should emphasize the word "state" rather than the word "perfection." That is to say, a religious by his vows is not consecrated to pursue perfection as his personal or even class prerogative, since all Christians aspire to perfection. But he is obliged to pursue it in a special "state," that is, as one who has freely assumed a permanent and active share in the public responsibilities of providing leadership in the Christian community by making himself the least and the servant of all.

It has not been my intent in the present chapter to sermonize religious superiors. Most of them get sufficient badgering in the ordinary exercise of their office. My quarrel is not with persons but with any speculative attempt to transform the responsibilities incumbent upon religious superiors into arbitrary power over the lives of their fellow Christians. This corresponds, of course, to the responsibilities of subjects to treat those upon whom the ultimate responsibility for decision making rests, with the charity, love, and honesty that their office demands. Superiors are human beings like everyone else and need all the love and support their communities can offer them. But superiors are public persons whose decisions affect the lives of other human beings. Hence responsible subjects can no more acquiesce automatically in their every decision regardless of its consequences any more than they can automatically repudiate every official directive as an arbitrary infringement of their liberty by an alien power structure. Nor can the subject avoid the burdens of cooperating creatively with concerned and enlightened superiors in the burdensome process of shared decision making.

But effective leadership in service in the Christian community presupposes that community leaders have a clear ideal of the kind of community that Christ intended his Church to be. If, then, we are to understand the sense of purpose which motivates a religious vow of service, we must begin to explore in greater detail some of the chief characteristics which should distinguish a genuinely Christian community.

Notes

1. Dt 6:13–15;13:15.
2. Jr 33:21–22.
3. Jos 24:22–27.
4. Dt 13:5.
5. 1K 18:36;Am 3:7;Is 1:2;Ez 2:5;Jr 7:25.
6. Gn 12:4;17:2;22:1–17;26:24;Ps 105:6–9.
7. Ex 14:13–14;Nb 12:6–8;Dt 34:5.
8. 1K 8:24–26;2S 7:8–16;Ps 78:70–72.
9. Jr 7:25–26;Ez 34:23ff;Nb 18:1–2.
10. Is 48:19–20;30:9.
11. Ex 24:7–8.
12. Ho 6:6.
13. Jr 7:4–11.
14. Jr 7:25–26.
15. Dt 9:24.
16. Jr 31:33.
17. Ez 34:23–24;37:24.
18. Is 42:1.
19. Is 42:2–3.
20. Is 42:4.
21. Mt 12:18–21.
22. Is 49:1,5a;Jr 1:5.
23. Is 49:3–5b.
24. Is 49:6.
25. Is 50:4.
26. Is 50:5–6.
27. Is 50:7.
28. Is 50:10.
29. Is 50:11.
30. Is 52:14–15.
31. Is 53:2–3.
32. Is 53:8–9.
33. Is 53:4–7.
34. Is 53:10–13.
35. Ps 110:5–6;2:9.
36. Ps 14:2–3.
37. Jn 1:34.
38. Is 6:1–13;Jr 1:4–10;Ez 1:4–2,15;Is 40:1–8.
39. Is 42:1.
40. Is 49:3.
41. Ps 2:7.
42. Ps 2:7–8.
43. Is 11:1–5.
44. Is 11:7.
45. Mt 4:1–11.
46. Lv 16:10;17:7;Is 34:11–16.
47. Jr 2:6;4:20–26.
48. Jg 20:26;Est 4:16.
49. Dt 8:2–3.
50. Dt 6:16.
51. Ex 17:7.
52. Jn 4:34.
53. Mt 21:43;Jn 8:31–36.
54. Jn 5:29–30;Mk 14:62;Mt 26:64–65;Lk 22:68.
55. Mk 10:43–45;Is 53:10.
56. Mk 1:22ff;Mt 5:20ff.
57. Jn 5:29–30;Mt 9:1–8;Mk 2:1–12; Lk 5:17–26.
58. Mt 17:24–27.
59. Mk 2:28.
60. Mt 8:8ff.
61. Mk 4:41ff.
62. Mk 10:43–45.
63. Mt 16:21–23.
64. Mt 20:25–28.
65. Mt 20:26–28;Mt 18:1–4;Lk 14:7–11;17:7–9.
66. Lk 16:13;Mt 6:24.
67. Mt 10:28–31.
68. Mt 16:24–26.
69. Jn 13:1–5;12–16.
70. Lk 22:25–27.
71. Jn 14:30–31;15:12–14.
72. Jn 18:36.
73. Jn 3:16–18.
74. Mt 26:27–29.
75. Mt 28:10–20.
76. Rm 1:5.
77. Rm 11:32;5:19–21;7:14–16,21–23; Heb 10:8–10.

78. Rm 8:19–23.
79. Rm 12:9–13.
80. Ac 2:42–47.
81. MG 5,645C,653A,692A.
82. MG 1,236A,277B,281B.
82a. MG 31,884C,888B.
83. ML 22,1080.
84. ML 33,964.
85. ML 36,274.
86. ML 36,504,277;37,1205.
87. MG 34,421D;cf.MG 82,56A;ML 54,336B;ML 77,16A.
88. ML 49,183C,185B.
89. MG 88,717B.
90. MG 65,389C.
91. DS 893.
92. DS 1165;cf.1230.
93. DS 2265–2269.
94. *Decree on the Bishops' Pastoral Office in the Church,* 35.
95. *Dogmatic Constitution on the Church,* 37.
96. *Ibid.,* 21.
97. *Ibid.,* 27.
98. *Ibid.,* 12.
99. *Decree on the Appropriate Renewal of the Religious Life,* 5.
100. *Dogmatic Constitution on the Church,* 46–47.
101. *Ibid.,* 45.
102. *Decree on the Appropriate Renewal of Religious Life,* 14.
103. *Ibid.,* 14.
104. Mt 15:1–9;23:1–36.
105. Murray, *op. cit.,* pp. 424–425.
106. Stanislaus Lyonnet, S.J., "St. Paul: Liberty and Law," in *Contemporary Spirituality* (New York: Macmillan, 1968),p.3ff.
107. McNaspy, *op. cit.,* pp. 87–90.
108. Karl Rahner, S.J., "Some Reflections on Obedience," in *Contemporary Spirituality,* p. 126.
109. *Ibid.,* p. 131.
110. *Ibid.,* p. 135.
111. John L. McKenzie, S.J., *Authority in the Church* (New York: Sheed & Ward, 1966), pp. 137–138.
112. Orsy, *op. cit.,* p. 151.
113. *Ibid.,* pp. 146–152.
114. *Ibid.,* p. 97.
115. Cf. McNaspy, *op. cit.,* pp. 88–96; Orsy, *op. cit.,* pp. 174–178.

V

The Christian Community

The people of Israel were conscious of being separate from the Gentile nations. Moreover, this separation was for them more than a fact; it was a moral imperative. They knew that it was their faith in the God who had gratuitously chosen to set them aside as his portion which had first drawn them together as a people.[1]

They also knew that election by the living God brought with it unique moral and religious responsibilities: for to be holy, to be set apart from the nations in one's way of life, was for the devout to live in the very likeness of the God who had chosen them and who was himself everlastingly set apart from the gods of the nations by his power, his fidelity, and his vitality.[2]

Moreover, it was by his continued actively salvific presence in the midst of his people that Yahweh renewed historically their special consecration to him; for it was in moments of crisis, when he actually saved them from their enemies, that he ratified in spite of their sins his sanctifying choice of Israel as his own, manifested the fidelity of his covenanted word, and assured his people that they did indeed remain "the community of Yahweh."[3]

On the other hand, since by the Sinai covenant the people of God had ratified this same divine election in all of its consequences, the sign and criterion for holiness in the true believer, i.e., for his being truly set apart and consecrated to God, was his fidelity to the terms of the covenant. For if Yahweh had initially revealed himself as a God who saves by summoning his people from Egypt, it was by his covenant that he had manifested to them through his servant Moses, his specific intentions in their regard. The truly holy Jew was, then, inevitably a man of the decalogue, faithful to the orthodox worship of the one, true God and concerned for the rights of his covenant brothers.[4]

But the holiness of God's people demanded more than lip service to the law. The burden of the prophetic message was, as we have seen, that ritual holiness alone was not enough. The truly holy man must fear Yahweh with all his heart and prove his holiness by his lived fidelity to the covenant in spite of every tribulation.[5]

Christian Election

The Christian community was, in its own way, equally conscious of having been chosen by God; and they were equally aware that such divine election brought with it serious moral responsibilities. But with the passage of time they also become increasingly conscious of specific differences which set them apart even from the Jewish community. For the sanctifying call which had created the Christian community had come to them from the lips of God's only Son.[6] From those same lips they had heard and begun to understand the scope and meaning of God's final and definitive offer of love to men. They had learned that they were the salt of the earth, the light and leaven of human society.[7]

As salt, they must not lose their savor; they were, then, committed by their acceptance of the divine call in Christ to retain a consciousness of their specific identity as a Christian community. "Do not," Paul warns, "model yourselves on the behaviour of the world around you, but let your behavior change modelled by your new mind."[8]

But as light and heaven, they knew that holiness was not to be measured in terms of isolation from the rest of men. Membership in the new Israel also brought with it the willingness to act as docile instruments of grace in the spread of God's kingdom to every corner of the earth.[9] In other words, one of the ingredients essential to the true savor of Christianity was that it remain actively involved in the task of transforming the world according to the pattern of the Christian ideals of gratuitous sharing, universal love, and service revealed in the life, death, and glorification of the Lord Jesus. Thus, the militant and zealotically oriented universalism which had begun to emerge in late Judaic thought was replaced in Christianity by a communal commitment to continue the salvific mission of universal service begun in Christ.

Moreover, it was in Jesus' faithful accomplishment of his messianic mission as God's servant that the Christian community recognized both its call and its covenant. For just as the divine call proclaimed by the Lord differed from the call of Israel in the explicit universality of its scope and in its abdication of political and coercive power as a means of establishing God's kingdom on earth, so too the covenant of the cross differed from the conditioned and revocable Sinai covenant in the fact that from God's point of view his salvific and sanctifying commitment to men had become, in and through the Christ event, both historically irrevocable and everlasting. Moreover, the new covenant was both of these things precisely because it was indeed a covenant of atonement, of reconciliation, of gratuitous love and forgiveness—a covenant, that is to say, which is the ultimate incarnate revelation of a divine longing to forgive which precedes both the sin of man and his repentance, which is willing to take upon itself the consequences of human malice, and which is simply *there* as an enduring salvific fact for any man who is willing to open his heart to the reality of Christ in a response of faith, confidence, love, and repentance.

The Christian community, therefore, felt no need to demand of God a constant renewal of his sanctifying fidelity to them by intervening again and again in the course of human events in order to crush their enemies beneath their heel. They realized that compared with the event of the risen Christ such interventions would be of limited salvific significance even if they should occur and that, anyway, they should be willing to love and forgive their enemies as Christ had. Moreover, their faith in Jesus told them that from God's viewpoint at least their consecration to him had been accomplished once and for all in the death and glorification of the Lord. All that was needed now was to mediate God's atoning love to each man, to confront him authoritatively and prophetically in the name of Christ with the enduring forgiveness that was his, if he would only turn to God in the spirit of faith and love. And to this end the lived kerygmatic proclamation of the word culminating in the sacramental act of eucharistic sacrifice was enough.

In other words, the first Christian community was aware of the fact that it had been summoned into existence by the service of atonement, of universal reconciliation and forgiveness embodied in the life, death, and glorification of Jesus. They also recognized that any human response to this final initiative of God in human affairs brought with it specific moral and religious obligations. Membership in the kingdom, in the community of reconciliation which Jesus had come to found, presupposed a willingness to accept as the ideals of one's life a whole complex of basic human attitudes toward God and toward one's fellow man—ideals drawn from the teachings of Jesus and from reflection in faith on the meaning of the Christ event, ideals whose purpose is the very constitution of a community of genuine service of the living God. Dedication to the service of God through the faith and love of Christ is, therefore, nothing else than active dedication to the cooperative graced enterprise of bringing the Christian community into being.[10]

Teachings of Jesus: Guidelines for Community Living

The formal teachings of Jesus as they are preserved for us in the gospels enunciate clear guidelines for the cooperative task of building up the Christian community. The ideal Christian community must first of all be one in which each member is at the service of every other.[11] It is a community of unrestricted hospitality, one which welcomes everyone with equal generosity, even the least of all, in the name of Christ.[12] It is a community which reverences each individual as one for whom God is personally concerned and hence, one in which each member is careful to avoid causing the least harm to any other member.[13] It is a community of reasonable men in which every effort is made to right wrongs which may occur by rational discussion and arbitration.

But it is also a community which is willing to count as its members only those who are genuinely dedicated to living the ideals of service.[14] Moreover, it is a community of unlimited forgiveness, whose acceptance of Jesus' own mission of atonement implies the willingness of each of its members to take upon himself the evil consequences of the actions of others without renouncing his love for them, even as Jesus himself had done in his own dealings with men.[15] It is a community dedicated to the genuine service of God in the image of Christ, however others may judge of its actions.[16] It is a community in which each individual is so concerned with the correction of his own failures and limitations that he is loath to pass judgment on his brethren.[17] It is a community which is concerned to exclude from its midst opinions and doctrines which are incompatible with the revelation which has taken place in Christ.[18] It is a community which is content to face adversity in peace of soul and in fidelity to its basic commitment to serve God by living and proclaiming fearlessly the truth his Son came to teach.[19] It is a community willing even to run the risk of losing its life for the sake of the Lord and of his mission in order to find that life again in him.[20] It is an expectant community stretched out in its aspiration for the fulfillment of all things in Christ and on the alert for the day of his final coming.[21]

Within such a community, the basic ideals of gratuitous sharing, of universal love, and of service provide radical centers which not only immediately ground and unify the attitudes of each Christian in his dealings with God and with his fellows, but also mediately, i.e., through the response of each individual in faith and love to the event of Christ, ground and unify the community itself.

Christian Hospitality

Sharing, for instance, in its formally ecclesial dimension is frequently presented under the rubric of hospitality. What is supposed to distinguish true Christian hospitality, where it does exist, from ordinary human hospitality is that it be undertaken as a sign and an expression of one's faith in the new covenant in Christ and hence that it bear the stamp of his universal and gratuitous love for men. Christian hospitality is not the cult of gracious living for its own sake, or even for the sake of personal, family, or social ties alone. It is, in its extremest form, a Polycarp cheerfully hosting the police who have come to drag him off to martyrdom.[22]

Needless to say, the ideal of hospitality had also been an important factor in the Old Testament view of what constitutes humane social relationships. But for the devout Jew religious belief was present as an additional important motive governing the social dealings of Israelites with their fellows. In the book of Leviticus, for instance, tolerance and cordiality toward strangers are presented as another way for the devout to recall with gratitude their own liberation from a foreign land through the intervention of a merciful God.[23-25]

Reenforced by the teachings of Jesus, the practice of hospitality took on even richer religious connotations among the first Christians. In his preaching the master had identified the "stranger" of the Old Testament with himself[26] and had further identified himself with the disciples he was sending into the world.[27] The true follower of Jesus learned, therefore, that he must share his hospitality with equal generosity to all, even to the least, as though each guest were the Lord himself.[28] As a result, Christian hospitality took on a new eschatological meaning. To welcome the Lord in the person of a guest came to be seen as an anticipation of the welcome which the Christian community would extend to the Lord in his own person on the day of his second coming. And the joys of unstinting hospitality were looked upon as an anticipation of the messianic banquet planned for the last day, when the Lord himself would return to minister in a final love feast to those who had received him with generosity.[29,30]

It is no wonder, then, that hospitality was a virtue demanded in a special way of all of those whose special mission it was to act as servants of the whole community. Apparently, a significant lack of hospitality could even disqualify a possible candidate from the office of president of the community.[31-33]

Labor as an Expression of Christian Service in Love

But commitment to the Christian ideal of sharing implies more than the commitment to a universal and selfless hospitality. For it also implies a commitment to personal labor so that one will indeed be in a position to share the good things of this life with others—in Paul's words, so that one may "be able to do some good by helping others who are in need."[34] Moreover, implicit in this same willingness to work is a number of closely related religious and moral attitudes. There is, first of all, a concern to avoid being materially burdensome to the very community that one is committed to serve.[35] Second, there is a fundamental respect for the property rights of other people.[36] Third, work with a view to serving others precludes both cut-throat competition and the egocentric desire to "get ahead" as the ultimate goal of one's labor.[37,38] Finally, labor so motivated is able to avoid all the foolish illusions of self-sufficiency which so easily accompany preoccupation with profit and with the gratifications of financial success.[39]

Needless to say, Christian reflections on the meaning and purpose of work as defined by its relationship to the ideal of gratuitous sharing must be read in the context of Old Testament thinking on the subject. In the Old Testament, however, work does in fact take on a certain ambiguous character when viewed in its relationship to man's ultimate salvation. On the one hand, it is regarded as both natural to man and fully compatible with his original state of blessedness.[40] On the other hand, as a result of Adam's fall from grace and consequent separation from the God who is the source of all life, human labor is reduced to the drudgery of struggling to wrest the means of survival from the recalcitrant earth.[41] Fallen man labors under the shadow of death in a struggle for life which he is sure at last to lose.[42]

Moreover, in a society vitiated by human arrogance and pride, human labor is degraded by every form of economic exploitation.[43-46] Nevertheless, the calloused exploitation of human labor by the unscrupulous and the proud is in fact the degradation of a human activity which possesses an inherent dignity and purpose of its own. From the hands of the laborer come objects of beauty and utility to embellish human life.[47]

Even more, work is seen as being an integral element in God's salvific plan for his people. The exodus from Egypt is nothing else than Israel's passage from a state of forced labor at the hands of powerful exploiters to the free service of the living God.[48] In other words, human labor finds its first redemption from the social consequences of man's own sinfulness by being regulated according to the prescriptions of the Sinai covenant.[49] And upon such labor Yahweh extends his blessing.[50]

Jesus in his own teaching insists on a proper hierarchy of values in human work: he insists that the labor of man has more than merely temporal significance and that the ultimate goal of one's labor must, therefore, look beyond the limits of this life.[51] Work, in other words, will find its *ultimate* redemption by becoming work for the kingdom of God, for the eschatological community of common sharing, gratuitous love, and service that he has come to found.[52] Needless to say, work of this sort will demand constant self-abnegation rooted in the conviction that the only way to save one's life is to be willing to squander it in the day-to-day service of God and of one's fellows.[53] Such labor is nothing else than the expression of the atoning, reconciling love of Jesus's disciples for one another in his name. And thus, it is a sign too of his own love for men and of the covenant of atonement which he has concluded with his Father and with them.[54,55]

It is also clear that Jesus himself had expected hard work from those who dedicated themselves to the service of the word; the images he used to describe the apostolate were in fact drawn from the back-breaking labor of the common man of his time.[56] Such labor, he warned, demands of men the willingness to die and to be reborn. For, on the one hand, it is the gratuity with which such apostolic work is undertaken that transforms it most effectively into a sign and proof that one's service of others is indeed undertaken in the name of Christ. On the other hand, the ultimate goal of such labor is the new creation itself, the final accomplishment of the reign of justice and of peace begun by Jesus when he founded this eschatological community of service and atonement as a newly covenanted Israel.[57]

The Classless Community

Finally, in addition to hospitality and labor for others in the name of Christ, commitment to the ideal of gratuitous sharing implies also a determination not only to eliminate effectively from the community every personal and social inequity in the use of material goods, but even to establish a community in which the very existence of class distinctions is intolerable.[58-64]

The Ecclesial Dimensions of Love

Fundamental though it is, the sharing of one's external possessions is only one way of expressing one's personal concern for others in Christ's name. Ideally it is the expression of a deeper charity whose purpose is to build up a community of faith and love by means of such gratuitous sharing. Charity may, however, also find a more direct form of personal expression without focusing on the use of external goods as such. And when it does, it falls less under the rubric of gratuitous sharing, and more under that of universal love. Needless to say, such rubrical distinctions are more a question of emphasis than of strict logical exclusion. Since, however, the commitment to religious living has many aspects, there is some use in calling attention to that very fact by arranging interrelated clusters of ecclesially oriented attitudes under different conceptual headings, even though these headings themselves merely express different facets of an integral commitment to service.

One is struck in reading the documents of the New Testament at the immense scope of personal relationships which the first Christian writers find implicit in the ideal of Christian love. We are told by Paul that it binds together every other virtue;[65] and by John, that it contains every other commandment of God within itself.[66] For the limited purposes of these reflections, however, the hymn to love in first Corinthians will serve us as a basic unifying text.[67]

"Love is never boastful or conceited; it is never rude or selfish." A community united by service in love possesses a common purpose and a common mind. Its common purpose is to seek the interests of others rather than one's own; its common mind, the mind of Jesus himself, who became the least of all in order to found that eschatological community of mutual service which is the Church. Such a common mind and common purpose exclude every expression of personal conceit and every manifestation of the egotistical desire for self-advancement.

"Love is patient and kind." For Paul patience is more than just another human virtue. It is a visible proof of the living presence of the Spirit of God in any community.[68] Moreover, Paul seems to be most immediately conscious of the horizontal, ecclesial dimensions of patient living; for he lists as its sister virtues: gentleness, humility, selflessness, and mutual tolerance.[68a,69]

"Love is never jealous." Paul associates jealousy (*zelos*) with feuds, factions, and wrangling within the community.[70] Viewed in its ecclesial consequences, then, it is the exact opposite of patience, kindness, and mutual tolerance. It is a disruptive force pitting Christian against Christian, group against group, slogan against slogan, as though Christ had been "parcelled out" to individuals or to sects as their private possession instead of being what in fact he is, the atoning bond of reconciliation uniting all to one another in love.[71-78]

"Love does not take offense and is not resentful." In writing to the Colossians, Paul observes that anger, ill-temper, spite, abusive language may indeed be compatible with the loose morality of pagan cults, but that such conduct is incompatible with a Christian's commitment to mutual and selfless service of others in faith and love.[79] Christian love is an atoning love which demands of men the same divine attitude of unwearied forgiveness which Jesus himself revealed in his passion and which the Father ratified in glorifying him as Lord.[80]

"Love takes no pleasure in other people's sins but delights in the truth." Christian love is realistic love. It is not grounded in a romantic idealization of human nature and conduct. And while it refrains from judging the subjective guilt of any individual,[81] still it is also careful in attempting to evaluate the deeds of men to call different kinds of human conduct by their proper names. Moreover, the believer can afford to be thus realistic precisely because his faith has freed him to acknowledge his own human salvific solidarity even with the worst of sinners and simultaneously to extend to such a one in Christ's name the hand of gratuitous friendship and forgiveness.[82] The true disciple of Jesus does not, then, as some of the American transcendentalists once did and as some contemporary social protesters are prone to do, demand the presence of integrity in others as a precondition for loving them. For the true believer is aware that for him to place any such condition upon his offer of love to others is to exchange a genuinely Christian commitment for the fundamentally egocentric cult of a loveless integrity.

In a word, one of the advantages of being a Christian is that one need never delude oneself about how bad things really are. The enduring need of each man for redemption is integral to the Christian vision; and a commitment to one another in a love which is both creative and redemptive is rooted, not in the illusory dream of an already faultless and spiritually triumphant community, but rather in the clear consciousness of that universally common and enduring salvific need. Thus, in his second letter to Timothy, Paul warns his friend to expect the worst in attempting to shepherd the people of God through the tribulation of the latter days.[83]

But at the same time as he acknowledges that the worst is always possible. Timothy is also to remain patiently committed to his task of building up a genuine community of service in the image of Christ. Moreover, he must do this, precisely because his own commitment to the ideal of service is not ultimately grounded—any more than Christ's was—in his personal success in the apostolate, or in the adequacy of men's response to his pastoral mission, but in Timothy's own faith in Christ's unshakeable fidelity to him.[84]

"Love is always ready to excuse." The clarity of vision which a love grounded in faith demands, however, never justifies any reaction to another's failure other than immense compassion and an understanding that is free from every trace of condescension. Indeed, the perfection which Jesus demands of his followers must be manifest in the first instance in the universality and comprehensiveness of their forbearance.[85] It is this compassion together with the honest acknowledgement of one's own proneness to fall which grounds the disciple's willingness to leave all judgment ultimately in the hands of a compassionate Lord.[86-88]

"Love is always ready to trust, to hope and to endure whatever comes." Ordinarily in Sacred Scripture, confidence in God and faith in him are two aspects of the same reality: God is the rock, the one person on whom a man can rely in every crisis.[89] Although the hymn to love in First Corinthians does not exclude such vertical confidence in the Almighty, Paul once again seems to lay greater stress on a more explicitly horizontal dimension to this basic Christian attitude. Our confidence in God must also inspire us to confide in *one another,* to trust *one another.*

Moreover, such mutual trust takes many forms and imposes very concrete obligations upon a community. Thus, in writing to the Romans, Paul insists that Christian love must manifest itself in a constant respect for the demands of individual consciences and that this respect must make one careful never under any circumstance to lead one's brother to violate his conscience, even in those cases when another's moral scruples, viewed more objectively, would seem to be groundless.[90]

Mutual trust also presupposes mutual honesty. Those who are committed to the ideal of service in love must be willing to speak the truth to one another in all simplicity.[91] There is, then, no place in a community founded on faith in Christ for lying, deceit, slander, or backbiting.[92,93]

Moreover, if to love in the image of Christ is to be willing to place one's confidence even in those who can all too easily betray one's trust, then implicit in the will to love is full and conscious acquiescence in the consequences of that risk. And, therefore, love which is ready to trust and to hope must also be ready to endure.[94-113]

Public Service in the Community: The Defense of Liberty

Because it is a community of service, the Christian community is, as we have just seen, a community of gratuitous sharing and universal and atoning love. But because its service of God and of men is grounded in the event of the resurrection, it is also a sacramental community which comes into being as a result of the fact that certain members of the community have received authority from the risen Christ to mediate to each person who comes into the world the Lord's own commitment of atoning love.[114] We have also seen in the preceding chapter that to accept the burden of exercising that sacramental authority implies the willingness not only to abdicate coercive power over men but also to accept the responsibility of conducting oneself in the community as the least of all, the servant of all. For Paul, therefore, as he reflected on the difference between such a sacramental community and one founded either on the event of the Sinai covenant or on the cult of pagan gods, this much at least seemed quite clear. Response to the atoning love of Christ through baptismal incorporation into the Christian community should be experienced by every man, Gentile and Jew alike, as a liberation. For the Gentile it was a liberation from the tyranny of passions which drove him to disregard the consequences of his acts upon himself and others.[115] For the Jew it was liberation from the minute observances of the Mosaic code as well, prescriptions which could, indeed, condemn a man before God but never of themselves justify him.

Hence, on the once hand, Paul warns Gentile converts at Galatia against submitting to re-enslavement to the Mosaic law through circumcision at the hands of more conservative-minded Judeo-Christians; for those rule-ridden people apparently felt that circumcision was an indispensable complement to the sacrament of Christian initiation. Implicit in this warning is, of course, the notion that for a Christian justification comes, not through fidelity to ritualistic practices, even when those practices are legally sanctioned, but by the vigor and sincerity of the faith and love which is embodied in his sacramental living, i.e., by the robustness of his response to God's prior and liberating commitment of atoning love, as a member of a sacramental community of service.[116]

On the other hand, Paul is always equally insistent that the liberty which comes with the law is not license; for license is enslavement to one's selfish desires and to the forces of evil which are opposed to God.[117]

There is, therefore, a vital tension in the ecclesial responsibilities which stem from the mission of the eucharistic priesthood to serve others in the name of Christ. On the one hand, there is the serious responsibility of seeing to it that the people of God never become overburdened by unnecessary legal prescriptions and decrees. Indeed, it was this precise pastoral principle which was consciously operative in the apostolic decision at Jerusalem not to impose the obligations of the Mosaic code upon Gentile converts.[118] Moreover, this same apostolic decree merely took to its logical and inevitable conclusion Jesus's own diatribes against the nit-picking legalism of the Scribes and Pharisees.[119] In other words, by supporting Paul and his doctrine on the relation of faith and legal observances, the apostolic college simply made it clear that they had indeed understood the Lord's own teaching that the Sabbath is truly made for man, not man for the Sabbath. They had also manifested an equally clear awareness that any man unable to live by such a principle is unfit to serve the liberated people of a new Israel.[120]

At the same time, the decision at Jerusalem was also evidence of a firm belief on the part of the apostles that their priestly authority, in virtue of the prophetic mission implicit within it, entailed a serious responsibility on their part to preside over and direct the various charismatic movements which arise within the community.

Public Service: The Discernment of Spirits

Indeed, the first Christians had been quick to discover that not every man who claims to speak in the name of God actually possesses the spirit of Christ. And with this discovery, there arose the felt need within the group for some criterion by which to distinguish true prophecy from false. The community found the norm it sought in the event of Christ itself. It is John, perhaps, who best articulates the insight: "It is not every spirit, my dear people, that you can trust," he writes. "Test them to see if they come from God, there are many false prophets, now, in the world. You can tell the spirits that come from God by this: every spirit which acknowledges that Jesus the Christ has come in the flesh is from God; but any spirit which will not say this of Jesus is not from God, but is the spirit of antichrist, whose coming you were warned about."[120a]

The first letter of John was written relatively late in the apostolic era; and the apostle is apparently most concerned as he writes about the threat posed to Christian belief by certain pre-Gnostic sects. In the apostolic community, threats to the integrity of belief had come, predictably enough, from two different quarters. The first alarms were sounded by those Judeo-Christians whose legalistic consciences had attempted to impose on the rest of the community rigidly formalistic attitudes incompatible with the free service of the new covenant. Paul had spent much of his life combating this particular abuse. But by the time of John's first letter, this initial crisis had passed; the danger was mounting on a different flank.

It is all too clear from the letters of Paul that from the earliest days of his apostolate among the Gentiles, converts from pagan worship were all too apt to bring with them into the Christian community the unbridled enthusiasms of Oriental religions, the contentiousness of a decadent philosophical eristic, and the uncriticized presuppositions of Stoic or late Platonic speculations. As John views the first stirrings of what would later develop into the powerful Gnostic sect he is understandably disturbed. And though the crisis which evoked from him the remarks just cited was historically limited, the criterion which he articulates for discerning the truth or falsity of any prophetic word heard in the community is a timeless one. The measure of any human prophetic utterance, he insists, must always be the Word of God himself, who in his temporal life, death, and glorification is the incarnation of God's definitive message of salvation to men. For just as the worship of the Mosaic code had found its fulfillment in Jesus's own living sacramental act of service to God and men, so too the prophetic tradition, which had functioned in the old dispensation not only as a warning against infidelity to the covenant but also as an ongoing historical guarantee of Yahweh's enduring commitment to his people, was forced in the new dispensation to take second place before the sacramental event of the risen Lord. Since, however, it is the resurrection which grounds historically and fully the sacramental authority of the Church and since the eucharist among all the sacraments holds the primacy, the definitive, eschatological character of the salvation offered men in the resurrection demanded that the Church's normative prophetic word be its proclamation of mankind's salvation in and through its eucharistic words and actions. That is to say, the ultimate measure of the authenticity of New Testament prophecy must be its fundamental compatibility or incompatibility with all that is implied in the eucharistic act seen as man's basic sacramental encounter with the risen Christ. Inevitably, then, those in this eschatological community of worship who have received from Christ the responsibility of presiding over the public celebration of the eucharistic banquet must also be those who are ultimately responsible to the community and to God for correctly discerning the degree of authenticity present in any of the prophetic voices which are raised within the group.

Public Service: Pastoral Supervision

Paul's letters to Timothy offer some interesting insights into the way in which the apostle conceived of this pastoral mission of service to the community as a whole. First of all, Paul encourages Timothy not to be self-conscious about his youth as he goes about the duties of his office. (Paul seems to have valued other things than age in a community leader.)[121] Instead, Timothy is to "be an example to all the believers in the way you speak and behave, and in your love, your faith, and your purity."[122] He must treat the people he serves with the greatest tact and with sensitivity toward their age, sex, and station in life.[123] He must be "saintly and religious, filled with faith and love, patient and gentle."[124] This exhortation comes, moreover, from one who had regarded himself as "the least of all the saints," who preferred to glory in his own weaknesses, and who had exhorted the Corinthians to imitate him to the extent that he himself was imitating the servant of all Jesus Christ.[125] Finally, Paul warns his friend to be careful to keep rules and regulations in their proper place, remembering that laws are made for criminals not for good people.[126-130]

It had also been Paul's experience that the tendency to indulge in endless and futile philosophical eristics "corrodes like gangrene" any community in which it is allowed to go unchecked.[131] He, therefore, warns his young friend: "Avoid these futile and silly speculations, understanding that they only give rise to quarrels; and a servant of the Lord is not to engage in quarrels, but has to be patient. He has to be gentle when he corrects people who dispute what he says, never forgetting that God may give them a change of mind so that they recognize the truth and come to their senses, once out of the trap where the devil caught them and kept them enslaved."[132]

At the same time Timothy is not to lapse into intellectual inertia. Paul is most concerned that the young man be learned in the teachings of the apostles and in the Scriptures so that he may test any speculative and prophetic voices raised in the community against the solid rock of the written word and the apostolic tradition.[133] But while Timothy must make sure that the salt of the Christian message does not lose its savor, still, his ultimate concern must be to bless what is good, not to condemn; to teach the erratic with all patience, not to anathematize them; and to bring all Christians to a common fulfillment in Christ.[134]

In addition to presiding over the community's spiritual growth in the knowledge and understanding of Christ, Paul charges Timothy with the further task of supervising the development of administrative structures within the group. Read in the light of the community's subsequent historical development, the charge should come as no surprise. For if the basic authority of the Church is indeed sacramental and if the sacraments are to be the consecration as well as expression of a life of service to the community in the name and image of Christ, then one of the major problems of those who as priests are commissioned to exercise a leadership function in the active formation of the worshipping community must be to see to it that the ongoing development of administrative structures, which are the inevitable tools for the effective service of any group, remain fundamentally compatible in their constitutive character with the commitment of selfless and atoning love mediated to men in the sacraments and demanded by way of lived sacramental response not only of the community at large but in a special way of those who serve the community officially in the name of a loving and crucified Christ. It is to this end that Paul outlines for Timothy certain basic guidelines for the selection of elders and of deacons. Such guidelines, he feels, are demanded because the "nobility" of the work of pastoral service to the community precludes admitting anyone to such a responsibility unless that individual shows signs of being capable of truly living a life of selfless Christlike service.[135]

Finally, Timothy himself must serve the people of God with truly selfless love. Above all, he must scrupulously avoid any hint of profiteering in his labors for Christ. Paul writes: "Religion, of course, does bring large profits, but only to those who are content with what they have. We brought nothing into the world, and we take nothing out of it; but as long as we have food and clothing, let us be content with that."[136]

There is, of course, another ecclesial aspect of the service of God which needs careful consideration, namely, the service of worship. But it is important and comprehensive enough to merit treatment in a chapter all its own.

The Patristic Age: The Emergence of Separate Communities

There is no evidence in the New Testament for the existence of small "religious" communities within the larger community of believers. At first glance one might be tempted to discern such a community in the apostolic college itself or perhaps in the charismatic calling of consecrated virgins and widows. The twelve apostles did seem to enjoy some sort of special status among the first disciples; and widows were in some sense "set apart" from the rest of the community. But on closer inspection, one is led to the conclusion that the special status of the apostles consisted precisely in their mission of service to the other disciples as the least and littlest of all and that what distinguished them was not their segregated mode of life but their peculiar mission to the community as a whole. Nor does there seem to be any evidence that initially at least widows or virgins gathered together in separate communities in order to live out their special charismatic calling.

On the contrary, not only did the formation of separate religious communities begin in earnest only in the fourth century; but when such communities did in fact emerge, they came about as the result of very definite historical circumstances. Both the fact of their late origin and the peculiar circumstances which gave rise to these communities had considerable impact upon patristic reflection on the meaning and purpose of community living in the religious life.

Gregory Nazianzen, for instance, is careful to link cenobitic institutions with the eremitical movement. He tells us that the hermits of Egypt had a threefold purpose in retiring to solitude. They sought to withdraw from the world; to live for God rather than for others who live in the body; and to avoid the companionship of all but God.[137] If Gregory is correct (and we have no reason to doubt his accuracy), the eremitical movement seems to have taken its origins at least in part from certain anti-social and anti-physical tendencies in the Egyptian religious community. To put the matter a bit facetiously, had God himself been a hermit to fit Gregory's description, it seems scarcely likely that the incarnation would have ever taken place.[138]

Unfortunately, however, the Egyptian hermit's solitary quest for transcorporeal transcendence eventually led to excessive and bizarre ascetical practices. The first organization of the fathers of the desert into communities was, in part at least, the result of a felt need to place a reasonable check upon the self-maceration of those hermits who took flight from people and from the body a little too seriously. In part, these communities were also the result of a gnawing Christian suspicion that in a religion of love there is something unsatisfactory about the quest for total solitude and separation from one's fellow man.[139-141]

There are, however, moments when one wonders whether or not the defenders both of solitude and of social contact are carried away by their rhetoric.[142]

In all events, there can be no doubt that the eremitical origins of monasticism did help give to the latter movement a strong contemplative bias. Jerome, for example, recommends the cenobitic life over the eremitical because he finds in community living, with its opportunities for spiritual direction and with the unavoidable curbs upon sensuality and pride which the needs of others place upon each monk a surer means of achieving genuine union with God.[143,144]

But if this was indeed the case, then our problem is a relatively simple one. We must investigate what modifications, if any, the ascetical ideals espoused by these first religious brought to the original biblical notion of the nature and purpose of community living. In attempting a very sketchy and schematic answer to this question, we shall limit our reflections to the biblical themes discussed in the earlier portions of this chapter.

Monastic Hospitality

To begin with, the cultivation of hospitality remained a prominent factor in the monastic tradition from the very beginning. Not only is it repeatedly recommended as an ideal, but we have ample evidence that monks were accustomed to extend the warmest welcome even to perfect strangers. Moreover, to this day, *venit hospes, venit Christus* has remained a cherished motto in monastic communities throughout the world.[145,146]

Rufinus, however, indicates the existence of a certain tension between the monastic contemplative ideal and the human contact demanded by the actual practice of hospitality. One joined a monastic community in order to find freedom from distracting conversation, he notes, in order to remain turned to God without the comfort of human companionship, to attend to one's own soul, and in that state to await the kingdom of God.[147] Hence, under the circumstances it was to be expected that uninhibited human contact with outsiders would pose certain problems. To be sure, in many communities monks in transit whose conversation would be likely to edify were occasionally granted the privilege of taking full part in the life of the community. But Rufinus also notes the practice of excluding even strange monks from the monastery proper if there were reason to suspect their attitudes or the edification of their conduct. Moreover, on a day-to-day basis, regular contact with travellers or with people living in the vicinity of the monastery tended to be limited to a few trusted elderly monks who would serve as the community's contacts with the outside world or to the doorkeeper whose job it was to exclude undesirables from the monastery and to minister in the name of the community to any guests who happened to be stopping over. The guests, however, stayed in special rooms separated from the monk's cells and from the ordinary life of the community.[148]

In other words, while the monks continued to cherish in a practical way the ideal of universal hospitality, their quest for contemplative transcendence meant that it was sometimes necessary to delegate the actual practice of hospitality to a chosen few who acted as hosts in the name of the community. Needless to say, the practice of such hospitality-by-proxy is nowhere to be found in the New Testament itself.

In addition, under the influence of the monastic movement, the universality and gratuity of Christian hospitality also underwent certain concrete practical modifications, at least in the sense that levels of preferential treatment came to be meted out to individual guests according to their degree of personal association with the contemplative ideal espoused by the host community.[149-151]

The Patristic Tradition: Monastic Labor

The closed nature of the contemplative community also brought to patristic reflection certain modifications of the biblical notion of work as an expression of and means to common sharing. Work for others in the name of Christ, was indeed one of the chief motivations behind the first formation of cenobitic communities. We have already noted Basil's suspicions of any work whose sole purpose was the fulfillment of one's own personal needs.[152] Similarly, Augustine insists that the distribution of one's possessions to the poor which precedes entry into a religious community implies an active willingness to bear thereafter one's share of the labor that is necessary for the community to remain self-supporting to the extent that that is humanly possible. And with Pauline hard-headedness, he gives instructions that any monk who refuses such labor should be denied the support of the monastery until his hunger brings him to his senses.[153]

But it would be a mistake to imagine that the labor of the monks was always directed exclusively to the support of the monastery itself, although understandably enough this seems to have been their most immediate preoccupation. Rufinus, however, recounts the concern of monks to share the fruits of their labor with the poor and the needy, even with those who lived at great distances.[154]

We may, therefore, discern two consequences for Christian reflection on the religious significance of work which emerges from the formation of closed contemplative communities. First of all, work tends to be conceived most immediately as work for the support of the other members of one's own religious community and only afterwards as work for the Christian community at large. Second, there is at least initially an unfortunate tendency, which is repeatedly opposed in the writings of the Fathers, to regard the quest for contemplation and physical labor as either unrelated or as incompatible. Moreover, the various efforts of the Fathers to resolve the tension range from the extreme of identifying private contemplation with a salvifically fruitful form of activity possessing of its nature genuine ecclesial dimensions, to identifying manual labor itself with prayer, to insistence that God is pleased with neither prayer nor work unless both are done in the measure approved by one's superiors.[155-158]

The Monastic Tradition: Classless Communities

From the first, the monks were concerned about eliminating every kind of class distinction from their religious communities. Chrysostom, for example, points out that in the monastery true nobility is measured not by externals, like fine dress and the signs of office, but by virtue, self-control, submission to God's law, and inner freedom from the domination of pleasure.[159-163] What is perhaps new in patristic thought on religious community is the feeling that monastic communities, precisely because they tolerate no distinctions of persons, are more authentically Christian than the larger community of the baptized. Chrysostom, for instance, also writes that as a result of living in a classless community of mutual service, monks find salvation a much easier task. But he also warns that for the same reason their lives are not necessarily more meritorious.[164]

The Monastic Tradition: The Ecclesial Dimensions of Love and Service

As we have already seen, the ideal of mutual service and love in Christ's name was one of the principal motives behind the formation of religious communities. At the same time the fact that these communities were contemplative in their aim and relatively isolated from the Chirstian community at large gave a special flavor to early monastic understanding of the meaning of that same mutual love and service.

First of all, there is a tendency in the pertinent texts to conceive the contemplative love of God in his transcendence as the true goal of all of one's activity. Augustine, for instance, never seems to tire of repeating that the soul can find its rest only in the

God who is its goal.[165] At the same time, prayer itself is often conceived as a privileged means of achieving a measure of divine union even in this life.[166,167]

Within the context of contemplative living, then, one of the chief manifestations of fraternal charity came to be the mutual assistance religious gave to one another in the task of achieving personal union with God through prayer. Needless to say, this common quest for contemplation necessarily placed certain restraints upon ordinary human manifestations of love and friendship.[168]

Similarly, one encounters not infrequently the notion that one's fellow religious, whether intentionally or not, provide one with a useful means for practicing that mortification which is an integral part of the contemplative ascent to God. Needless to say, this tendency to speak of the members of one's community as an important instrument for acquiring those inner dispositions of heart which are a prerequisite for true contemplative union with God finds no parallel in the pages of the New Testament itself.[169-170]

Inevitably, too, the closed character of the first contemplative communities limited in practice the actual scope of the service and love that its members could concretely cultivate. Most immediately, though not exclusively, religious were expected to serve one another within the confines of the monastery itself. Indeed, as we have seen, mutual service among the members of a community was from the beginning one of the chief duties incumbent on every religious.[171]

At the same time, Augustine notes that the crying needs of the Church could at times appear relatively remote to men and women isolated by their quest for contemplation from the rest of the Christian community. Though personally drawn to a contemplative life, he writes to Abbot Eudoxius urging him and his monks to be ready to come to the aid of the Church should the need arise. He concludes: "Do not, then, prefer your leisure to the needs of the Church; for if no good men are willing to minister to her in her labor, you will find your own delivery obstructed."[172]

Finally, there is also a tendency among the patristic writers to identify the suffering necessarily implied in the service of God with obedience itself. Pseudo-Macarius, for instance, writes: "Abnegation of soul, however, is never to seek one's own will, but to subdue self-will and do unceasingly the word of God, to use it as a good steersman, who pilots the congregation of the brethren to the port of God's will."[173] Similarly, the *Sayings of the Fathers* teaches that obedience takes the place of the afflictions that one must undergo in order to reach the kingdom of heaven.[174]

The Magisterium: The Ecclesial Dimensions of Sharing

Prior to the nineteenth century, a large number of the official pronouncements of the Church about the ecclesial dimensions of Christian sharing were concerned with the legitimacy and effects of almsgiving.[175-178]

Another dominant official concern was the ability of almsgiving to benefit the dead. The Waldensians had opposed the notion that the giving of alms actually benefited souls in purgatory; and their position had been roundly condemned.[179] In 1274, the Second Council of Lyons had insisted that the dead can indeed be helped by alms;[180] and both the Council of Florence and Sixtus IV in an encyclical letter had reiterated the doctrine.[181]

The Council of Florence, moreover, had also taught explicitly that alms can satisfy for the effects of one's own personal sin; and Trent had made the same point definitively.[182]

Finally, in the late seventeenth century, the laxist attempt to redefine "superfluity" of possessions so as to absolve the rich from any obligation whatever to share their goods with the poor was also condemned, by Pope Innocent XI.[183]

These pronouncements of the magisterium serve as a useful thermometer for measuring the attitudes toward the gratuitous sharing of wealth which were prevalent in the Christian community in different eras. The decrees suggest that although belief in the ecclesial dimensions of almsgiving had indeed endured even during the late Middle Ages, as a result of growing preoccupation on the part of Christians with divine punishment for sin in the life to come, the basic purpose of almsgiving had assumed a dominantly other-worldly character. That is to say, it was seen all too often primarily as an efficacious way of shortening punitive suffering in the fires of purgatory. At the same time, the official ecclesiastical defense of the practice of almsgiving as a value for the living Christian community had taken the rather limited form of vindicating medieval institutionalizations of the religious profession of poverty. Finally, the laxist effort in the seventeenth century to dismiss almsgiving as impracticable suggests an even deeper indifference toward the plight of the poor on the part of baptized Christians. It was in effect a theological rationalization for existing aristocratic and bourgeois apathy toward the misery of the downtrodden by transforming that attitude into a curious ethical imperative.

Christian Sharing: The Reform of Economic Society

The industrial revolution and its social and political consequences began to re-alert Church leaders in the nineteenth century to the monstrous injustices which had resulted from the irresponsible use of private capital. In their social encyclicals, the Popes show a vital concern for correcting the economic ills of their times. They seek to strike a balance between the extremes of laissez-faire individualism and of economic collectivism. Against the latter they affirm man's natural right as a person to ownership; against the former, man's duty to use property responsibly and with regard for the personal rights and basic needs of other men.[184-188]

But even though these documents show an acute and perceptive sense of the social dimension of ownership and of the social obligations inherent in the use of material goods, their chief concern is with right order in civil and economic society. Hence, as important as they are they cannot be taken as a full and adequate expression of the purpose and use of property within an ideal Christian community. It is one thing to secure justice in the civil order; it is much more to use material goods in order to build up a community founded on the principle of open-ended and gratuitous sharing with all in need. It should, then, come as no surprise if in the latter case significantly greater sacrifices are demanded of the disciple of Christ. In this context it is perhaps worth noting that Vatican II reminds religious that their concern to share freely with one another should not be restricted to the members of their own community or even to the poorer houses and provinces of their own order or congregation, but that religious must contribute generously from their resources to the needs of the Church as a whole and to the needs of the poor in the places where they live.[189]

The Magisterium: Christian Hospitality

The ideal of Christian hospitality has for the most part been ignored in official documents of the Church. Hospitality to strangers is, however, commended in the documents of Vatican II as being the mark of the truly Christian family.[190] And in *Populorum Progressio* Pope Paul reminds Christians of their duty in faith to show special hospitality to those from foreign lands, especially to foreign students from the developing nations and to migrant workers.[191]

The Magisterium: The Dignity of Labor

In the case of labor conceived as a Christian ideal, there are, however, some interesting texts in the statements of the magisterium. Interestingly enough in the controversy with the Protestant reformers, ecclesiastical authorities were careful to avoid condoning idleness on the part of religious. For instance, the carefully hedged condemnation by the Council of Constance of Wycliff's propositions that religious should work for their living instead of begging is an interesting example of the embarrassment of Church leaders who have been forced into the position of condemning the inaccuracy of a thesis whose more moderate formulation might have elicited their positive support. Thus, the bishops condemn the first part of the proposition (that monks should work for a living) on the basis that it implies that *all* monks are idlers, and the second part (that monks should not beg) for being simply erroneous. Taken together, the two parts of the condemnation would seem to imply that mendicants should earn the right to beg by working hard to support themselves as far as possible by their own sweat.[192]

The most frequent references to the purpose of labor, however, occur, as one might expect, in the papal encyclicals. In *Rerum Novarum,* for instance, Leo XIII characterizes labor as being both personal and necessary. It is personal because it appertains intimately to the person who performs it, is proper to him, and should benefit him; it is necessary, since man depends upon the fruits of his labor for life itself.[193] Subsequent papal decrees expanded this leonine doctrine.[194-197]

Vatican II: Toward a Theology of Work

In addition to papal decrees on the social rights of working men and women, the documents of Vatican II show a vital pastoral concern with the meaning and salvific dimensions of human labor. By way of general exhortation, the bishops remind Christians everywhere of their obligation to work for the elimination of suffering and injustice from human society. The bishops single out for special concern the aged, the migrant worker, the refugee, abandoned and illegitimate children, and the hungry. The bishops also call upon all Christians to oppose whatever destroys or diminishes human life, such as murder, genocide, abortion, euthanasia, suicide, mutilation, suffering in any form both of soul and of body—as well as whatever diminishes human dignity—such as arbitrary imprisonment and deportation, slavery, prostitution, living conditions which are sub-human, working conditions which degrade the laborer.[198-203]

Seeking to concretize these abstractions in action, the bishops, conscious of their responsibilities as leaders, outline a series of goals and programs for protecting the dignity of human labor in contemporary society. They insist first of all that laborers be made vitally aware of their right to culture and education.[204]

They demand the removal of economic inequalities in national and international society without violence to the rights of persons or to the national characteristics of each country. In particular they call for help to farmers in the production and marketing of their produce, for social measures to protect family life, for the elimination of every kind of labor which reduces man to a mere tool of production, for an end to every form of unjust economic discrimination against classes or races of men whether in wages or in working conditions.[205] They re-affirm the duty incumbent on every man to labor and the consequent right that is his for the chance to fulfill that duty in society. They condemn every form of economic slavery and insist on the right of every human person to develop his abilities, his personality, his resources and potentialities, to enjoy sufficient leisure and rest, and to cultivate a familial, cultural, social, and religious life. The bishops affirm both the right of every man to belong to a labor union without fear of reprisal and the obligation of every union to represent its membership truly, to contribute to general economic growth, and to seek the settlement of grievances by arbitration, before resorting to strikes.[206]

The bishops exhort those who labor and whose work is often burdensome to seek by their toil not only to perfect themselves, aid their fellow citizens, and raise both the whole of society and creation itself to a higher degree of perfection, but also to seek in their labor to imitate by lively charity, joyous hope, and willingness to share one another's burdens the Christ who "roughened his hands with carpenter's tools and who in union with his Father is always at work for the salvation of men." Thus, by their labor itself, they will grow in a truly apostolic sanctity.[207]

Finally religious are reminded that they too are subject to the same law of labor which is binding upon all men. But as men vowed to the imitation of a compassionate Christ, they must brush aside all undue concern for themselves in providing for their own needs and by sharing liberally with others must entrust themselves instead to the providence of their heavenly Father.[208]

The Magisterium on Social Class

The basic biblical belief that a Christian can make no distinctions based on social class in his dealings with his fellow men is reflected indirectly in some of the official documents of the magisterium. In 873, for example, John VIII wrote the princes of Sardinia urging them, in virtue of their obligation as Christian men and of their hope for a better reward in heaven, to set their slaves free.[209] In 1537, Paul III, at the request of the Archbishop of Toledo, intervened in an effort to protect the Indians of Central America and of the West Indies from enslavement and exploitation by the conquistadores. The fact that the Indians of the new world were pagans, the pope insisted, in no way justified their enslavement and deprivation of life, liberty, and property "since they are men and therefore capable of salvation."[210] Gregory XVI in 1839 condemned the black slave trade, especially in Latin America;[211] and in 1931, Pius XI repudiated the Marxist concept of "class warfare" as a means of achieving a just social order.[212]

In the documents of Vatican II, the bishops deplore the imbalances that persist in the contemporary social, economic, and political structure. They acknowledge that mankind has never had such wealth, resources, and economic power at its disposal as it has today; and yet they observe with sorrow, a "huge proportion of the world's citizens continue to suffer from hunger, poverty, and illiteracy. Politically the world is divided into armed and opposing camps, while social, political, economic, racial, and ideological disputes divide men one from the other."[213]

At the same time, the bishops affirm the Church's active concern for the oppressed and suffering masses of humanity and her desire to relieve them in their need.[214] They deplore the myopic efforts of both capitalists and communists to find solutions to man's social problems based exclusively on economic principles, which fail to take account of man's human and religious needs.[215-217]

Finally, religious are instructed to eliminate class distinctions so that there is only a "single category" of religious in any community.[218]

Varieties of "Christian Love"

Theological errors concerning the meaning of Chrsitian love condemned over the centuries by the magisterium have inevitably reflected the intellectual preoccupations of the age in which the condemnation occurred. The condemnation of Eckhart in 1329, for instance, seems to be concerned to establish the principle that there are, indeed, degrees of love and that God must always remain the supreme object of human concern.[219] The contrast, however, between this early condemnation and later pronouncements during the seventeenth and eighteenth centuries is interesting; for while the fourteenth-century condemnation seeks to vindicate the transcendent aspects of Christian love, the later condemnations are equally concerned to counteract the excessive transcendence of jansenistic and quietistic interpretations of the meaning of charity and to insist more strongly on the immanent dimensions of love.[220-239]

These condemnations also manifest a realistic sensitivity on the part of the teaching Church to some disturbing movements which developed in the theory and practice of Catholic piety. Post-tridentine "devotion" showed all too often an alarming tendency to dissociate the love of God from the love of one's neighbor and in the process not only to convert the love of God into a Platonic flight from the present world, but also to conceive of Christian love in increasingly subjectivistic terms as though it were merely a quality inherent in the individual Christian instead of an essentially relational (i.e., social and ecclesial) reality as well, one that opens one out in joy to both created and uncreated reality. If we are to believe the first letter of John,[240] the death of both the love of God and the love of neighbor which finally found verbal expression in laxist "piety" would be the logical outcome of such a dissociation.

Vatican II: The Ecclesial Dimension of Love

The documents of Vatican II made a concerted effort to reinstate fully and explicitly the ecclesial dimensions of Christian love. The Council Fathers remind us that mere Church membership is no guarantee of salvation unless membership also finds expression in a love which responds to the grace of Christ in thought, word, and deed.[241] The bishops, moreover, are careful to link the love of God intimately with the love of neighbor. They remind us that Jesus' supreme act of love for his Father consisted in his dying for us on the cross and that belief in him demands an active involvement with the needs of the men and women for whom he died.[242, 243]

The Council Fathers are, moreover, at pains to spell out in some detail precisely what the love of our fellow man in Christ's name entails. It implies, first of all, an active recognition of the dependence of men on one another within society and an active concern that every man enjoy the food, clothing, and shelter necessary for a truly human life. It means, the bishops insist, active commitment to the ideals that every man have the freedom to choose a suitable state of life, to found a family, and to provide for the care and education of his children; that every man enjoy the chance for employment, the advantages of a good reputation and of the respect of his peers; that every man have access to the information he needs to guide the course of his life intelligently and responsibly; that every man be free to act according to his conscience, provided he respects the rights of others; that the privacy of every man be protected; and that he enjoy the freedom he needs to worship God as his conscience dictates. In a word, love of others in the name of Christ demands active commitment to the collective human task of improving the social order either as an individual or as a member of a group enterprise.[244]

Hence, to love others in the name of Christ also implies the willingness to respect and love those who think differently from oneself in social, political and religious matters. While the believer must repudiate error where error does in fact exist, he must nevertheless be scrupulously careful by the way in which he deals with those of other opinions and of other faiths to respect their fundamental dignity as human beings and their right before God to live according to their conscience provided they manifest reciprocal respect for the rights and needs of others.[245]

To love others in the name of Christ means to work in order to transform the institution of the family into a genuine community of love. The Christian family will be a sign of the savior's presence in the world by union of all the members of a family with one another in prayer and in belief and especially by the loving union of husband and wife, by their generous fruitfulness, by their solidarity and fidelity, and by the spirit of loving cooperation which should characterize Christian famliy life.[246-248]

For those who have received special grace, to love others in the name of Christ means to lead an active and affective life of apostolic celibacy; for both priests and religious[249,250] must carry one another's burdens. A true and thriving fraternal love among the members of a community will leave them to give thanks to the love of God which has thus gathered them together.[251] The bishops also insist that even though religious should love God before all else and should seek to "develop a life hidden with Christ in God," their very dedication to God must give rise and "urgency to the love of one's neighbor for the world's salvation and the upbuilding of the Church." For the religious's commitment to Christ is mediated by the living Church, and this very mediation demands a loving commitment to the service of the Church as the necessary and logical consequence of loving commitment to Christ.[252]

To love others in the name of Christ means active involvement in all forms of the lay apostolate. This apostolate, the bishops insist, calls out to "all of the faithful," as the necessary consequence of their acceptance of the law of love taught and lived by Christ. It demands of all who are involved in it not only the continual exercise of faith, hope, and love, but also requires preferential involvement in apostolic works which embody in a special way the love of one's neighbor in Christ's name.[253]

To love others in the name of Christ means to be a peacemaker, to labor to disperse the threat of war which will overshadow humanity until men return to the Christ who shed his blood in order to reconcile them with one another.[254]

To love others in the name of Christ means active involvement in ecumenical work. It means to labor in order to level all the barriers which divide men from one another, whether those barriers exist within the Christian community itself or in society at large. Moreover, the bishops warn, to encourage the kind of dialogue which is needed for the reunion of all Christian peoples demands of every peacemaker self-denial, unstinted love, yearning for unity, a willingness to grow toward maturity in faith and love, and a sincere effort to live the message of the gospel.[255]

To love others in the name of Christ means to give support both to the missionary activity of the Church, which must itself be an expression of love and of a desire to share with all men the spiritual goods of this world and the next, and to Christian education, not only by creating the proper religious atmosphere in Christian homes, but also by making Christian schools into institutions in which full personal development in truth and in the love of God are effectively inculcated.[256]

Finally, to love others in the name of Christ means to be willing to treat every man, be he Christian or not, as one's own brother and as one who has been fashioned in the image of almighty God.[257]

The Magisterium: The Priestly Mission of Service

The Christian community is a servant community, dedicated to the service of God in a worship which includes and presupposes the active service of others in the name of Christ. It follows, therefore, that those who exercise a leadership function in the community must lead all others in the service they render freely and gratuitously in the name of Christ.

Prior to Vatican II, the declarations of the magisterium are concerned to vindicate the double fact both that priestly ordination does indeed involve a special mission and office within the community and that this mission derives from Christ himself and not from the men and women whom he came to save. This priestly mission is consistently presented under the familiar rubric of preaching the good news in the name of Christ, sanctifying men through the administration of the sacraments, directing the Christian community's life of service to God and to others in Jesus's name.[258-260]

Thus, both in the decrees of Trent and in official Church documents of the eighteenth and nineteenth centuries, official declarations on the meaning of the priestly ministry remain concerned not only with the divine origin of Church authority but with the proper subordination of authorities within the Church's hierarchical structure.[261, 262, 263, 264, 265]

Finally, both Pius XI and Pius XII reaffirmed the sacramental function of the ordained priest within the community, insisting that the ordained minister of Christ bears the person of Christ by being empowered to function as the latter's personal delegate,[266] that he is not, therefore, a mere delegate of the community but acts in the name of the community precisely because by his ordination he acts in the name of Christ and is thus constituted a real mediator between Christ and the people of God. The community of the faithful, Pius insists, does not "sustain the person of the divine Redeemer" in the same manner as the priest, that the community is not a conciliator between itself and God, and that it cannot, therefore, enjoy the same sacerdotal office as the priest.[267]

One must, however, turn to the documents of Vatican II to find the fullest official explanation of the meaning and purpose of the priestly mission within the Church. Not only do these documents provide needed perspective for understanding the meaning of papal primacy by balancing it with the doctrine of collegiality, but they also spell out in concrete detail much of what is involved in the pastoral mission of serving the servants of God.

The bishops attempt to resituate the teachings of Pius XII concerning the mission of the priest in a larger theological context. They remind us that all the faithful are indeed "a holy and royal priesthood," but that within this priestly community not all exercise the same function. Not all have the power to offer sacrifice or to remit sins, but only those who are so configured to Christ the High Priest that they may act in his name as Head of the mystical body, namely, bishops and to a lesser extent priests, whose mission it is to assist the bishop in his priestly office.[268]

Moreover, just as insistence on the priestly mission of the whole Christian community provides an expanded context for interpreting the meaning of the priest's own mission, so too earlier insistence on priestly authority is balanced in Vatican II by a new insistence on the obligations which are consequent upon the acceptance of the priestly office. Whoever is sacramentally configured to the Head of the mystical body is solemnly bound to move among the people of God as one who serves them and is truly concerned for their needs, as one who comes to minister, not to be ministered to.[269]

The priestly mission of service remains, however, prophetic and challenging. Its purpose is the glory of God, which "consists in this: that men knowingly, freely, and gratefully accept what God has achieved through Christ and manifest it in their whole lives." Those who exercise the priestly office contribute to the extension of God's glory when they engage in prayer and adoration, in the prophetic proclamation of God's word, in offering the Eucharist, in administering the other sacraments, and in performing any other works of service proper to their ministry.[270]

Vatican II: The Service of Religious

Religious are those believers who are most intimately associated with the labors of those who exercise a priestly mission of prophetic service within the worshipping community.[271] By their vows, religious enter into a special relationship with the rest of the believing community: They are consecrated to the task of implanting, strengthening, and spreading the kingdom of Christ throughout the world by prayer and works of service[272] and to doing so with a selflessness which shows that they regard the kingdom of God as a value which is superior to all earthly considerations.[273]

Two consequences would seem to flow from the professional association of religious with the hierarchy's mission of apostolic service. On the one hand, at an immediately practical level, religious should be able to function smoothly and effectively within the apostolic team headed by their bishop.[274-280] On the other hand, the mission of religious men and women within the Christian community must partake of aspects of both the priestly and the lay apostolates without sharing fully in the sacramental status of the hierarchy.

Community Living: The Manual Tradition

Manual asceticism has few reflections to offer on the meaning of community as such. Its preoccupations are with the individual, with his inner purification under grace from the remnants of personal and original sin, with his acquisition of appropriately Christian virtues and attitudes, and with his personal approach to God through prayer. Needless to say, all of these are perfectly valid and justifiable goals without which no Christian community can exist. In the matter of community, therefore, the fundamental objection to be raised against a manual approach to community is not whether the goals it implicitly sets for a religious community are worthwhile, but whether through a less individualistic approach to religious living there might not be equally effective, or even more effective, way of achieving those same goals. For we badly underrate the Holy Spirit if we imagine that his inspirations are exhausted by our ascetical manuals.

But even though the manual tradition remains relatively

silent on the subject of community, its silence is not absolute. When it does speak about community, however, its approach tends to be rule-oriented, authority-oriented, and contemplative in its bias.

Needless to say, insistence upon the need for rules in community living can no more be sniffed at and dismissed than the need for personal contemplation. Some kind of regularity in one's life may well be for many people, even for many who resist it most, the only effective way to ensuring fidelity to prayer, efficiency in one's apostolic work, and a sense of purpose and of mission in one's life. And failure to put such regularity into one's life may indeed, as manual asceticism warns, be one of the contributing factors in this or that individual's loss of vocation.

But one may concede all of these points and still not concede the basic presupposition about community which one habitually encounters in a manual approach to the subject, namely, that total fidelity to the written rule and to its legally authoritative interpretations is the ultimate basis on which to build a religious community. If the analysis of the preceding chapter is correct, to accept the rule of one community rather than another as an ordering principle in one's life is to insert oneself into a developing ascetical tradition with a view to understanding its basic motivations and to contributing as far as possible to its advance both speculatively and practically. True fidelity to the rule, then, is fidelity to its ultimate purposes, to the inspired vision which originally gave rise to its historically conditioned set of normative regulations. Moreover, one can pledge one's fidelity to that vision only to the extent that it is itself compatible with the vision of Christ himself and with the existing needs of the Christian community.

Moreover, as we have already seen, sacramental authority with all the responsibilities it implies is indeed constitutive of the Christian community, so much so that without it the community as such would cease to exist. But if, on the one hand, we attempt to attribute to the non-sacramental use of authority the same self-validating characteristics as its sacramental use, and if, on the other hand, we seek to make such misconceptions of authority the ultimate basis of our day-to-day community living, then we are indeed perversely building our religious houses upon sand rather than on rock.

Finally, the historical development of religious communities, the magisterium of the Church, and theological reflection on the Christian ascetical tradition, all make it quite clear that an individualistic quest for contemplative ascent to God without reference to the service of others in Christ's name can never be the ultimate constitutive purpose of Christian community living.

Preliminary reflection on the limitations of the manual tradition thus leaves us faced with two important and rather basic questions: How concretely are we to conceive the constitutive purpose of a religious community? And how does prayer relate to that ultimate purpose? We shall postpone any attempt to answer the second question until the following chapter. The first question alone will, however, provide more than enough difficulties to occupy us for the remainder of this one.

The Search for Alternatives

The current disrepute of the legalistic mind in many segments of the Christian community has led to speculative attempts to provide some other ground than rule-observance as the unifying purpose of the religious community. The result has been the proposal of two antithetic community ideals, which might be labeled the "functionalist" ideal and the "personalist" ideal.

The functionalist ideal seeks to fill the moral vacuum created by manual asceticism's nominalistic approach to rule-observance with a practical sense of accomplishment. And indeed to the extent that manual asceticism treats rule-observance as an end rather than as a means, it does in fact effectively deprive religious life of any lived sense of purpose beyond regularity for its own sake. One of the clichés of a manual approach to community living is, for instance, that the ideal community is the perfectly observant community.

The functional ideal of community is, on the other hand, more situationally relative. It regards the rule as at best one useful guide among others for discovering the will of God in any given situation. That is, it seeks to alleviate the purposelessness consequent upon a nominalistic attempt to absolutize fidelity to written law by insisting instead upon a realistic, situationally motivated sense of purpose as the common bond uniting the members of any given community. The resulting community is, therefore, in the first instance at least, that of a task-oriented community united by its cooperative attempt to get a particular job done. In other words, it is the apostolic task in hand which justifies the community in its existence and is the cohesive force binding its members to one another.

But for many religious this "functional" ideal of community living is almost as alarming as a legalistic one. It summons up the spectre of an impersonal business corporation. Anti-functionalists find little in common between an association of people for the pragmatic accomplishment of some task and the ideal of a truly Christian community. The Church is not, they argue, General Motors Corporation. They fear the substitution of an impersonal cult of efficiency for the impersonal cult of uniform rule-observance. They fear that a task-oriented community will almost by definition seek to use human beings as mere means to the accomplishment of its ends rather than to recognize that every person must be treated as an end-in-himself.

The "personalist" ideal of a religious community is, therefore, an attempt to provide an alternative to both a "functional" and a "rule-oriented" ideal. The *raison d'être* of a religious community, it insists, is neither efficiency nor uniformity. It is the establishment of inter-personal community among its members. That is to say, religious come together in a community in order to establish deeply personal relationships of mutual understanding, love, and trust; to settle for anything less is to acquiesce in an ideal of community that is less than Christian.

Still, the "personalist" ideal of community is not itself beyond all criticism. When viewed as an alternative to the "functionalist" ideal, it seems at first sight to deprive the religious community of an important aid for the establishment of interpersonal relations. One of the Fathers of the Church once counseled that if one would have men love one another, one should have them build a tower together. One cannot establish realistic "I-thou" relations in a vacuum. To be dedicated as a community to a common apostolic work ought, then, to encourage rather than to inhibit interpersonal relations among its members. Even the husband-wife relationship in marriage has a certain "task-orientation," namely, the cooperative upbringing of children.

By the same token, the exponent of a "rule-oriented" approach to community living might object to a functionalist that written rules are nothing else than the written expression of the felt common apostolic purpose ideally motivating the members of a community, and to a personalist that some form of institutionalized common living is necessary as the social context in which interpersonal relations may be allowed to develop.

All of these mutual recriminations have their point. For if rigid emphasis on written rules does tend to depersonalize community living and to deprive it of a sense of purpose, in their extreme forms both a functionalist and a personalist approach to community can—the one by its pragmatic situationalism, the other by its sense of the concrete immediacy of human relationships—tend to develop into a destructive anti-institutionalism which is opposed in principle to any regularized expression of community life whatever. Moreover, an extreme functionalism which values efficiency more than the personal human needs of the people whose labor produces that efficiency can indeed have as depersonalizing an influence on community living as pharisaical legalism. The personalist approach can, on the one hand, become as devoid of purpose as any legalism if it transforms the formation of "I-thou" relations into the exclusive end of community living. In other words, while extreme functionalism successfully compensates for the purposelessness induced by an extreme legalism and while extreme personalism compensates for the impersonalism also induced by the latter, nevertheless, on the one hand, neither functionalism nor personalism in their extreme forms compensates simultaneously for both of these chief deficiencies of extreme legalism. On the other hand, both extreme functionalism and extreme legalism tend to overlook the positive values inherent in the reasonable institutionalization of human life.

Service: The Integrating Factor

Clearly, then, what is needed is an approach to community living which combines the positive values of all three positions while simultaneously avoiding as far as possible their tendency to a certain myopic narrowness.

The complex ideal of service proposed in the preceding chapter would, we would suggest, seem at first sight to fill the bill. To the personalist it gives the assurance that the *raison d'être* of a religious community is indeed the establishment of an association of people who are bound together mutually in an attitude of gratuitous, forgiving, and atoning love. To the functionalist, it offers the further comforting assurance that that love-commitment is empty and meaningless unless it finds material embodiment in the gratuitous sharing of material goods, i.e., unless it finds active expression in a cooperative community effort to serve those of its members and those in the Christian and human community who are in greatest need. For to the extent that a religious community is actively and lovingly need-oriented, it is task-oriented as well. Finally, to the exponents of a rule-oriented asceticism, it gives the assurance that some kind of institutional structure is inevitable in any essentially sacramental community. But it insists upon the need to exercise constant vigilance over non-sacramental institutional structures in the Church so as to ensure, to the extent that it is humanly possible to do so under grace, that the latter do indeed mediate and embody quasi-sacramentally both in their purpose and in their active implementation, the same commitment of divine atoning love mediated to men in the formally sacramental use of ecclesial authority. For shared participation in the apostolic mission of service of the eucharistic priesthood remains historically and situationally an open-ended one and is in fact capable of any number of personal and institutional embodiments.

The Constitutive Tensions of Community Living

In his book on the religious life, Fr. Örsy has been at pains to point out that the decree on the religious life approved at Vatican II has rendered obsolete some very traditional ascetical categories. Thus, the insistence of the bishops that all religious communities are both apostolic and contemplative has made any attempt to distinguish communities into contemplative, apostolic, or mixed quite pointless. As Fr. Örsy insists, if every community is both contemplative and apostolic, then all are mixed. He himself settles for a distinction between "enclosed" or "cloistered" communities and "apostolically active" ones.[291] The distinction would seem to be in many ways a useful one. On the other hand, both terms suggest already existing canonical structures; and since our present intent is more theoretical and ideal than factual and canonical, we should perhaps avoid the use of such terms and speak instead, much as the Council Fathers themselves seem at times inclined to do, of an unavoidable and dynamic polarity which is operative within every religious community.

That is to say, a religious community comes into being as the result of the simultaneous presence within it of two divergent forces: the one centrifugal, the other centripetal.

In the earliest communities, it is the centripetal force, i.e., the impulse to form separate communities within the larger Christian community which is predominant in religious living. The formation of distinct communities was, as we have seen, a relatively late development in Christianity and was partly a result of the need to bring order into the eremitical movement. But the survival and subsequent evolution of distinct communities within the larger worshipping community indicates that the movement had deeper spiritual roots than curbing the ascetical excesses of the hermits. For there can be little doubt that behind the formation of Christian religious communities has always been to some extent the charismatic response of the devout to the presence within the larger community of a significant number of nominal believers. Such nominal belief, it is felt, is due not only to the personal failure of individual Christians but also to the antipathy which exists between authentic Christian values and those which motivate much of secular society. The centripetal tendency operative in the religious life takes the form, therefore, of a cooperative effort to form a community in which not only the concrete personal ideals of its members but the community structures which form their life together are directly inspired by the Christian ideals of gratuitous sharing, unrestricted love, and service.

In other words, the formation of distinct religious communities within the larger Christian community results from a felt consciousness on the part of Christians both that society at large and to a certain extent the lives of Christians who must acquiesce in existing social structures remain largely motivated by the pursuit of power, of possession, and of enlightened self-interest, and that the attempt to live as a Christian while simultaneously ordering one's life to fit the social patterns which are the institutionalized expression of such ideals does in fact place one in the position or running a constant risk of compromising one's most basic religious beliefs.

Thus, viewed centripetally, the formation of a religious community has a certain utopian quality about it. Yet it is, perhaps, in its utopian desire to labor in spite of existing obstacles to realize now the kind of community originally envisaged by Christ that the positive eschatological dimensions of community living, the dimension of hope, of confidence in the operative grace of God, is most strikingly manifest.

We should, however, note at once that if the desire to form a religious community is in certain aspects utopian, its utopianism is also a realistic one. For it arises out of a consciousness of the collective sinfulness of men and of disorder in the structure of human society. It has, moreover, no illusory dreams either about the total innocence of those who are dedicated to its realization or about the inevitability of success. Thus Christian utopianism has of necessity a hard-headed practical dimension about it to balance its idealism. For it is also the expression of a belief that unless a significant number of Christians provides the collective public witness which is involved in the effort to construct such a community based upon explicitly Christian ideals, the larger community, faced as it is with the need of conforming to the demands of a Christian or even an anti-Christian environment is apt to lose consciousness of its own *raison d'être* as a community.

There are, therefore, two extremes to be avoided in the structural renovation of a religious community. The first would be to seek to derive community structures unreflectively or indiscriminately from the contemporary secular society in which it exists; for unless a religious community can find some way of embodying socially its specifically Christian motivations, it loses all reason for existence as a community. The other extreme to be avoided is too rigid or too exclusive an adherence to past social structures which have traditionally served the purpose of mediating a community of sharing, love, and service. In other words, the re-structuring of our communities cannot be reduced to a mere exercise in secularization. It must be from first to last an exercise in imaginative re-Christianization.

Needless to say, the word "imaginative" is crucial. Exclusive emphasis upon the centripetal factor in religious community living can, for instance, not only lead to exaggerations and abuses; but those very abuses if left unchecked could conceivably lead to the effective de-Christianization of the community in which they exist, no matter what the external religious trappings which such a community might manage to preserve. Exaggerated emphasis on the pursuit of individual personal contemplation especially in an apostolically active order can also lead to the erection or preservation of artificial social barriers between the religious community and the larger worshipping community. Or it can on occasion produce a holier-than-thou attitude among "professional" religious in their dealing with "worldly" Christians. And such artificial barriers and hardened attitudes can easily lead to claims of privilege within the worshipping community for vowed over unvowed Christians.

In this context it may be useful to note a tendency in some Protestant circles to speak of religious orders and congregations as the "Protestants" of the pre-reformation era. There is some truth to the suggestion. Religious orders, as we have noted, often do come into being as the result of a felt need to reform or improve the worshipping community in some respect. Clearly, however, one significant difference between religious life and the Protestant movement is the willingness of the former to undertake its reforms within both the institutional and the sacramental structure of the worshipping community. Religious life does, however, share with Protestantism one of the hazards of the reform mentality: namely, that it is often very difficult to express dissatisfaction with the religious conduct of the larger worshipping community without adopting the condescending attitude of the spiritual snob. Needless to say, religious communities in which such attitudes may chance to exist have in point of fact lost the very sense of purpose which ought to have called them into existence as communities. For if a religious community is to justify its own separate existence within the larger community, it can do so only by actually being a community of genuinely self-effacing service, not only within but for the larger servant community.

It follows, therefore, that the centrifugal, or outward-looking, factor operative in the constitution of a religious community is not only not incompatible with the centripetal thrust which originally motivated its formation; but it is even demanded by the latter. For if a religious community is to be faithful to its constitutive purpose, as a Christian religious community, it must look lovingly and forgivingly beyond itself in a selfless desire to serve the human and spiritual needs of men.

But if the dangers of overemphasis on the centripetal factor in community living can lead to abuses like sanctimonious pharisaism and the pursuit of class-privilege, overemphasis on the centrifugal factor can produce abuses all its own, not the least of them being a spiritually shallow activism, impatient of prayer and of serious study, content exclusively with stop-gap solutions to serious problems, and uninterested in the patient reform of the recalcitrant institutional structures that cause the problems with which the community is concerned.

Fortunately, of course, there are many other options open to religious community than the extremes of becoming either sanctimoniously pharisaical or mindlessly activistic. And in point of fact, the simultaneous presence of both centripetal and centrifugal factors in the constitution of religious communities merely reflects, as in fact it should, the same tension that is operative in the larger worshipping community. As the new Israel, the Christian community must preserve its identity in a non-Christian and sometimes in an anti-Christian environment. But it will lose an essential element of its specifically Christian identity if it attempts to remain itself by splendid self-isolation from the rest of society. As the salt of the earth, the Christian community cannot lose its savor; nor on the other hand can it keep its savor if it ceases to be the light of the world and returns to a pre-Christian concept of a chosen people. One significant difference, however, between the larger worshipping community and the religious community is that in banding together to order their lives on any explicitly Christian basis, the members of the religious community assume the added obligation of preserving a real openness in love not only to the secular world of men, as does the larger worshipping community, but also to the worshipping community itself, for whose sake it exists.

Symbols of Service or of Class Privilege?

The first obligation incumbent upon the members of a religious community is, therefore, the serious one of seeing to it that their peculiar status as a separate community of service within the larger worshipping community does not lead to the establishment of artificial class barriers segregating them from other Christians or, worse still, setting them above their fellow believers. Like the members of the eucharistic priesthood whose coworkers they are, the members of a religious community must be conscientiously concerned to see to it that their mission of service with its inevitable involvement in the leadership structure of the Church does not become transformed into an excuse for the assumption of class privilege. As servants of the servants of God in the image of Christ, the only "privilege" they can claim is that of becoming the least of all, the slaves of all.

In this connection it is useful to recall that a certain ambivalence can attend traditional symbols of service, like religious habits or clerical dress. Such symbols are intended to be the visible insignia of the mission of service of the eucharistic priesthood and of those who share in its pastoral responsibilities. Although the scope of that mission remains generically fixed by the will of Christ, the effectiveness of the external insignia which symbolize its purpose must fluctuate with historical circumstances. Ideally, however, religious or clerical dress should express the solidarity of those who wear it with the people they serve, especially with those among God's people who are in greatest need.

There can be little doubt that one reason for the growing dissatisfaction of priests and religious with clerical dress and standardized religious habits, even apart from the cult of artificial uniformity which such dress symbolizes, is that it also suggests to many, rightly or wrongly, the acquiescence of the one who wears it in the existing ecclesiastical power structure with the "clericalized" attitudes that such acquiescence implies. Clearly, to the extent that habits and Roman collars serve to establish and to perpetuate such artificial social and psychological barriers between the people of God and those who are seeking to serve them, standardized clerical and religious dress becomes self-defeating, an obstacle to service rather than an aid, and should be abandoned at need for more effective and perhaps less obtrusive signs of service—like, for instance, a simple pin or medal or ring.

At the same time, there is no reason why the wearing of "secular" dress by priests and religious need be conceived as a concession to galloping "secularism." On the contrary, it can and in many instances should be the expression of a concern to reestablish the Christian ideal of solidarity between the people of God and their leaders in mutual and self-abasing service. Hence, any attempt to reaffirm by one's "secular" mode of dress the socially classless character of the sacramental community is not to secularize that community but to seek to purge it of fundamentally un-Christian elements and in a very real sense to work for its re-Christianization.

On the other hand, one cannot simply assume that clerical or religious dress will in every instance be more of a hindrance than a help in the fulfillment of the mission of service of the eucharistic priesthood and of those associated with it. What is needed is not a new "secular" rigidity in dress but a situational flexibility. Religious should be able to adapt their mode of dress to the needs of those with whom they deal. In dealing with the young or with the professionally liberal Christian, it will, for instance, often be helpful to avoid the use of habits and Roman collars. In dealing with more "traditional" Catholics, a religious or priest is likely to find that secular dress produces the same alienation that the standardized habit does in the case of the more professionally liberal.

Finally, it goes without saying that the partial or total abandonment of standardized dress in a community should not lead to the establishment of a rich or a poor class, a well-dressed and a shabby class, within the same religious house. Under ordinary circumstances, the avoidance of ostentation or of tasteless flamboyance in dress should, however, be able to be left to the good sense of religious and priests themselves and, where that fails and the good of the community is at stake, to commonsensical budgeting and to the tactful and balanced vigilance of local superiors.

Community Hospitality

The communal practice of hospitality among religious is another aspect of community living which deserves critical review, especially in centrifugally oriented communities whose preoccupations are more actively apostolic.

It would seem that the practice of "hospitality by proxy" which grew up in the early contemplative communities still has a place in religious communities whose chief preoccupation is the service of worship. One clear service rendered by such communities is to provide centers of worship to which the members of the larger community can come in order to find peace, spiritual refreshment, and an atmosphere of prayer and recollection. It is, therefore, in the interests of both the religious community itself and of the service they render to others that certain precautions be taken that the practice of hospitality not disturb the community's own prayerful recollection. One has the distinct impression today, however, that it is precisely the communities most oriented toward the service of worship who are best known for their Christian hospitality.

But if "hospitality by proxy" is not an anomaly in such communities, it often is a very real anomaly in action-oriented communities, which by seeking to preserve artificially the social barriers of an earlier, more contemplative age endow their carefully cloistered homes with the air more of an embattled fortress than of an open center of gratuitous and gracious hospitality.

If one has any actual doubts on the last score, one would do well to observe the behavior of the ordinary lay person on those rare occasions when the cloistered portcullises fall and he or she is actually ushered into the dining room of a religious house to be "entertained" by the community. If our layman is typical, the very thought of such an ordeal is liable to bring cold sweat to his brow and to the palms of his hands. Equally interesting is the reaction of many religious to the unexpected intrusion of an "extern" into their midst at a "closed" social gathering of the community. Communities vary considerably, of course, but it would not, I would suggest, be altogether unusual for a significant number of the members of almost any given community to react to such an intrusion with all the ease and grace of Increase Mather at a witches' sabbath.

I myself witnessed not long ago a little comic scene in which a religious who had become accustomed to live in an open community in which "externs" were actually welcome at all meals had had the temerity to invite a friend to a social gathering of a different community of which he was only a temporary member. As soon as the "extern" appeared, the superior, once he and his community had recovered from the initial shock of seeing their perimeter penetrated, called the offending religious over, reprimanded him on the spot for his unseemliness, and ordered him to remove the guest at once, since, as the superior clearly explained, an "extern" had no right being in the community's "private Home." Such an incident may not occur frequently; not every subject is as innocently brash as this one. But it typifies, one may suspect, the siege mentality of many religious who, even though they are actively associated with "externs" for most of the day, boggle at the thought of making them welcome in their dining room or chapel on any kind of regular basis.

But if the religious community exists in order to provide the larger worshipping community with a paradigm of what the ideal Christian community ought to be, then every religious community ought to exercise leadership in the practice of a genuinely Christian hospitality as well. That is to say, the religious community as a community should actively open its doors to others, not from a merely humanitarian motive, but as a profession of faith in the Christ who is present in each of his little ones, as a sign of hope and confidence that he will himself on the last day welcome into his Father's home those who have welcomed the least of his brethren in this life, and as an expression of a truly gratuitous love whose gratuity is manifest in the unrestricted character of one's hospitality and in the concern to take in those who are in fact in greatest need.

Needless to say, even active religious have a very real need for recollection and for a certain amount of privacy. But sufficient privacy may be preserved or even ensured by regulation if necessary, while allowing the free access of "externs" of both sexes to the chapel, dining room, and recreation area of a religious house.

Moreover, the pastoral advantages of active religious returning to this earlier ideal of Christian living are potentially many. The practice, for instance, could do much to break down the artificial social barriers which do in fact exist in many Church-run institutions between lay and religious faculty and staff. It could also be used as an effective means of making foreigners and needy persons feel that they are fully accepted as members of the Christian community. Contact within the community with a variety of persons could help break down the narrow isolationist attitudes of some religious toward "the world" and make religious more conscious of the needs and interests of the larger community of which they are members.

But more is needed than the mere lowering of external barriers. What is needed is a certain broadened understanding of the kind of hospitality which genuinely Christian, and therefore religious, community living demands. The present practice in religious houses of freely welcoming the members of one's own congregation or, occasionally, of other congregations is commendable; but there is serious room to question whether it alone measures up to the ideal of Christian hospitality. Viewed objectively, such hospitality cannot help but smack, despite the best intentions, of a certain cliquishness. It is equally commendable but insufficient for a religious community to share its leftovers with the needy; but such attempts at Christian sharing can all too easily smack of impersonality or even of condescension. What is really needed is a basic shift in attitude on the part of religious themselves toward the very idea of a religious community. What is needed, especially in the case of active religious, is to begin to conceive of their communities as actually having a serious obligation to witness as a community to the universal openness and cordiality of Christ. What is needed, therefore, is for religious to think of their houses less as bastions of holiness to be defended from the world and more as centers of hospitality in which any person is genuinely welcome in Christ's name, regardless of his personal merits and deserts.

The unrestricted hospitality of individual religious houses

should, needless to say, find a parallel in the institutions run by any given order or congregation. Any institution run in Christ's name not only should be open to all, but should also show special concern for the foreigner, for the needy, for the handicapped, for the social outcast.

There is no doubt but that the practice of more open hospitality can place a financial burden upon a religious house or congregation. It may well happen, therefore, that the real test of a religious community's willingness to accept in a meaningful way the ideal of hospitality taught by Christ himself will be the willingness of its members to make the material sacrifices that are necessary to make such hospitality financially feasible.

But if religious are, in virtue of their leadership function in the community, expected to show a signal communal example of openhanded hospitality, then, a fortiori the leaders of religious, their superiors and their members of the eucharistic priesthood, ought themselves to be people who are not only outstandingly hospitable, but who can stimulate the communities they lead to discover effective ways in which to embody their shared desire to welcome any human being freely in Christ's name.

Labor for Service

Once we conceive of the meaning of the first vow of religion in the active, dynamic terms of gratuitous sharing, it is easy to see why not only hospitality but also labor with a view to sharing is one of its fitting ecclesial expressions. At the same time, it should also be clear by now that even though the "poor man" in the Christian sense of the term is one who works for the sake of others in Christ's name, it is not true to say that anyone who simply works is ipso facto such a "poor man." All depends on the motive which inspires the work, the way in which it is performed, and the gratuity with which its fruits are shared with others.

That is to say, religious should work because they desire to avoid placing unnecessary financial burdens upon the very people whom they have been called by God to serve. In this respect, Paul is, of course, the Christian model who first comes into mind; he made tents so that he could preach the gospel gratis and by so doing better mediate to others the gratuity of God's love for them in Christ.

Religious should also work because they desire as Christians to have something that they can share freely with others in Christ's name. They should not, therefore, work to acquire and accumulate material possessions but in order that others may share freely in the fruits of their labor. Unless, therefore, the hard work done by religious is matched by the effective sharing and distribution of the fruits of their labor, it will inevitably lead to their own growing material wealth and subtly undermine the effective pursuit of the ideals of gratuitous sharing to which they are vowed.

Religious should work for the house and congregation of which they are members and for the Christian community at large because they look upon all such labor for the sake of the kingdom as an expression of their faith in Christ, who founded and sustains the worshipping community for whom they spend themselves, and as an expression of their hope and confidence in his promises and of their love for one another in his name. Moreover, like Paul, religious may also administer funds and property of considerable value provided they do so for the sake of the whole community and provided they are answerable to the community for the Christian manner in which they discharge their administrative responsibilities.

Finally, religious should work tirelessly for the sake of the kingdom because they accept labor for their own religious community and for the larger worshipping community as an act of atonement for sin, i.e., as an opportunity under grace to seek to right the disorders which exist in the world and in oneself, by spending oneself physically and spiritually in using material goods selflessly in order to mediate a Christian community of mutual and gratuitous love and concern in Christ's name.

All of this is clear enough. But the problems which presently trouble religious are not so much whether they should work but rather the precise form that their labor for Christ should take. Moreover, recent theological emphasis on the lay apostolate has further complicated the question. Nowadays, priests and religious frequently find themselves working side by side with Catholic laymen of considerable talent and zeal, whose technical competence and skill at the work in hand may in fact exceed that of the religious themselves. As a result of such experiences, religious often find themselves faced with the very basic question: Why become a priest or a religious at all, if I can as a layman perform identically the same job as I now perform as a religious, e.g., teaching, research, social work, etc., with the same, or perhaps in some instances, even greater effectiveness than now? Does not the layman work at his job for Christ? Doesn't his labor promote the spread of the kingdom?

Job vs. Call

These questions are, of course, rooted in the same fallacy, namely, that a religious vocation is simply a job to be accepted or rejected according to the same pragmatic criteria that one would accept or reject any other job. Being a religious is no more merely a job than being a father of a family. It is, as Fr. Örsy has insisted, a call from God, a call, that is, to assume certain ecclesial responsibilities in a community of atoning love, responsibilities which are generically pre-determined but which allow for a multiplicity of concrete modes of embodiment. Thus, just as the father of a family accepts publicly in his marriage vows certain concrete, stable responsibilities in love to his wife and children, so too the religious by his vows has assumed certain stable, public responsibilities of leadership and love within the larger worshipping community. Thus, just as for the father of a family, his job provides one important means among others to mediate his love to his family and to fulfill his moral obligations as breadwinner for his wife and children, so, in an analogous fashion, the religious should find in his job, not the essence of his vocation, but the context within which he is expected to live up to his public responsibility of exercising leadership in the formation and fostering of a worshipping community of truly gratuitous and universal love and sharing. His success as a religious or as a priest is not, therefore, measured essentially by job-success but rather by his success in loving others unrestrictedly and gratuitously in Christ's image and by his constant concern to do whatever is in his power to unite his coworkers and all those with whom his job places him in human contact in a truly Christian community of worship and of service.

Moreover, in this context it might be worthwhile to note in passing that an important aspect of a priest's and a religious's stable public leadership function within the environmental context provided by his job is the encouragement and support of any manifestation of personal Christian leadership on the part of the lay Christians with whom he works.

Ideally, then, a religious should be both good at his job and good at forming and encouraging the growth of a Christian community among those with whom he works. But it is quite possible that a religious might be less than completely successful or efficient at his job but extremely successful as a religious by the constancy and quality of his love and by his constant readiness to serve whenever possible as an effective catalyst in the formation of a worshipping and explicitly Christian community among the human community of labor of which the priest or religious forms a functioning part.

Religious as Breadwinners

But can a religious, like the father of a family, also be in any sense a breadwinner? In a poverty of non-possession or of passive dependence, it would be difficult to supply any coherent theoretical justification for the compatibility of such a role with a religious profession of poverty. But in a poverty of active gratuitous sharing, no such theoretical difficulties arise. Every order has younger, retired, or sick members who are in need of financial support. The religious who works in order to share freely the financial fruits of his labor with his fellow religious who are in need does indeed function as their breadwinner in some real sense. Nor is there theoretically any reason to restrict the breadwinning function of working religious to the support of the members of their own house or congregation. The ideal of gratuitous sharing would theoretically allow any working religious to be the breadwinner for any person in genuine need.

In point of fact, of course, in many orders and congregations the active members do in fact already contribute to the support of their younger, sick, and aged brethren. It may, however, depending on persons and circumstances, be desirable for such financial support to be more personalized instead of accomplishing it through the levying of a general "man tax" or some similar administrative device. Why, for instance, could not a religious activity laboring in the apostolate assume conscious personal responsibility to provide out of his wages material support for a particular younger member of his community still in training or for the medical care of some particular elderly religious? The consciousness on the part of the working religious of his personal responsibility for the support of one or more of his brethren and the awareness of personal indebtedness on the part of the religious being supported could, in certain instances, effectively bind the individuals concerned closer to one another and could perhaps throw a useful bridge across the generation gap where it does exist.

Community Support of Vowed Christians

But if, ideally, religious ought to be self-supporting, so as not to be a financial burden upon the people of God and upon one another, one cannot preclude the possibility of religious being supported directly by the worshipping community or by their order or congregation when such a financial arrangement seems under the concrete circumstances to be more advantageous. As laborers for the kingdom, i.e., for the growth and nurture of the Christian community, priests and religious have a strict right to such material support, provided, of course, that the priests and religious in question do in fact spend themselves on some important or worthwhile labor. Moreover, religious so supported by the worshipping community must be careful to see to it that their self-gift in labor is not conditioned upon their receiving a pre-determined financial compensation when such insistence would compromise the genuine gratuity of their service. Indeed, ideally the loving and sincere reticence of priests and religious in demanding material compensation as a pre-condition for their labor ought to go hand in hand with the free and heartfelt desire of the people they serve to see to it that such labor for the kingdom is in fact not only justly but lovingly compensated, as the mark of the work-relation of priests and religious to the worshipping community which most distinguishes it from the financial relationship of employer and employee in civil and economic society.

The fact that religious by their vow of obedience share in the public responsibility of providing leadership in service within the Christian community makes it also fitting that they should have some share in the responsible disposition of the material means available to their particular community or congregation. There should, therefore, be in every religious community regular open discussion of budgeting and finances with a view to determining whether the material resources of the community are being used in as Christian a manner as they might be. Although in larger communities ultimate responsibility should remain with the superior, open discussion of finances in every community should provide a useful measure of the extent to which budgeting effectively meets the needs and aspirations of the community and of those they are publicly dedicated to serve. It should also help to create in each individual member of a religious community an awareness of the financial headaches involved in running an order or congregation as well as a greater consciousness of their personal obligation to use material goods as an expression of their own commitment to gratuitous sharing in Christ's name.

The Choice of Labors

The fact that labor in religious life ought to be an expression of gratuitous sharing entails as a consequence that certain types of apostolic work are concretely more compatible than others with the ideals of religious living. Although every kind of labor, as the documents of Vatican II remind us, can be transformed into a gift of self when it is performed in a spirit of faith and love, the labor of those who are publicly dedicated to providing leadership in service within the Christian community ought in a special way to be need-oriented. The documents of Vatican II have, moreover, provided some useful guidelines for determining what are the apostolates of greatest contemporary need. A preliminary listing might include: catechetics, or the sound instruction of the faithful in Christian doctrine in a manner which is also adapted to contemporary needs and problems; the education of youth; social work of various forms, especially among those who are in greatest need; the study and support of family life and of marriage; care of the sick and the needy; the aid and defense of the laboring classes; the public defense of basic human rights for all men, especially for the poor, the ignorant, and the alien; the fostering of economic and social justice; peacemaking, or the breakdown of bigotry and of divisions among men; the quest for world peace and for international accord; ecumenical work; missionary activity and aid to developing nations; scholarly research in all fields but especially in philosophy and theology and their related disciplines; the problems surrounding the population explosion; intelligent opposition to agnosticism and atheism; communications and the fine arts; the problems of urbanization. One might also include any form of work which would tend to transform the human and Christian community into the ideal classless society that Christ himself envisaged.

Needless to say, any such listing of areas of apostolic service is bound to be incomplete. The criterion for deciding whether priests and religious should become active in these or in any other legitimate areas of human labor and endeavor is, at the concrete level, a complex one. It is not reducible merely to a question of the talents and competence of individuals alone, although the diversity of apostolic needs should provide fruitful fields of work for almost any individual to exploit his or her personal talents, training, and expertise. Besides the individual factor, however, one must also consider the extent to which there is need for the presence of official Church leadership in the field in question. For as a result of their official involvement in the responsibilities of public leadership in the community, the active presence of priests and religious in any line of work inevitably signals out that the field of labor in question is of official concern to the Christian community. Since, moreover, the leadership function of priests and religious derives ultimately from the immutable sacramental structure of the Christian community, and not from any prevailing personal and social attitudes toward Church leadership and its mission, the significance of the affirmation of ecclesial concern present in the involvement of priests and religious in any area of human endeavor is not dependent upon shifting popular religious attudes. Once made, it is simply there to be recognized by anyone who is willing to do so. Revisions of the given apostolic commitment of a specific religious group, must, however, be collectively discerned through the cooperative effort of all its members. Provincial and regional congresses organized for this purpose under professional guidance are an important instance of the kind of creative leadership demanded of today's religious leaders. Open community forums can serve a similar function within individual religious houses.

The Divided Community

Perhaps one of the most alarming problems confronting contemporary religious is the polarization of the membership of some congregations and communities into liberal and conservative factions. In this matter as in many others, religious communities serve as an active thermometer of the more general problems confronting the larger worshipping community. Where this polarization has in fact taken place, both the challenges and opportunities to practice a truly atoning love within a religious community are magnified beyond all ordinary measure; and the need for a Christian discernment of the spirits at work within the community becomes all the more pressing.

The norms for discernment and for the formulation of one's conscience in such circumstances elaborated by Paul in First Corinthians are still as relevant as when he wrote them. Now as then any "prophetic" voice raised in a religious community—be that voice the voice of change or the voice of stability, the voice of youthful enthusiasm or the voice of cautious experience—is radically suspect to the extent that it seeks to prolong jealous factionalism rather than to find the means needed to reconcile all divisions and jealousies through the healing power of love. No voice raised in a community, whatever its age or whatever its supposed "orthodoxy" or lack of it, can claim to possess the Spirit of Christ if its words and tone are boastful, conceited, rude, or selfish. No voice which is grudgebearing, quick to take offense or bitterly resentful speaks with the Spirit of Christ.

Those who speak with the Spirit of Christ seek to found the purpose of their community and the relationship of its members in truth; they, therefore, value the facts of any situation above the established position of any institution or of any individual, themselves included. At the same time, they are more concerned to understand the experience and views of others in real depth before attempting to pass even tentative judgment either upon the authority grounding those views or upon their truth. Conscious of the example of Christ, they are unwilling to pass judgment on the motives of any individual and when necessary seek instead to excuse as far as possible their external conduct. Those who speak with the Spirit of Christ are willing to trust the other members of their community, even when such trust may lead to personal suffering and sacrifice on their own part; and they are willing to take the risk involved in facing both the future and their fellow Christians with a hope and joy in their hearts that is rooted ultimately in their confidence in God. Those who claim the Spirit of Christ must scrupulously respect the consciences of their fellow Christians and a fortiori of their fellow religious with whom they come in daily contact. Once again the Pauline solution to the conflict in the early Church between the meat-eaters and the vegetable-eaters is peculiarly applicable to many of the concrete problems of renewal confronting us today. In his day the massive influx of Gentiles into the Christian community brought with it a free-wheeling approach to the worship of God that was opposed to the more ordered and ritualistic religion of the Judaeo-Christian; and conflicts of conscience between Gentile rigorists and laxists had raised much the same problem.

We might, for instance, paraphrase the principles that Paul then brought to bear upon the problems in the community in the following manner: (1) No Christian can invoke blind fidelity to the externals of religious life and worship as sufficient basis for resolving definitively such religio-moral conflicts. The passover of Christ has freed us from bondage to law-oriented religion and introduced us to a love-oriented religion which preserves in a higher synthesis the essence of the law and goes far beyond it in love. For a Christian, therefore, any approach to the resolution of conflicts within the community must begin with the question: What is the loving, not what is the legal, solution to the issue? (2) Being theoretically correct in such a religio-moral dispute cannot by itself serve as sufficient grounds for the conduct of disputing Christians toward one another. Both the Christian legalist and the Christian anti-legalist are equally open to the fallacy of assuming that the opposite is the case. But for either to do so is to substitute the cult of moral self-righteousness for Christian love and to ignore for the sake of self-vindication the more fundamental obligations of Christian living. (3) Disputing Christians who pass judgment on one another have themselves good reason to tremble at the thought of the divine judgment. (4) It is incompatible with the law of love to treat those who are scrupulous or morally rigid and rule-oriented with bitterness or condescension, or to force them to violate their over-tender consciences. It is equally incompatible with the law of love for those who are rule-oriented, scrupulous, or morally rigid to force their over-sensitive consciences on those who are of a more liberal mind. (5) Scrupulosity, moral rigidity, and inflexible adherence to written laws are often symptomatic of a weakness of faith; for the rule-ridden person can all too easily come to place more confidence in his personal fidelity to a prearranged pattern of behavior than in the saving power of Christ. (6) No community, therefore, can claim to bear the name of "Christian" which does not allow within itself every kind of legitimate diversity of conscience in disputed or in trivial religio-moral questions for such mutual tolerance and forebearance is clearly demanded by the law of love whatever the ultimate solution to the disputed point may ultimately prove to be. (7) Finally, no community can claim the name "Christian" which does not manifest in practice a tendency and loving concern for the faith-needs of the morally rigid and scrupulous.

Christian Love and Narcissism

Reflection on the different historical attempts to define the Christian meaning of love ought to alert contemporary religious to the dangers latent in taking too partial a view of this "form of all the virtues." To oppose the love of God to love of one's fellow man or to the commitment to any kind of legitimate human endeavor, to conceive of love as self-destructive immolation which excludes the desire for any divine or human reciprocity, to conceive of love as excusing one from strict moral responsibility, as devoid of an essentially ecclesial dimension, as purely immanent or as purely transcendent—to do any of these things is to substitute a caricature of love for Christian love itself.

Now, if the present age is capable of generating its own distortion of Christian love, that distortion may well take the form of the ascetical negative to the quietist doctrine. That is to say, our most popular substitute for Christian love in the sixties and seventies may well turn out to be, not destructive self-immolation, but its direct opposite: the cult of a basically narcissistic need-fulfillment. Everyone, of course, needs love and everyone needs to experience the external signs of affection. But the need for love is not yet love itself; and if religious become too exclusively preoccupied with relating deeply, intensively, and interpersonally with others, they may find that they have little psychic interest or energy left for actively seeking to love those with whom they cannot relate deeply, intensely, and interpersonally. Unfortunately, however, love of such persons is one of the precise forms which the unrestricted and gratuitous love of religious ought to take, if it is to be as truly unrestricted in its scope as it is supposed to be.

To be sure, a religious who finds it impossible to seek to love others gratuitously and unrestrictedly can often be suffering from some deeper emotional disturbance, which deserves compassionate love, attention, and care. But a community in which the love of its members has ceased to be genuinely unrestricted has ceased to that extent to be a truly Christian community and has become instead a closed clique. For to equate love exclusively with the intensity of fulfilling interpersonal experience is ultimately to transform "love" into a divisive rather than a unifying force. Intense interpersonal experience can be shared ordinarily only with a limited number of persons. There is nothing wrong with such sharing in itself; but love among religious in the explicitly Christian sense of active, gratuitous, compassionate concern for others in Christ's name must encompass and inform both the more intense, non-romantic, interpersonal relationships and their opposite, just as in a larger context it must be capable of encompassing both married and celibate love. Nevertheless, just as rape would be impossible if sex were synonymous with love, so too if "turned-on" relationships were simply identical with love, manifestations among the mutually "turned-on" of overt or covert hostility toward those who prefer to remain more emotionally "turned-off" would be equally impossible. Unless love can manage to take in every type of individual it is not fully Christian.

Challenge of the Small Community

Perhaps even more serious than cliquishness resulting from the attempt to fulfill unfulfilled affective needs is, however, the danger of irreconcilable liberal and conservative factions within the same religious community. That there should be liberals and conservatives in the same community is not only inevitable;

it is fundamentally healthy, provided both liberals and conservatives are willing to tender one another a mutual respect and a willingness to listen and to dialogue. It is only when the dialogic relationship between the two groups breaks down through hostility, dishonesty, and selfishness, that they are transformed from interest-groups into factions.

It is precisely in such moments as these that small communities can work upon religious like the lure of the promised land. Small communities can, of course, provide genuine possibilities for community living impossible in larger religious houses. Heenan, for instance, has argued that small task-oriented communities can because of their small numbers offer possibilities for deeply personal group interaction impossible in a large religious community. They can, he feels, limit the likelihood of psychological sanctions within the group, challenge each member to contribute personally to community life, be more mobile than large communities, and offer more meaningful opportunities for common worship.[292] The ideal of such small communities is most certainly an attractive one, provided two important reservations are kept in mind. First, like the large community, the success of a small community is radically dependent on the attitudes and problems of those who compose it. The mere reduction of numbers and emphasis on task orientation will not necessarily produce deep interpersonal relations. In certain instances, it may even aggravate hostility and increase the psychological sanctions which community living in any form can impose on its members. Second, if communities are screened to include only those who are emotionally compatible. small "compatibility communities" can in fact sacrifice to intimacy and efficiency a dimension of personal and spiritual growth that comes from contact with a variety of persons, viewpoints, interests, and emotional types. Contact with incompatible people may not always be pleasant, but it can in many instances be both broadening and profitable for both parties. What is gained in successful small communities is, of course, a feeling of personal intimacy and of belonging and a greater opportunity for spontaneous, personal sharing. Only the circumstances, needs, and possibilities of the prospective members of a religious community can determine the community structure best suited to a given religious. It is, therefore, of considerable importance that a variety of options among kinds of communities be available to superiors and subjects alike.

Indeed, the only point I wish to make here is that it is naïve to suppose that the size and structure alone of any religious community will solve the human conflicts that inevitably accompany any experiment in community living. New structures merely provide a predefined context within which to work at the human tensions and conflicts which will inevitably arise in the course of social contact. The fact of the matter is that there are advantages and disadvantages to almost any kind of community structure. While large communities provide a variety of human contacts, they can veer toward impersonality and superficiality in social relations. Nevertheless, deep personal friendships are far from impossible in a large community. By the same token, small communities may foster greater intimacy; but they can also veer toward cliquishness, especially when those who join them seek to do so merely as an escape from the burden of bearing with fellow religious whose attitudes and beliefs are abrasive. Yet no one can in fairness claim that cliquishness is the inevitable product of small communities. Changes and new experiments in the structure of community living in this country are certainly desirable; but they will be of little avail unless they are accompanied by a change of heart, by a rebirth within our communities of a truly open, unrestricted, and gratuitous love.

These remarks are not, then, intended in any way to discourage small communities but only as a plea that the members of such communities take care to preserve attitudes and goals compatible with a commitment of atoning love. A community, whatever its size, must maintain an unrestricted openness in membership. Once this point it conceded, then it becomes obvious that there should be in any order or congregation a variety of community structures flexibly adaptable to the personal and apostolic needs of its members. Indeed far greater, not less, experimentation in the adaptation and evaluation of new structures for community living is demanded than we have experienced up till now.

Community Leaders in a Community of Service

The guidelines set down by St. Paul for the leadership in service of a servant community are as relevant now as when he wrote them in the first century. Community leaders must by their example embody the Christian ideals they seek to inculcate in others by actually serving others in the name and image of Christ. They must be men and women of outstanding love, faith, and purity. They must exhibit tact, patience, gentleness, and human sensitivity in dealing with others. They must be men and women who are conscious of their own human faults and weaknesses. They must realize that the law was made, not for good people but for criminals, and that Christ came to free us from blind subservience to law. They must be men and women of intellectual interests, students of the Christian tradition, learned and spiritual enough to test the validity of the prophetic voices that arise in each community while simultaneously preserving a scrupulous respect for the consciences of other people. They must be peacemakers, who are concerned to heal the breaches in the community rather than join in futile eristics. They must be hospitable and concerned to share freely of their means with others. They must be responsible in their management of community funds and publicly accountable to the community for their stewardship. And they must avoid all semblance of profiteering in the exercise of their office. Finally, they must be men and women of prayer concerned to see to it that every aspect of their lives is compatible with the love-commitment made in baptism and in their public assumption of leadership responsibilities in the community and renewed in every eucharistic act.

The temptation of Christ in the desert ought to alert contemporary religious to the dangers which lie in the path of anyone who seeks to follow the way of service, be he superior or subject. For since no servant is above his master, the contemporary religious can expect to be tempted, as Christ himself was, to self-reliance rather than to reliance upon God, to a pragmatic rather than to an absolute faith-commitment, to a leadership of coercive power rather than to one of atoning love.

The first of these temptations we will treat in the following chapter. The second and third, however, are pertinent to our present discussion.

The Lure of Pragmatism

American society is success-oriented. Pragmatists at heart, we tend to place great value on what works. Pragmatic in our ethics as well, we tend to place great stress on values which are directly experienced. Our best thinking tends to be problem solving, finding the right means to effect the limited goals that confront us in any given situation.

As a result, we are easily tempted to transfer our pragmatic presuppositions into the religious sphere as well and demand of our orders and congregations a high degree of efficiency as a condition for associating ourselves with them and their work. In fact, not a little tension in American religious life arises, we would suggest, out of an attempt to judge one's religious vocation by crudely pragmatic standards.

At first flush, however, there would seem to be some point to putting one's vocation to some kind of pragmatic test. Entry into the religious life or priesthood is never a forced option. Since, however, any person faced with the possibility of several vocational options needs some kind of criterion of value to guide his choice, why not use a pragmatic one? Especially with recent emphasis on the lay apostolate, neither religious life nor the priesthood seems to be the only way of serving both God and the Christian and human community. Is not the basic vocational question, then, how can I personally serve God most effectively: as a priest, as a religious, or as a layman, whether married or single? And how can I answer such a question except in terms of the foreseeable consequences of each of these possible options?

Moreover, what is true of vocation in general would also seem to be true of the choice of a specific order or congregation. How judge one's suitability for membership in one religious community rather than another except in terms of the practical consequences of choosing membership in the one community rather than the other? How evaluate one order or congregation over another except in terms of the efficiency with which it runs its institutions or conducts its works of service?

And why, a thoroughgoing pragmatist might insist, should one stop the process of evaluation at the question of vocation? Why not apply the pragmatic test to Church membership as well? Should not the Church which God blesses be the most successful, the most efficient, the most up-to-date? Isn't that what is behind the *aggiornamento* in Roman Catholicism: up-dating the Church so that it can meet the stiffer competition of other world religions, sects, and secular society?

Needless to say, it is at this point that the sensitive Christian ought to begin to wince at the above chain of reasoning. Surely, an *aggiornamento* based exclusively on naturalistic motives of enlightened self-interest can scarcely bear the name of Christian. Moreover, in an American context, there can be little doubt that the cult of efficiency all too often presupposes an ethical frame of reference which places a premium upon externally verifiable material success. But for a Christian, does not the Sermon on the Mount turn most of our success-criteria topsy-turvy? How reconcile an ethics of success, or even a pragmatic ethics of shared consummatory experience with the inspired precepts of Christ: blessed are the poor, blessed are they who mourn, blessed are you when men shall hate you and persecute and revile you? or with that simple directive: if you would be perfect, go, sell what you have, give it to the poor, and come follow me? How reconcile it with the Pauline admonition that among Christians there must be no competition, but each must seek to follow Christ in making himself the least, the servant of all?

On the other hand, one can scarcely maintain that failure is the goal of the Christian community. Christ our Lord gave every indication of having been deeply disappointed by men's failure to respond to his message and to join the new Israel which he felt himself sent by the Father to found. No one can hold up inefficiency as the ideal, let alone as the measure of the supernaturality, of Church-run institutions.

Unraveling the Confusions

The confusions implicit in these questions are multiple; and we must begin to attempt to unravel some of them.

Some of them are logical. Ever since Peirce formulated the pragmatic maxim for the clarification of ideas: "Consider what effects, that might conceivably have practical bearings, we conceive the object of our conception to have. Then, our conception of these effects is the whole of our conception of the object."[293] Philosophers have been trying to decide what it means and how to use it. Logical analysts have dissected it. James brought to it a distinctive flair for practical activism. Dewey read it from the viewpoint of his own peculiar naturalistic immanentism. Royce exploited it for his own religious idealism. Peirce himself seems to have had second thoughts about the precise meaning of the maxim as his own philosophy became less positivistic and more metaphysical.

If, therefore, the development of American thought provides any kind of criterion, then clearly the pragmatic maxim, when viewed as a purely logical principle, is compatible with a variety of world views: with a Peircian realism, with a Jamesian supernaturalism, with a Roycean idealism, with a Deweyan naturalism.

Of all the philosophical versions of pragmatism, however, the popular, non-technical meaning of "pragmatic" is probably closest to James's pragmatic philosophy, although James's thought is in fact far more sophisticated than any commonsense "pragmatism." Still, when most Americans speak of being "pragmatic," they are concerned with the concretely practical consequences of a given theory, hypothesis, or choice. By contrast, Peirce himself was most concerned with its logical consequences and with its speculative and metaphysical implications.

One thing, however, seems quite clear: As a logical principle, there is certainly no necessary connection between the pragmatic maxim and a naturalistic position in theology and ethics. That naturalistic pragmatism may invoke the pragmatic test at a logical level is, of course, undeniable; that only naturalism may do so with consistency is questionable in the extreme.

Moreover, whatever interpretation one may choose to put upon Peirce's original formulation of the pragmatic maxim, one can scarcely deny that the pattern for conceptual thinking which he articulates in his "Neglected Argument for the Existence of God" ought, as he himself insists, to be present at least ideally in "every well-conducted and complete inquiry."[294] According to Peirce such an enquiry when seen in its basic logical structure has three complex stages. The abductive stage begins with the observation of some phenomenon which disappoints one's speculative expectations in some way and, therefore, demands better explanation. The search for an explanation leads the mind to a thorough examination of all the phenomena which are conceivably relevant to the question and to the formulation of as many plausible hypotheses as possible concerning the relation of the problem in hand to the other elements of one's experience.

The second stage of enquiry consists in the logical explicitation by the use of deductive reasoning of those consequences which in strict logic flow from the proposed hypothesis.

The third and final stage of enquiry is the testing of the proposed hypotheses and their logical consequences against the available data and the selection through the process of verification of that hypothesis which most accords with the structure of experience. One can scarcely object to the exercise of such "pragmatistic" care in the resolution of one's conceptual difficulties, especially if one refuses to restrict positivistically one's understanding of observable "phenomena" to "external," sensible phenomena alone. In this specific logical sense, therefore, any man can indeed be a "pragmaticist."

Three points are, however, worth making. First, the acceptance of such a "pragmatistic" logic leaves the enquirer open at a religious level to the experience of transcendence, to the experience of a virtual infinity in man which is integral to the structure of experience, and ultimately to the affirmation of the reality of a God. Second, it does not necessarily commit one to an ethics of expediency or of immanent value alone. Such ethical theories must stand or fall on the basis of their logical consistency and on the basis of their adequacy to the structure of the whole of human experience.

Third, although the faith-commitment is experientially testable up to a point, in the sense that the events of salvation do illumine certain aspects of one's experience of the mystery of man, it demands more than the mere acceptance of revelation as a plausible hypothesis for verification. The faith-commitment is absolute and it is personal. It is personal in that it terminates at the person of Jesus as the revelation of the Father and giver of the divine Spirit. It is absolute in the sense that it is rooted in man's unconditioned acceptance of God's own irrevocable love-commitment revealed in Christ. In other words, the believer not only accepts Jesus's own unique consciousness of his person and mission and the apostle's uniquely privileged and unrepeatable experience of the risen Christ as the normative and immutable measure of any account of man's relationship to God. But such is his confidence under grace in the truthfulness and love of the God who has revealed himself in Christ that he never questions either the person or the truthfulness of God's own Son.[295]

The unconditioned character of the faith-commitment is not, however, a substitute for clear thinking. To be sure, the person and message of Christ are partly mediated to us in words. And as a result, the confidence of faith does indeed extend to the words of divine revelation proximately and mediately, but not ultimately, since the believer's ultimate confidence lies in a God we cannot verbally encompass. But while the believer's confidence under grace in the fidelity and truthfulness of God is in principle absolute, his confidence in himself and in his present limited grasp of the meaning and message of Christ can never be absolute. There is no conceptual formula which expresses faith in Christ, however valid that formula may be recognized to have been when seen in the context of the limiting historical circumstances which gave rise to it, which cannot be verbally reformulated or conceptually explicitated and qualified. That is to say, there is no valid formula of belief for which we can claim that its theological implications have been wholly exhausted.

Hence, where the problem confronting the believer is not the truth but the meaning of the divine message revealed in Christ, there can be little doubt that "well-conducted and complete" theological enquiry will follow the general logical pattern outlined by Peirce in his "Neglected Argument." In other words, faced with the realization that one's present personal conceptual formulation of the meaning of divine revelation is in some concrete instance inadequate to the precise problem which confronts one, a person who wishes to resolve in faith his theological difficulties other than by the stubborn reaffirmation of his original position or by an appeal to authority has little choice but to investigate as thoroughly as possible the human and salvific data pertinent to the problem he is facing, to survey the possible theological explanations of those events, and to test each possible explanation by explicitating its logical consequences and by measuring it and its consequences against the available pertinent data. Moreover, if the believer is quite honest with himself, he must undertake the process of investigation with an acute consciousness of his own personal theological fallibility and with a desire to profit from the experience and from the reflections of other members of the community of intelligent belief of which he is a member.

These schematic reflections on the possible place to be accorded to a "Peircian" logic within a theological reflection which is the product simultaneously of one's confidence in the truthfulness of God and of one's consciousness of one's own personal limitations and fallibility in grasping the full implications and meaning of the divine message can perhaps throw some light on the nature of a religious vocation considered precisely as the concrete embodiment of a faith-commitment.

As we have already seen, a vocation is not a job; it is a grace, a call from God to love him in men in a specific ecclesial modality. Hence, the three traditional signs of a vocation are as good a yardstick as they ever were for judging whether or not one has such a call. The traditional theology of vocation maintains that one who has a vocation to the religious life or to the priesthood must freely and inwardly desire it, must be physically, mentally, and spiritually fit for his calling, and must be accepted by the community he or she aspires to join.

These conditions are neither arbitrary nor unrelated. For without the inner desire, without the lure of divine grace, there can be no vocation. But what precisely is a religious called to do? If the analyses of the preceding chapters are correct, a religious is called to assume the responsibility of leading the Christian community in the service of God by bearing official public witness to the unrestricted and gratuitous character of Christian love by the freedom and openness with which he shares whatever he has with others even to the point of suffering personal want, by the joy with which he welcomes any man in the name of Christ, by the generosity with which he labors for the sake of others, by the zeal with which he opposes social injustice in Christ's name, and by the selflessness with which he embodies the Christian ideal of service through atoning love. Finally, he is one who feels the importance of doing all of these things as a public profession of the common faith of the Christian community and, therefore, feels called to do them publicly in the name of Christ, as a sign of the presence of his Spirit in the midst of men, and in the name of the sacramental community of worship and of service which Christ came to found.

The graced desire to hear such witness and the acceptance and confirmation of that desire by the community itself are, therefore, integral to a vocation to the priesthood or the religious life. The second of the traditional signs does nothing more than give the limiting condition of any vocation: It must be humanly possible under grace for an individual to learn to bear such public witness to the gratuity and unrestricted character of Christ's love.

As we have seen, the unconditioned character of the act of faith derives from the fact that the believer's ultimate ground of certitude is the truthfulness of a self-revealing God. Its inner conceptual dynamism is rooted in the finitude and fallibility of the individual human understanding. The unconditioned character of a vocational commitment derives from the fact that it is a love-commitment made in Christ's name, which, therefore, partakes of the absoluteness of his own love-commitment to us. Its inner dynamism derives from the fact that it commits a person to seek under grace the embodiment of an ideal of love which cannot be completely embodied in any single act of love; nor, men being the historically limited and morally imperfect beings that they are, can it be perfectly and exhaustively embodied in any single life of love. That is to say, much as the indissolubility of Christian marriage through the initiative of the contracting partners themselves derives from the fact that theirs is a love-commitment made in the name and image of Christ, which must like his be an absolute and unconditioned commitment of atoning love, so too the public ecclesial commitment to unrestricted love embodied in a life of gratuitous sharing and atoning service, being a love-commitment made in Christ's name, is also absolute and unconditioned, though non-sacramental, and hence, once made, is indissoluble by the vowed Christian who promises it to God. Since, however, both of these ecclesially sacralized commitments demand intelligent and life-long embodiment, a practical dynamism of loving service analogous to the theoretical dynamism of theological conceptualization demanded by the faith-commitment is necessarily implicit in the acceptance of a specific vocational call to love others in Christ's name and image.

But precisely because a vocational commitment is a call to love, fidelity to it cannot be contingent upon mere job success or pragmatic efficiency. The distinction made earlier in this chapter between a vocation and a job is, therefore, really a crucial one. A job-commitment is fundamentally pragmatic; it is a commitment to do some *thing* rather than to love some one. Now, there can be little doubt that it makes little or no sense in terms of task-oriented efficiency either to attempt the impossible or to persevere in the face of evident failure. But to devote one's life to a lost cause, to persevere in spite of failure can be and sometimes is the only available expression of a love rooted in faith precisely because love does not count the cost and does not make measurable success the condition of one's self-gift.

Still, there are limits even to love's toleration of failure. For love can be content to fail only when failure is compatible with love itself. When, therefore, a task or job is undertaken as an expression of loving concern for the needs of the beloved, love cannot seek the failure of such a task or culpably allow its total or partial disruption to take place and still continue to be love. But a genuine love-commitment made in Christ's name can tolerate the failures of a task undertaken in love for the sake of the beloved only when such failure or its partial amelioration is beyond the control of the lover and when the task in hand is the only concrete means available to meet the beloved's needs.

Perhaps the application of these abstract principles to a concrete apostolic work frequently undertaken by contemporary religious will help to clarify them. The unrestricted character of a religious's love is manifest, as we have seen, in its need-orientation. Unrestricted love is not bound to one person, but is bound to seeking out those whose need is greatest. Under the presupposition, then, that a given task undertaken by a religious community is genuinely need-oriented (think, perhaps, of an educational project in the inner city), for the members of the involved religious community to undertake the project publicly, i.e., as a witness to the unrestricted character of Christ's love, places each member under the serious obligation of using every effective means available to make the project a success. But precisely because the project is an expression of a Christian commitment of atoning and gratuitous love, even though for the religious involved maximum efficiency at an individual and at a community level must be one of the goals of the project, such maximum efficiency cannot be the precondition for personal involvement in the project as long as an inefficient expression of love is in the given circumstances better than none at all. Dissociation from the project on the basis of its inefficiency can, then, be justified on at least two conceivable grounds: (1) consciousness of the existence of some greater need which should take precedence over the present project and which the religious in question are capable of fulfilling; (2) the degeneration of efficiency in the running of the project to the point where the work in hand is no longer recognizable as a mediation of love. On the other hand, when the latter circumstance is not verifiable, even though a given project is plagued by many human and bureaucratic inefficiencies, continued involvement in it in the hope of improving it and the service it renders to those in need is often the only way for a religious to witness in the concrete circumstances in which he or she finds himself to the fact that the work in question is not merely an impersonal job-commitment, but is in fact a deeply personal commitment and a labor of love.

The Lure of Power

The second great temptation of those publicly consecrated to the service of the Christian community is the temptation to transform leadership into power. It is, of course, clear that public commitment to the service of atoning love precludes the actual use of physical violence as an apt means to the establishment and nurture of a genuine Christian community. But it is also equally clear that Church leaders are seldom in a situation in which physical violence constitutes a real option. The temptations to convert leadership in loving service into the pursuit of power over others are, however, subtler and more pervasive than the temptation to brute force. More often the temptation takes the form of the failure of official Church leaders to embody the ideal of loving service which they have assumed the public responsibility of seeking to inculcate in others as in themselves.

The temptation can, for instance, take the form of selective blindness to particularly disagreeable community needs whose fulfillment depends upon the consent and/or interest of the official community leader. Like those who passed by the man who had fallen among robbers, there are few human beings who do not discover rather early that it is sometimes very easy to do violence to the needy by simply ignoring them. Moreover, the human necessity that cries out for the compassion of an official community leader need not necessarily be physical. Denying others needed psychological attention or even needed affection through inaction and indifference on the official's part can often be even more exquisitely and violently painful than ignoring their physical suffering.

Selective blindness may also be transformed into selective deafness to anything that does not agree with one's own preconceived view of the universe. Particularly susceptible to this disease are those of a dogmatic cast of mind, (and who among us does not have his or her dogmatic moments?), people who will tolerate only one view of God, man, the world, and human conduct. Often partial victim of inadequate theological, spiritual, or emotional development, the selectively deaf leader seeks to impose arbitrarily his own patterns of belief and conduct upon the legitimate freedom of those he is bound to serve by making them into his own spiritual image. A meat-eater himself, he is convinced that every intelligent person must be brought to conform to his own dietary convictions, although he is, of course, most careful to explain to every conscientious and protesting vegetarian dependent upon his decision how grieved he is that the immutable will of God does not allow the vegetarian to be himself. "My decision that you become a carnivore," the dogmatic community leader protests, "cannot be my will since I am grieved by my need to make it. Nor can it be your will, since you are protesting against it. Therefore, it must be God's will." The leader in the Christian community who so conducts himself uses his office to do subtle but quite effective violence to those he is committed to serve in love.

The violent consequences of such spiritual deafness are, moreover, manifold. Such consequences may, for instance, consist in a refusal to consult the people one has the responsibility of serving in any really effective way concerning their own needs, or in a refusal to recognize the existence of difficulties that arise in the course of community living, or in withholding from those one is appointed to serve information that would make them conscious of human, cultural, and spiritual need of which they are presently oblivious, or in conceiving obedience as being in all cases blind obedience, or in failure to respect the freedom of those one has assumed the responsibility of serving, or in attempting to make their responsible decisions for them either personally or through legislation, or in refusing to air in public important administrative problems like the details of financing or the question of collective goals or supporting or not supporting the vested interests of existing institutions, or in refusing to learn from a humanized version of modern administrative techniques, or in ignoring a consensus of informed, expert, and responsible opinion, or in vindicating one's authority over those one should seek to serve without acknowledging one's responsibilities to them, and so on.

Some particularly subtle forms of spiritual deafness consist in assuming a pose of benevolence while simultaneously retaining complete control over the means of real power: for example, by granting trivial liberties while keeping the means to legal or psychological coercion tightly in one's grasp, or by using the vocabulary of renewal without implementing the reforms which genuine renewal demands.

Closely akin to spiritual deafness in the violence of its effects is culpable ignorance in a community leader. One who assumes the responsibilities of leadership also assumes the responsibility of seeking and gaining all the factual and theoretical information pertinent to the needs and problems of those he serves. Decisions taken in ignorance fail only by lucky chance to do violence to those whose lives are affected by it. Here too one can multiply examples: to seek to resolve a dogmatic or theological controversy in ignorance of the progress and meaning of contemporary theological reflection; to seek to resolve a moral question troubling the consciences of Catholics without informed regard to the moral circumstances of their lives and without due regard to the legitimate disagreement among moral theologians; to fail to consult expert opinion in the resolution of problems or, once it is consulted, to ignore it; to fail to establish and maintain effectively open communications with those one has assumed the responsibility of serving; to refuse to delegate responsibility to those who are more competent to discharge it and to seek instead to pass judgment on matters in which one is personally incompetent even to weigh expert advice; to perpetuate bureaucratic structures which keep one in ignorance of information necessary to the effective service of the people of God.

There are still other ways of doing subtle violence to those one is publicly dedicated to serve. Pusillanimity is one: e.g., to refuse out of fear or irrational conservatism to take prudent risks in meeting the needs of those who are dependent upon one's actions. Favoritism is another: e.g., to direct one's service not by need-oriented love but by personal affinity and preference. Blackmail is a third: e.g., to refuse to serve others gratuitously but instead to place an arbitrary price in the case of certain individuals as a precondition to showing active concern for them in Christ's name. Intimidation is another: e.g., to play upon the insecurities of others in order to prevent them from making demands upon one's time and services. Ambition is another: e.g., placing one's advancement in the ecclesiastical bureaucracy before one's obligation to speak the truth or to meet the less popular needs of God's people. Hypersensitivity is another: e.g., to allow resentment of criticism and of personal affronts to stand in the way of a forgiving concern for the needs of the offender.

This catalogue of different ways of transforming leadership in service into power over the lives of others is, of course, only partial and impressionistic. But the reader can, no doubt, make his own additions to the catalogue. What is common to all of the items listed, however, is an attempt on the part of the community leader to impose his personal viewpoint and limitations arbitrarily upon the legitimate freedom of those he is vowed to serve.

Needless to say, these abuses of one's leadership role in a community of service should not be restricted to religious superiors or to the clergy alone. Such abuses are possible in the case of any religious or of any Christian publicly appointed to a position of responsible service in the community, in his dealings with those whose lives are affected by the manner in which he discharges his responsibilities, and by the decisions which he takes.

Clearly, then, appointment to any position of leadership in

the Christian community whatever its degree of positive responsibility (i.e., acceptance into the hierarchy or into a religious order or congregation or personal acceptance of public responsibility for some community service) demands a person who at least aspires to really rare and truly Christ-like qualities. For not only must such a person be prepared to deal with others as a member of a community of graced, but fallen and finite men, but he must also be one who can lovingly help the community to maintain its own Christian sense of identity in matters of both faith and morals—not by autocratically demanding immediate and blind assent to a catalogue of dogmas and regulations but by seeking to make the mysteries of Christian doctrine and life reasonably acceptable to the people he serves. For Christians imbued with a nominalistic mode of thinking or with an autocratic medieval or baroque image of Church leadership, the way of blind assent will, no doubt, seem more appealing and pastorally efficient than the way of Christ. But such tactics can scarcely be reconciled with the Pauline injunction to Timothy to "do all with patience and with the intention of teaching," or to "be gentle when he corrects people who dispute what he says."[296]

There can be little doubt, however, that individuals can on occasion perform actions that may demand a public declaration by Church leaders of their abandonment of the ideals and beliefs of the Christian community as a means of avoiding more serious scandal. But there can also be little doubt that Church laws governing due process in such instances are presently inadequate to prevent the occurrence of autocratic and unjustifiable official disciplinary actions. Since the autocratic and unjust exclusion or punishment of a member of the community is the most effective way to undermine this important aspect of Church discipline and since on occasion the right of Church leaders to exercise such authority responsibly may indeed be a crucial factor in the community's preservation of its Christian self-identity, it is in the interests both of the people of God and those who serve them that adequate legal provision be made in the community for the protection of Christians and their reputations from unjust and sometimes slanderous innuendos concerning their good standing in a community, which result from their being officially, autocratically, and unjustifiably excluded from the community or from the legitimate exercise of their office within the community, with all the defamatory consequences that such an action necessarily entails. Particularly vulnerable are theologians and other community leaders who engage in legitimate and responsible theological debate concerning the meaning of Christian belief and concerning the binding force of certain disputed aspects of Church discipline.

Notes

1. Dt 7:6.
2. Lv 19:2;1S 6:19;HO 11:9.
3. Ex 33:12–17.
4. Ex 20:1–17;Dt 22:1–4;23:20; 24:19.
5. Dn 7:18–22.
6. Jn 15:16.
7. Mt 5:13.
8. Rm 12:1.
9. Mt 28:18.
10. Ep 4:10–13.
11. Mt 18:4.
12. Mt 18:5;Jm 1:9–10;2:8–9.
13. Mt 18:6–14.
14. Mt 18:15–18.
15. Mt 18:21–35.
16. Mt 6:1.
17. Mt 7:1–5.
18. Mt 7:15.
19. Mt 10:28–33.
20. Mt 3:37–39.
21. Mt 24:42.
22. Lk 14:12–14.
23. Lv 19:33–34.
24. Ps 49:12–13.
25. Dt 10:18–19.
26. Mt 26:35.
27. Mt 10:40.
28. Mk 9:37.
29. Lk 12:37.
30. Rv 3:20–22.
31. Tt 1:7–8;cf.1Tm 3:3–4.
32. Lk 14:21–24.
33. Jn 14:2–3.
34. Eph 4:28;cf. Rm 12:11.
35. 1Co 9:17–18;Rm 13:8,10; 1Th 5:4
36. Eph 4:27.
37. Ph2:3–4;Jm 3:16.
38. Col 3:5–11.
39. Jm 4:13–17.
40. Gn 2:15.
41. Gn 3:19.
42. Pr 21:25.
43. Jr 22:13;Jm 5:4.
44. Am 5:11.
45. Si 33:25;2S 12:31.
46. 1S 8:10–18;1K 5:27–32.
47. Si 38:24–39.
48. Ex 20:1–2;Dt 5:15.
49. Lv 19:13;Dt 14:29;16–15.
50. Ps 128:1–2.
51. Jn 6:27.
52. Mt 6:33.
53. Lk 9:24.
54. Jn 13:34–35.
55. 1P 5:2.
56. Mt 9:37;Jn 4:38.
57. 1P 2:10;Rm 8:19ff;Ep 1:10; Col 1:16–20.
58. Jm 1:27;Rm 12:13;1Th 5:14.
59. Rm 12:16.
60. Jm 1:9–10.
61. Jm 13:5–6.
62. Jm 2:8–9.
63. Jm 2:2–4.
64. Col 3:9–11.
65. Col 3:12–17.
66. 1Jn 5:2–4.
67. 1Co 13:4–7.
68. Gal 5:22.

68a. Eph 4:7;cf. 2P 4:5–7.

69. Jm 1:2–4;23–25.
70. Ga 5:19.
71. 1Co 1:11–16.
72. Ep 4:31–2.
73. Ep 5:1–2.
74. Jm 4:11–12.
75. Ep 2:1–11.
76. 1Co 14:29–33;37–38.
77. 1Co 13:1;14:3–4.
78. Col 4:5–6.
79. Col 3:5–7.
80. Col 3:13.
81. Rm 14:13.
82. Jn 8:1–11.

83. 2Tm 3:1–5.
84. 2Tm 4:1–2;8.
85. Mt 5:7.
86. Mt 7:1–5.
87. Jn 3:16–21;1Jn 4:7–14.
88. Lk 11:23.
89. Is 26:4;30:29.
90. Rm 14:14–15.
91. Ep 4:25.
92. 1P 2:1;Jm 3:18;4:11–12; Eph 5:4–5;Col 3:9;Jm 1:19–21; 4:11-12; 3:18.
93. Jn 13:1–20;Lk 22:47–48.
94. Ac 15:5–29.
95. Ac 15:28.
96. Ac 15:28.
97. 1Co 8:1–6.
98. 1Co 9:7–9.
99. 1Co 10:6–13.
100. 1Co 10:28–29.
101. 2Tm 4:2.
102. 1Co 10:23–24;cf. Rm 14:15.
103. 1Co 9:19–23.
104. 1Co 8:7–13;9:23–30.
105. Rm 14:1–3.
106. Rm 14:7–12.
107. Rm 15:1–4.
107a. Rm 15:7.
108. Rm 14:5.
109. Ep 5:1–2.
110. Ep 5:3–4.
111. Ga 5:19;Ep 5:3–4;Col 3:5.
112. Ep 5:22–6:9.
113. Rm 12:6–8.
114. Mt 28:19–20.
115. Rm 1:16–2:24.
116. Ga 5:1–5.
117. Ga 5:13–24.
118. Ac 15:28.
119. Mt 23:23–26.
120. Mk 2:27;Mt 16:5–12;23:4;1Tm 1:8–11.
120a. 1Jn 4:1–3.
121. 1Tm 4:14.
122. 1Tm 4:12.
123. 1Tm 5:1.
124. 1Tm 6:11.
125. 1Co 11:1;Ph 3:17;2Th 3:7.
126. 1Tm 1:8–11.
127. 1Th 5:19–22.
128. 2Th 3:15.
129. 1Co 5:9–13.
130. Tt 1:10–11.
131. 2Tm 2:16–17.
132. 2Tm 2:23–26.
133. 2Tm 1:13–14;3:14–16.
134. 2Tm 4:2–8.
135. 1Tm 3:1ff;Tt 1:7–9.
136. 1Tm 6:6–8;cf.1P 5:1–4.
137. MG 35,1101D.
138. MG 35,413C.
139. MG 31,928C,933A.
140. MG 35,1101D;36,576C.
141. ML 16,1153D.
142. MG 12,540B.
143. ML 22,1077,1080.
144. MG 35,721C;ML 22,1080.
145. ML 21,443C.
146. ML 21,418D.
147. ML 21,389.
148. ML 21,439C.
149. MG 34,1101C.
150. ML 49,483B,486C.
151. MG 65,133A.
152. MG 31,928C.
153. ML 40,564.
154. ML 31,440B.
155. MG 65,141D.
156. ML 40,564.
157. MG 78,256D.
158. MG 65,253B.
159. MG 47,366.
160. MG 47,388.
161. ML 40,572;ML 33,961.
162. ML 33,961.
163. ML 49,1135A.
164. MG 47,376.

165. ML 38,651;32,659;32,795;32,848; MG 93,1508A.
166. MG 11,444C;32,289C;ML 49, 801A;MG 79,1173C;88,1129A;90, 929C.
167. MG 79,824D;ML 40,446.
168. ML 21,444C.
169. ML 49,1136B.
170. ML 49,1138B.
171. ML 37,1729.
172. ML 40,576.
173. MG 34,421D.
174. MG 88,1640C.
175. DS 844.
176. DS 1170.
177. DS 1174,1184.
178. DS 1491.
179. DS 797.
180. DS 856.
181. DS 1304,1405.
182. DS 1713.
183. DS 2112.
184. DS 3726–3727.
185. DS 3965,3942.
186. *Pastoral Constitution on the Church in the Modern World,* 69.
187. *Ibid.,* p.71.
188. *Populorum Progressio,* 51.
189. *Decree on the Appropriate Renewal of the Religious Life,* 13.
190. *Decree on the Apostolate of the Laity,* 11.
191. *Populorum Progressio,* 67.
192. DS 1174;cf.DS 1184.
193. DS 3268.
194. DS 3733,3735–3737.
195. DS 3947,3960.
196. *Pastoral Constitution on the Church in the Modern World,* 68.
197. *Populorum Progressio,* 69.
198. *Pastoral Constitution on the Church in the Modern World,* 27.
199. *Ibid.*
200. *Ibid.,* 34.
201. *Ibid.,* 35.
202. *Ibid.,* 60.
203. *Ibid.,* 67.
204. *Ibid.,* 60.
205. *Ibid.,* 66.
206. *Ibid.,* 68.
207. *Dogmatic Constitution on the Church,* 41.
208. *Decree on the Appropriate Renewal of the Religious Life,* 13.
209. DS 668.
210. DS 1495.
211. DS 2745.
212. DS 3741.
213. *Pastoral Constitution on the Church in the Modern World,* 4.
214. *Dogmatic Constitution on the Church,*24.
215. *Pastoral Constitution on the Church in the Modern World,* 63.
216. *Decree on the Ministry and Life of Priests,* 6;*Decree on the Missionary Activity of the Church,* 20;*Declaration on Christian Education,* 9;*Decree on the Appropriate Renewal of the Religious Life,* 13;*Decree on the Apostolate of the Laity,* 8.
217. *Pastoral Constitution on the Church in the Modern World,* 69; *Decree on the Bishops' Pastoral Office in the Church,* 12, 13.
218. *Decree on the Appropriate Renewal of Religious Life,*15.
219. DS 975.
220. DS 1530,1561,1578.
221. DS 1561.

222. DS 1548.
223. DS 1931,1937,1970.
224. DS 1938.
225. DS 2307.
226. DS 2323.
227. DS 2458.
228. DS 2447.
229. DS 2444.
230. DS 2351.
231. DS 2355.
232. DS 2357.
233. DS 2359–2361.
234. DS 2369.
235. DS 2373.
236. DS 2021.
237. DS 2106.
238. DS 2110.
239. DS 2111.
240. 1 Jn 4:20.
241. *Dogmatic Constitution on the Church*,14.
242. *Ibid.*, 42.
243. *Ibid.*, 50, 51.
244. *Pastoral Constitution on the Church in the Modern World*, 26.
245. *Ibid.*, 28.
246. *Ibid.*, 48.
247. *Ibid.*, 47.
248. *Ibid.*, 51.
249. *Decree on Priestly Formation*, 10.
250. *Decree on the Appropriate Renewal of the Religious Life*,5.
251. *Ibid.*, 12,15.
252. *Ibid.*, 5,8.
253. *Decree on the Apostolate of the Laity*,3,4,8.
254. *Pastoral Constitution on the Church in the Modern World*, 78.
255. *Ibid.*, 92;*Decree on Ecumenism*, 6, 7.
256. *Decree on the Missionary Activity of the Church*,7,11;*Declaration on Christian Education*,3.
257. *Declaration on the Relationship of the Church to non-Christian Religions*,5.
258. DS 761.
259. DS 1771.
260. DS 1771.
261. DS 2592–2597;2603–2610.
262. DS 3064.
263. DS 3115.
264. DS 3308.
265. DS 3804.
266. DS 3755.
267. DS 3850.
268. *Decree on the Ministry and Life of Priests*,1–2.
269. *Dogmatic Constitution on the Church*,27.
270. *Decree on the Ministry and Life of Priests*,21,25.
271. *Decree on the Bishops' Pastoral Office in the Church*, 34.
272. *Dogmatic Constitution on the Church*,44.
273. *Ibid.*, 45.
274. *Decree on the Bishops' Pastoral Office in the Church*, 35.
275. *Ibid.*,16.
276. *Ibid.*,14.
277. *Ibid.*,16–17.
278. *Dogmatic Constitution on the Church*,28.
279. *Decree on the Ministry and Life of Priests*,4–6,9.
280. *Decree on the Appropriate Renewal of Religious Life*,5,18,23.
281. *Decree on the Ministry and Life of Priests*,3; *Dogmatic Constitution on the Church*,46.
282. *Dogmatic Constitution on the Church*,43.
283. *Ibid.*, 31, 33, 36.
284. *Ibid.*, 35.

285. *Decree on the Appropriate Renewal of Religious Life*,5; *Dogmatic Constitution on the Church*,44.
286. *Dogmatic Constitution on the Church*,36.
287. *Decree on the Apostolate of the Laity*,3;*Decree on the Appropriate Renewal of Religious Life*,5.
288. *Decree on the Appropriate Renewal of Religious Life*,5; *Decree on the Apostolate of the Laity*,3;*Dogmatic Constitution on the Church*,37–40.
289. *Decree on the Apostolate of the Laity*,10–14;*Dogmatic Constitution on the Church*,44,46–47;*Decree on the Appropriate Renewal of Religious Life*,2,3,5,6, 17, 20; *Decree on the Bishops' Pastoral Office in the Church*, 33–34.
290. *Decree on the Apostolate of the Laity*,16;*Decree on the Bishops' Pastoral Office in the Church*, 33–35.
291. Örsy, *op. cit.*, pp. 271–282.
292. Edward Heenan, "A Quest for Religious Community," *Woodstock Letters*, xcvi (Summer, 1967), pp. 300–301.
293. C. S. Peirce, *Collected Papers*, C. Hartshorne and P. Weiss (eds.), 8 vols. (Cambridge, Mass.: Harvard, 1960), 5, 2.
294. *Ibid.*, 6, 468–472.
295. *Ibid.*
296. Cf. DS 3008.
297. 2Tm 2:25;4:2.

VI

The Prayer of Involvement

No really adequate account of prayer can be compressed into a single chapter of any book, especially not a book as elementary as this one. The purpose of these brief reflections is, therefore, quite limited. In them we shall attempt to explore some of the dimensions of a certain type of prayer, which we have named the "prayer of involvement." As in the case of more contemplative types of meditation, the prayer of involvement consists in opening one's mind and heart to the person and transcendent reality of God. But it is called the prayer of involvement precisely because it springs most directly from one's personal involvement in the work of spreading God's kingdom on earth, from one's existential commitment in faith and love to the living Christian community, and from an authentic concern to bring about its growth and progress through active dedication to the enterprise of service.

Old Testament Prayer

At the living center of much Old Testament prayer is belief in the covenant. The covenanted Jew prayed in his heart of hearts to the Lord of hosts because he was confident that Yahweh would indeed live up to the terms of the alliance he had once made with his people through the patriarch Abraham and his servant Moses. Hence, in moments of personal need and of public crisis the true believer called upon the God of the covenant with an assurance inspired both by his own sense of having faithfully kept the precepts of God's law and by a confidence that Yahweh could never be outmatched by one's own human fidelity.[1]

The prayers which mount up to God from his people are, then, in large measure prayers for deliverance—deliverance from one's enemies;[2] from the contempt of one's peers and from public disgrace;[3] from violence and oppression;[4] from the consequences of one's own sins;[5] from sickness;[6] from the melancholy burdens of old age;[7] from childlessness and sterility;[8] from the impious;[9] from suffering and death;[10] from slanderers;[11] from national disaster;[12] from the ravages of war;[13] from the anguish of soul which is the mark of the human condition;[14] from every form of misfortune.[15]

Covenant Prayer: Blessing, Petition, Adoration

If his petition is in fact answered the devout Jew responds vocally with praise and joy at this latest re-confirmation of his confidence in the Lord's covenanted word. Moreover, this vocal response to God's saving action seems to be conceived after the manner of an exchange of gifts between God and man in which both renew their covenant promises one to the other: God renews his word to man through the very favor granted, while man's return gift to God is both his faithful acknowledgement of the Lord's goodness and his rededication to the divine service.[16]

The prayer of blessing is, however, also interesting in that it illustrates the extent to which covenant prayer is rooted in a personal reflection on the sense and purpose of salvation history. The man who blesses God not only rejoices to experience every latest renewal of divine favor, but also sees in each new blessing from the Lord a reconfirmation of his whole religious heritage. Among other things, therefore, to bless God means to be willing to accept the full burden of the religious past of one's people, to be sensitive to the salvific meaning contained in that past and through a process of historical discernment to develop the ability to respond sensitively to the presence of God in all the good things of life.

Granted, then, the whole context of covenant worship, it was humanly inevitable that the devout Jew, who had obeyed the law and kept his side of the covenant bargain, would experience God's silence in the face of his need, God's failure to respond to his plea for deliverance as a severe test of his own belief in the covenant and in God's fidelity to his servants. Confronted with the silence and the absence of God, the petitioner experiences at times an almost indignant sense of his rights by the terms of the covenant to be heard; and his redoubled petitions not only press his case in the divine court but also constitute the puzzled renewal of his trust in an enigmatic God, who, to judge from appearances at least, would seem to be reneging on his covenanted word.[17]

Sometimes, though not always, this prayer of renewed petition takes on the character of what might be called a "prayer of impatient endurance." For though the prayer truly is the expression of renewed faith in Yahweh's ultimate fidelity, still, the petitioner's insistence on the legal terms of the covenant often introduces into his prayer an note of impatient, juridical pleading.[18]

It is relatively late in the development of Jewish belief, specifically in the book of Job, that Yahweh finally silences the impertinence and self-righteousness which could be latent in such a prayer.[19] The protagonist of the parable, Job, is a man of the land of Uz, not, therefore, a covenanted Jew. Yet by the testimony of Yahweh himself, Job is the faithful servant of the Lord without parallel anywhere on earth.[20] The sin of Job is to imagine that his service of God has in fact given him a legal claim upon the Lord. "Who can get me a hearing from God?" he complains in his misfortune after listing all the virtuous deeds to his credit. "I have had my say, from A to Z; now let Shaddai answer me. . . . I will give him an account of every step of my life, and go as boldly as a prince to meet him."[21]

But when he has been confronted with the power and the splendor of the Lord, Job, as the true servant of God that he is, confesses the folly and pride of trying to hold Shaddai to account for his management of the vast universe he had created.[22]

Yahweh's restoration of Job's fortunes after the latter's repentance is not just a literary flourish to give the story a happy ending. It is a reaffirmation of the final fidelity of the Lord to all who serve him well.[23] But the main point of the parable is clear enough: Belief in God's fidelity gives no man the right to question any concrete historical decision the omnipotent creator of the universe happens to make—not even when the course of events would seem, in human eyes, at least, to compromise God's equity in his dealings with his servants. In other words, the book of Job deprives the prayer of impatient endurance of its impatience. But in reducing it to a prayer of simple endurance the parable leaves the petitioner face to face with a mystery: Why does the Lord of the covenant choose to act with such apparent heartlessness toward those who serve him faithfully? For all its wrestling with the problem of evil, then, the book of Job concludes with a question rather than a solution, a question to which the reader is invited to respond with Job: "What can I reply? I had better lay my finger on my lips."[24]

As the protagonist of a parable, therefore, Job typifies the unresolved paradox of the man of faith whose suffering is in fact wholly unmerited and yet permitted by God. The paradox remains unresolved because the author of Job opts to reduce the problem of evil back into the mystery of God. Earlier biblical writers, especially the prophets, had, however, suggested a simpler explanation of God's silence. Rather than appeal to the divine transcendence, they had sought instead to excuse Yahweh's apparent indifference to the pleas of his servants by pointing to the experienced fact of human iniquity. That is to say, God's intermittent silence toward the prayers of his people became explicable if only one questioned the factual grounds of men's covenanted claim upon the Lord.[25]

Not even a personal sense of one's own innocence could serve as an infallible guarantee of one's justice before the divine judge; for could not God's silence be due to some past unrepented sin?[26] Or to one's share in the collective guilt of one's people?[27,28]

The Sense of Guilt

Thus, as we have already seen before in different contexts, one of the religious fruits of the experience of God's periodic silence to the prayers of his people—a silence which culminates in the final destruction of the kingdoms of Israel and Judah—was their growing explicitation of a sense of personal and collective guilt.

Moreover, this guilt-consciousness added in its turn two important dimensions to the practice of Old Testament prayer. The first was a feeling of immense wonder and joy at the phenomenon of a God who again and again freely chose to rescue his people in spite of their sinfulness, of a God who was in fact so often willing to keep his side of the covenant bargain in spite of his servants' failure to keep theirs. "Yahweh is tender and compassionate, slow to anger, most loving . . . he never treats us, never punishes us as our guilt and our sins deserve."[29]

Gradually, therefore, Israel came to recognize that the inevitable anger of God at the sinfulness of man is exceeded only by his compassion and his desire to forgive. Yahweh's message to his people in the midst of the idols of Babylon is simple and moving: "I have loved you with an everlasting love, so I am constant in my affection for you. I build you once more; you shall be rebuilt, virgin of Israel."[30]

Thus, the second important element which this sense of guilt, evoked by the silence of God and by the experience of human infidelity to the covenant, introduced into Old Testament prayer, consisted in Israel's ability to recognize the very absence of God as itself a call to repentance.[31-38]

This return to the God of the covenant could be either individual or collective. The practice of communal liturgies of penance culminating in a covenant renewal seems to have been present in some form at every period in the development of Hebrew belief. Often, the sense of collective guilt which motivated such a liturgy led the people to have recourse to an important religious leader to act as mediator between them and the God whom they had angered by their infidelity. Moses is, of course, the biblical type of such an Old Testament leader.[39-51]

Eschatological Longing

The psalms reflect in their own way this same development of Hebrew belief. In them, Israel's penitential longing for reconciliation with the Lord gradually takes on an increasingly explicit eschatological character.[52,53,54] It was, moreover, the longing of God's faithful remnant for the promised day of its final vindication which inevitably merged with the messianic hopes of post-exilic Judaism in order to find vocal expression in numerous prayers of immense reverence and hope, as well as of profound yearning and deep religious emotion.[55-61]

It is, however, interesting to note that even this eschatological supplication remains more or less explicitly covenant-oriented. For Israel the speedy advent of the day of the Lord meant nothing less than the conclusion of a new covenant to replace the broken tablets of the Mosaic alliance: "See, the days are coming—it is Yahweh who speaks—when I will make a new covenant with the House of Israel (and the house of Judah), but not a covenant like the one I made with their ancestors on the day I took them by the hand to bring them out of the land of Egypt. . . . No, this is the covenant I will make with the House of Israel when those days arrive—it is Yahweh who speaks. Deep within them I will plant my Law, writing it on their hearts. Then I will be their God and they shall be my people. There will be no further need for neighbor to try to teach neighbor, or brother to say to brother. 'Learn to know Yahweh!' No, they will all know me, the least no less than the greatest—it is Yahweh who speaks—since I will forgive their iniquity and never call sin to mind."[62]

Teaching of Jesus

The subject of prayer comes up frequently in Jesus' instructions to his disciples. He not only suggests to them things for which to pray, but also indicates what should be their inner attitude of heart as they present their needs to their heavenly Father.

For Jesus as for the men of the Old Testament, the most fundamental form of prayer is the prayer of petition.[63] But what strikes one repeatedly about the objects of petition which the master suggests is their explicitly eschatological character. Though the disciples are exhorted to pray for the fulfillment of their basic material needs (but not for wealth or luxury),[64] the master directs most of their petitions to the speedy accomplishment of his messianic mission. Thus, the disciples should ask the Father that all men come at last to reverence and serve their heavenly Father, that the eschatological kingdom of atonement which Jesus has come to found be established finally and definitively on earth.[65] They are to pray for the irreversible accomplishment of the right order willed by God through mankind's final reconciliation to him in obedience and filial devotion. They are to pray for the forgiveness of their own sins and for the strength to meet the test which will be theirs on the last day. They should pray for the enterprise of spreading God's kingdom on earth and for the greater involvement of men in the salvific endeavor of actively reaping the harvest of redemption that the labors of past ages had brought to its moment of fruition.[66]

The master is also quite clear on the basic attitude of soul which should characterize the prayer of the true children of God. The filial character of their prayers must manifest itself first of all in the absolute confidence with which they turn to their heavenly Father and in their unshakable certainty of being heard.[67]

In other words, to hesitate in prayer, to fail in any way in one's confidence of being heard is, by the reverse logic that is inherent in the faith commitment, to fail in one's own fidelity to the Father and by that very fact to fail in one's mission as his adopted son.[68,69]

This firm filial confidence of being heard by the Father—of ultimate vindiction at his hands—also motivates a second attitude of prayer, viz., that of perseverance. The Father's delay in answering our petitions should never disconcert his children or cause them to doubt his ultimate fidelity to them. Instead they should look forward with all the greater confidence to the full accomplishment of his salvific plan on earth through the final establishment of the messianic kingdom he has promised.[70]

At first sight, therefore, the would seem to be a certain initial antimony latent in the master's teaching concerning prayer. For on the one hand, the disciples are told not to expect in every instance the kind of immediately miraculous response to their petitions which Elijah received in his contest with the false prophets.[71] The Father may indeed delay his saving action. On the other hand, the master gives repeated assurance that the Father's answer will indeed come and that it will come "speedily." "Everything you ask and pray for," he teaches, "believe that you have it already, and it will be yours."[72]

The third quality of authentic filial prayer is repentance. Every son of Adam who seeks justification before God in prayer must make his own the entreaty of the publican, "God, be merciful to me a sinner."[73,74]

The fourth quality of heart which the master demands of those who would turn to his Father in prayer is the more horizontal attitude of mutual forgiveness. The Father who has offered his own forgiveness to men in the mission of his Son demands that those who claim to be his adopted children show the same kind of divinely inspired willingness to forgive one another in the name of God and whenever possible to take upon themselves, as Jesus himself had, the evil consequences of mankind's sinfulness.[75]

Absolute Confidence

Moreover, in addition to these four positive characteristics, the master is also careful to indicate some important negative norms for the practice of truly filial prayer. The true child of his heavenly Father ought to take care to avoid in prayer every manifestation of superstition, of meaningless formalism, of hypocrisy and ostentation.[76-78]

Interestingly enough, Jesus also demands the same kind of

unwavering confidence from those who turn directly to him for help as he had demanded of those who petition his heavenly Father for assistance. When, for instance, the father of the epileptic demoniac boy pleads with the master, "If you can do anything, have pity on us and help us," Jesus replies with the gentle but pointed rebuke, "If you can? Everything is possible for anyone who has faith." The requested miracle is then performed, but not until the father has responded with his own profession of confidence, "I do have faith. Help the little faith I have."[79-83]

If Jesus demands a positive and categorical faith from those who approach him in search of help, he also seems to find such faith irresistible when he does in fact discover it. The centurion at Capernaum, the woman suffering from a hemorrhage, the two blind men, the Canaanite woman—all evoke from him a spontaneous response of admiring praise which is rich in human warmth and encouragement.[84]

Prayer of Jesus

We should also take care to note that the master did not merely instruct his disciples verbally concerning prayer; he gave them an example as well. Moreover, one has the distinct impression from the gospel narratives that his personal prayer to the Father was, humanly speaking, fully integrated into his whole messianic sense of mission. That is to say, it is apparently his sense of messianic purpose which draws him to prayer, while the prayer itself strengthens him in his humanity for his work and gives him clarity and direction in the choices he must make. It is while praying that he first receives his saving mission of atonement on the banks of the Jordan.[85] He then begins the labors of his apostolate by retiring to the desert to pray; and there, in communion with his Father, he formulates the broad outlines of the kingdom he has come to found.[86] From then on we find him in prayer at all the critical moments of his apostolic career. Before leaving Capernaum to preach in the synagogues of Galilee and Judea, he once again retires into solitude in order to pray alone with his Father at dawn.[87] Before choosing the twelve men on whom he will rely to build with him a new Israel, he spends the whole night in prayer.[88] When the seventy-two disciples return rejoicing at their success in proclaiming the kingdom, his own joy bursts forth in a happy prayer of blessing.[89] After eluding the attempt of the crowds, following the multiplication of the loaves, to force him to be their temporal king, he retires to the mountains to compose himself in prayer.[90] Before the raising of Lazarus, in order to confirm the faith of those who have come to believe in him, he blesses his Father for always hearing his petitions.[91] In the atmosphere of increasing conflict and doom which surrounds his final ministry in Jerusalem, he retires regularly to the Mount of Olives with his disciples in order to pray.[92] At the last supper he pronounces prophetically the first eucharistic prayer[93] and then turns to the Father in a final supplication for those whom he has chosen, asking that they remain untainted by the world and that they become one with himself, with the Father, and with one another.[94,95]

Priestly Prayer of Christ

Moreover, the evangelists seem to have sensed that Jesus' life of apostolically oriented prayer reached a climax in the prayer which was an integral part of his suffering and death. The synoptic accounts of the passion all begin with his prayer in the garden, a prayer which is wrenched from his human heart in the extremity of his anguish and need, but which ends with the same profession of abandonment to the Father, the same refusal to test the Father's fidelity, the same repudiation of the way of coercive power with which he had begun his messianic career in the desert.[96-101]

Needless to say, the apparent silence of God in the face of Jesus' pleas during his passion must have placed immense strain upon the disciples' belief in the master's teaching concerning the efficacy of prayer. A strange kind of fidelity indeed this heavenly Father seemed to have. Worse still, precisely because the master had insisted all along on the filial character of his own and his disciples' relationship to God and on the divine longing to hear every petition addressed him by his children, the Father's silence and absence from the hill of Calvary posed an even deeper problem than the book of Job, which in contrast to the master's teaching on the fatherhood of God had insisted rather on his inscrutable power and on his kingly right to arrange his universe whatever way he may choose. Moreover, any appeal in the manner of the Old Testament prophets to the fact of man's guilt in the eyes of God as a way of explaining the Father's failure to act was, in Jesus' case, quite pointless; for who indeed could convict their good master of sin?[102]

The Eschatological Dimension of Jesus' Prayer

The mysterious resolution of such doubts and perplexities came, of course, in the disciple's confrontation with their risen Lord. The insight is best articulated by the author of Hebrews: "During his life on earth, he offered up prayer and entreaty, aloud and in silent tears, to the one who had the power to save him out of death, and he submitted so humbly that his prayer was heard. Although he was Son, he learnt to obey through suffering; but having been made perfect, he became for all who obey him the source of eternal salvation and was acclaimed by God with the title of high priest *of the order of Melchizedek.*"[103]

Several significant implications can be drawn from this key text. First, the author points out that the Father's response on Easter day to all of Jesus' prayers was proportioned to the latter's prior total abandonment on Good Friday of his life and mission into the Father's hands. The Father's reply to his Son's pleas for the coming of the kingdom demanded that Jesus' confident and unquestioning fidelity to his messianic call on the banks of the Jordan be "made perfect" by his final and complete immolation upon the cross. Seen in this context, then, the resurrection is nothing else than the Father's endorsement of that mission in the specific historical form in which Jesus conducted it. It is the enthronement of the incarnate Son, in the historical modality which his incarnation assumed, as the messianic high-priest, the universal mediator and atoning sacrifice for the sins of all men.

Second, the resurrection is the revelation of the full dimensions of the eschatological kingdom of service which Jesus had come to found. And these dimensions are complex in the extreme. To begin with, the Father's response to the Son's entreaties for the definitive establishment of a kingdom of atoning love upon earth was also his revelation to men of the fact that such a kingdom can never be brought to perfection either by human labors alone or even as long as the present order of creation continues to prevail. The world which we now experience, the people among whom we live, we ourselves are far too impregnated with disorder, with egotism and selfishness for the universal advent of God's justice to take the form of anything but a re-creation, a re-fashioning of the universe after the pattern of the risen Savior.

For a Christian discovers his full faith in God the creator in the glorious transformation of the flesh of God's incarnate Son. Only secondarily and mediately does he discover it in the Old Testament creation narratives. That is, the Christian believer finds an understanding of the meaning of creation in the ancient Hebrew accounts of human and of cosmic origins to the extent that these ancient narratives are themselves illumined and fulfilled by the Easter event.

Moreover, what the disciples began to realize in the light of that Easter dawn was the staggering fact that the kingdom of God for which they had been laboring and praying as members of the master's community of gratuitous sharing, unrestricted love, and service is itself nothing else than this same new creation in process of preparation.

Paradoxically, then, even though the Father's answer to all their prayers for the kingdom's arrival had indeed come "soon" as the master had promised, the kingdom itself had nevertheless assumed a character which they had little expected. Moreover, the concretely eschatological form which it had finally taken had itself become God's revelation to them not only of a whole new order of salvation but also of a whole new context in which they could begin to penetrate the real meaning of the theoretical and practical formation in a life of prayer which they had received at the master's hands. Thus, only when they were actually confronted with the risen Christ did they begin to comprehend the reason why the Father's response to the master's prayers for the accomplishment of his mission could not have taken the form of the twelve legions of angels that they themselves might have preferred, to prevent his suffering and crucifixion. The death of Jesus had been the inevitable precondition for the transformation of his mortal flesh into immortal glory. To have prevented his death would have been to forestall the arrival of his glorious enthronement at the right hand of God. But now, in the light of the Easter event, the disciples began to grasp that the human prayer and labor for the kingdom of God, as God envisaged that kingdom, had as its real purpose to prepare the extension of the consequences of God's abrupt and regenerative eruption into his creation to the whole material universe and to do so by actively involving this as yet unregenerate world in the mission of universal service and atonement which the Lord had inaugurated in the course of his temporal life and death.

Inevitably, then, the Father's "delay" in answering his children's petitions during the last age of salvation could conceivably, when measured in historical terms, extend until the universal resurrection, until the parousia of Christ. Such, after all, had been Jesus' personal experience in his dealings with the Father. And surely no disciple could expect to be treated better than his master.

Still, however long the delay, one could pray to God with absolute assurance of being heard, precisely because the glorification of Jesus, i.e., the Father's ratification of a new and eternal covenant of love in the flesh of his own incarnate Son, remained as mankind's guarantee of the Father's faithful will to save all who turn to him for help in Jesus' own spirit of unquestioning filial confidence and trust. For as the revelation of the Father's eternal and unshakable will to save all that exists by re-creating it in the image of the glorified Christ, the resurrection is every believer's assurance not only that his prayers for a share in the kingdom have already been heard by God long before he himself is moved to utter them, but also that the condition for his being heard is that he actually pray with the same absolute confidence as Jesus himself had demanded. For unless the believer pray in the same spirit of death-conquering trust as God's incarnate Son he can make no claim of truly being a child of God.

God's failure to answer our prayers at once may, of course, as the author of the letter of James warns, always be due to our failure to ask for anything but objects of selfish gratification.[104] The fact remains, however, that even the best of our prayers, one that is rooted in a faith strong enough to move mountains and cast them into the sea, may well have to await the parousia before those mountains will budge.[105]

But the resurrection had deeper implications yet for a Christian understanding of the meaning of prayer. For in its light, the disciples realized with new clarity drawn from the full and final manifestation of the incarnation itself that the mystery of God's dealings with men is, as the author of Job had dimly seen, inseparable from the mystery of God himself. All the paradoxes and perplexities articulated by Job had been subsumed into the tragic events surrounding the crucifixion of Jesus. And though they had not been explained away, they had received a kind of resolution by being again subsumed into the larger mystery of a God-made-man, whose faithful love for men was such that he preferred to let them kill him rather than destroy them with the sword of his wrath.

Moreover, having once glimpsed in the dawn of Easter the promise of a glory after death, the infant Church could never again be finally content with any lesser gift from God. In other words, once the disciples had begun to grasp the truly cosmic dimensions of God's salvific plan to remake the world in the image of his risen Son, they also began to recognize that no response of God to human prayers short of the final coming could ever be truly adequate to the real object of all man's inner yearnings. They began to see that at the basis of every human plea for deliverance addressed to God since the beginning had lain the more or less obscurely realized yearning of each man for his own resurrection and that this yearning which had found expression in innumerable prayers to God is itself man's response to the prior and completely gratuitous call from a loving God to share in the life of his glorified Son. What the resurrection had revealed to them, then, was that every man since the beginning had been living in an order of salvation whose full dimensions had finally been revealed in the glorification of Jesus. And though they continued to believe that there was, in principle, nothing to prevent God from intervening miraculously and spectacularly in human events, as he had in his previous dealings with Israel, and that the miracles of healing accomplished by Jesus in the course of his public ministry could indeed be wrought again in his name, nevertheless, such partial and temporary interventions of God had been quite eclipsed by the universal resurrection itself as the believing community's principal object of desire. Miracles might be all right for a start; but having once seen and touched the glorified body of the Lord, the first Christians could be content in their prayers with nothing less than the ultimate miracle, the new creation itself, the complete transformation of the whole material universe in the image of the risen Christ.[106]

More important still, their own ability to endure prayerfully the silence of God as Jesus had, by persevering as he had in an attitude of unshakable filial confidence and love in spite of every suffering and injustice, had itself become for them the sign that they did indeed possess the Spirit of Christ and, with his Spirit, his assurance of their own final share in risen glory.

In a word, the resurrection diminished both the importance and the necessity of pleas for isolated acts of spectacular divine intervention in human affairs. It diminished their necessity because in the new dispensation, individual miracles were no longer needed, as they had been under the revocable Sinai covenant, to assure men of God's continued commitment to them in spite of their sins: That assurance had been given once and for all in the resurrection of the Lord. It diminished their importance because such miraculous interventions were no longer as desirable as they had been, now that the new creation had been revealed. That the resurrection left the servants of God somewhat jaded in their petitions for deliverance, for they recognized that prior to the parousia all that any isolated miracle could accomplish was the restoration of an order of things still radically in need of final and total transformation in Christ. And so limited a good paled beside the promise of a personal share in the parousia itself.

But though the resurrection may have left the first Christians somewhat jaded, it did not leave them in any way apathetic about the value and importance of the things of this world. For in the light of the Easter event, they also realized that however much they might long for the second coming, the one unavoidable condition for their sharing personally in the glory of the risen Lord was their individual and collective willingness to become deeply involved in the enterprise of building up a community of "little ones" who, by living after the pattern of gratuitous sharing, unrestricted love, and service set by Christ during his apostolic career, might be to all men an anticipation and a prophecy of the glory still to come.

Even more, the new creation did not simply replace the old creation; it *transformed* the old creation. By choosing to transform this material world rather than annihilate it, God had manifested once and for all the inherent goodness and value of the present world in spite of its need to be purged of the effects of man's sinfulness and disorder.

Eucharistic Prayer

In other words, the resurrection completed the gradual transformation of the new Israel founded by Jesus from a praying to a eucharistic community. Jesus had, during his own public ministry, initiated the process of transformation by focusing his disciple's prayer of petition primarily upon the advent of the kingdom of God. Even their prayer for nothing more nor less than their "daily bread" implied a more basic petition for that inner poverty of spirit which was integral to membership in the kingdom as Jesus envisioned it. The resurrection completed the transformation by revealing the full eschatological, cosmic, and creative dimensions of the kingdom for which the disciples had yearned. In the post-resurrection community, therefore, petitions for the coming of the kingdom necessarily took the form of prayers for the coming of the parousia, for the participation of all things in the glory of the risen Christ, a glory already in process of preparation through the gift of the Spirit.

By the same token, resurrection-centered prayer was also of necessity a prayer of blessing, the thankful recall in faith and confidence of God's final saving intervention in human affairs through the mission and definitive revelation of his Son to men. The resurrection had, moreover, provided an essentially new context for understanding the purpose and meaning of the ancient Hebrew prayers of blessing. First of all, it had made apparent to the first Christians that all the past interventions of God on behalf of his people which such prayers traditionally commemorated were only promises and dim foreshadowings of the salvation revealed in the risen Christ. Moreover, when the Christian community was led by one who had priestly authority from the risen Christ himself to pronounce in the Lord's own name the blessing commemorating the central act of human salvation, the death and glorification of Jesus, then the very prayer of blessing, in and through the sanction and eschatological meaning given it through the person and event of Christ, took on a new, i.e., a genuinely sacramental, character. It became a communion with the body and blood of the risen Christ which mediated to men through the eucharistic signs and actions the Father's efficacious promise to those who serve him as his children, by remaining actively and lovingly united to one another in his Spirit, of the same inheritance of glory he had granted to his Son and true servant.

Moreover, the eucharistic prayer possesses such salvific efficacy precisely because it is a prayer of sacrificial atonement which renews in the name of Christ risen God's new and everlasting covenant of reconciliation with men. It differs from the Hebrew covenant renewals to the extent that the new covenant in Christ differs from the Sinai covenant in its regenerative efficacy, its irrevocability, and its universal and cosmic scope. That is to say, the eucharistic blessing is an act in which the Father's regenerative commitment to a sinful world, embodied in the glorification and enthronement of Jesus for the faithful accomplishment of the mission of universal and atoning love originally given him by the Father, is effectively renewed in and through the sacramental mediation of that same faithful and fatherly commitment to each of his adopted children, in an act which, as the sacramental reenactment of the death and resurrection of Jesus, demands of each man his personal and active rededication in faith and confidence to the enterprise of actively building up a community of atoning love, committed to the ideals of gratuitous sharing, unrestricted love, and mutual service in the image of Christ.[107]

Finally, because the new sacramental covenant is a covenant of atonement (at-one-ment, reconciliation) which demands the acceptance of the gratuitous forgiveness of God revealed in Christ not only as a revelation of grace but as the model of one's own willingness to take upon oneself the evil consequences of the selfishness and pride of mankind, its renewal demands of those who share in it not only the willingness to acknowledge their faults to God and to one another in simplicity and sorrow but also the determination to suffer the injustices perpetrated by their fellow men with the same kind of loving forgiveness as Christ himself had shown when he dwelt among us. And, indeed, had not the master demanded of those who turn to the Father in prayer not only confidence and perseverance but an enduring attitude of mutual forgiveness as well?

In other words, eucharistic worship is simultaneously the unification and the fulfillment of the four types of Old Testament prayer which we considered at the start of this chapter. To begin with, it is the Christian community's confident and persevering *petition* to the Father for the universal establishment of his kingdom on earth, that is to say, for the fulfillment of all things in Christ through the preparatory involvement of all men in the enterprise of service which is the sign and promise of the second coming.

The Eucharist is, in addition, the community's active renewal of the new covenant of divine reconciliation in Christ. It is, therefore, also a prayer of *penitential atonement,* the acceptance of the Father's gratuitous forgiveness, incarnate in the crucified and risen Lord and, through his Spirit, reembodied in the community's mutual forgiveness of one another in his name.

To the extent, therefore, that the eucharistic act demands of all who share in it the willingness to take freely and forgivingly upon themselves the consequences of the malice of others, the Eucharist is also a prayer of *Jobian adoration* in the face of the Father's inscrutable salvific purposes, a prayer of *simple and unquestioning endurance* in the face of every trial and injustice.

But most of all, the eucharistic prayer is a prayer of *blessing* of the God who, in the passion and glorification of his Son and in the mission of his regenerating Spirit, has revealed his willingness to take the consequences of our sinfulness upon himself and his longing to share with us the fullness of his life.[108]

The first letter to the Corinthians offers us some useful insights into the attitudes of the apostolic community toward the celebration of the Eucharist. First of all, it is quite clear that the first Christians approached the eucharistic banquet both as a sacrificial communion with the body and blood of their glorified Lord and as a judgment. As a sacrificial act which united them with God's only Son, the eucharistic banquet was also an effective source of union within the community itself.[109]

But though the Eucharist has as one of its purposes to unite true believers with one another by joining them sacramentally to Christ, it also separates them in their worship from men who continue to worship gods of their own making. To the extent, therefore, that the Eucharist continues the process of sorting out the children of light and the children of darkness, it continues the process of judgment begun in the passion and glorification of Jesus.[111]

But the eucharistic act is also a judgment upon the Christian community itself. For to celebrate the Eucharist is to "proclaim the Lord's death until he comes" with full consciousness of the consequences which belief in Christ entails for one's own conduct.[112] Otherwise, Christians shall, to their dismay, find themselves "eating and drinking their own condemnation."[113]

The passage is an interesting one, because it reflects Paul's conviction that participation in the eucharistic meal presupposes on the part of those who share in it an attitude of positive involvement in the enterprise of Christian service. Whoever partakes of the eucharistic banquet by that very act commits himself to the task of building up the Christian community through actions which express an atoning love and an active concern for others in the name of Christ. Anyone who misguidedly seeks to share in the supper of the Lord on any other basis is "eating and drinking his own condemnation."

Prayer in the Apostolic Church

Though the Eucharist is the archetype and focal point of Christian worship, its celebration did not exhaust the prayer life of the early Christian community. To judge from Luke's account in Acts, the apostles seem to have taken very seriously the Lord's command to pray always.[114] Paul for one exhorts the Ephesians to make it their custom to "pray on every possible occasion."[115]

Significantly enough, one has the empression that, as in the case of Jesus himself, the prayer of the first Christians both spontaneously expressed and actively reenforced their sense of apostolic mission to the world. We discover the apostles turning to prayer at all the critical junctures in their work for the kingdom: before the election of Matthias;[116] before the ordination of the first deacons;[117] in moments of persecution, for "boldness" in proclaiming the good news;[118] before confirmation of the baptized;[119] before the departure of missionaries to preach the word;[120] before the appointment of elders;[121] in moments of temptation.[122]

The apostles seem to have learned well the master's instructions to direct their petitions primarily toward the successful establishment of the kingdom. Their instructions are that Christians are to pray constantly for one another to remain steadfast in the face of every trial,[123] that they should pray as well for the success of those laboring to spread the good news,[124] for the Christian community's growth in understanding and in love,[125] and for God's forgiveness of their sins.[126]

Moreover, the Christian's absolute confidence of his petitions being heard must be rooted not only in his belief in God's promises[127] and in his fidelity to the Lord's commandments of faith and of love,[128] but especially in the Easter revelation of Jesus' divine power to save any man who turns to him in his need as well as in the intercessory efficacy of Jesus' role as unique mediator between God and man.[129] Seen in the light of Easter, the sufferings of Jesus themselves are transformed into an added assurance that we will receive from him a compassionate hearing. "For it is not as if we had a high priest incapable of feeling our weakness with us; but we have one who has been tempted in every way that we are, though without sin."[130,131]

But above all, the Christian community must constantly bless God and thank him for his graciousness in the gifts he has given to men. "Be happy at all times," Paul writes the Thessalonians, "pray constantly; and for all things give thanks to God because this is what God expects you to do in Christ Jesus." Christians should thank God for one another, for the mutual love and concern that unites them in Christ, for the gift of faith, for the assurance of God's love for them, for divine adoption and for the inheritance promised the children of God, for the gift of the Holy Spirit who is at work in every Christian actively building up the Church of Christ through the variety of the gifts he dispenses to its members.[132-136]

The close connection between apostolic work and a life of prayer is also manifested by the fact that no hard and fast distinction is made between them in the early Church. For the first Christians apostolic labor for the kingdom was itself regarded as an act of worship of God, while the prayers of the widows for the welfare of the community were also looked upon as an important act of service to the group.[137] Moreover, experience soon convinced the apostles that the real effectiveness of their apostolic labors demanded of them a certain amount of leisure for personal reflection and prayer. They discovered that no one could effectively serve a community of faith and of worship in a priestly capacity without first assimilating personally the message and the meaning of Christ.[138]

Finally, as far as the practical business of leading the Christian assembly in prayer was concerned self-conscious preoccupation with the nicely turned phrase was soon found to be more of a hindrance than a help to genuine prayer. Paul exhorts the Roman community, for instance, not to be too concerned when people express themselves poorly at common worship, since the Spirit of God within us presents our plea to the Father far more effectively than we have words to express it.[139]

The Patristic Tradition

The Fathers are careful to preserve a number of basic biblical teachings concerning prayer. They insist, for example, as Jesus had, that the God who searches hearts cannot be deceived by hypocritical prayers.[140] and that sincere prayer prefers to be secret.[141] They also insist on God's fidelity in hearing our prayers[142] and offer a variety of explanations why some of the things we ask for are not in fact granted. In many of these explanations one senses that the Father's pastoral concern to justify the ways of God to men and to discourage superstition in prayer sometimes led them in speaking of petitionary prayer to focus their attention almost exclusively on prayers for the good things of this world and that in the process the eschatological dimensions of prayer of petition discussed above received increasingly short shrift.[143-147]

The Fathers praise perseverance in prayer; but many are also perplexed about the precise meaning one should attribute to Jesus's injunction that one should pray always. Tertullian interprets the logion of Jesus as meaning that there are no privileged times or places for praying: All are equally good.[148] Origen suggests that to pray always means to live always in such a way that one's life is pleasing to God; but he suggests that one also set aside at least three periods every day for formal prayer.[149] Athanasius with less imagination associates perseverance in prayer with fidelity to the ritual praying of the psalter and with prayer at meals.[150] Basil, however, is dissatisfied with such a ritualistic solution and suggests (perhaps a bit idealistically) that praying always means constantly thinking about God, confessing him, and thanking him in all one does. He recommends specifically prayer before and while eating, prayer while dressing, prayer when retiring, prayer throughout the day, and prayer from time to time at night.[151,152] It is, of course, imaginative reflections such as these which prepared the way for the systematic practice of recollection and the presence of God and to the canonization of the hours of the office.

The Lure of Contemplation

What is also new in patristic teaching on prayer is the conscious and explicit quest for contemplation as something distinguishable from practical Christianity and in some respects superior to it. Gregory Nazianzen, who states the distinction with great balance, attributes its origin to Greek philosophy.[153]

But though Gregory insists on the interdependence of action and contemplation, the ultimate effect of distinguishing them is their mutual dissociation as horizontal and vertical aspects of the spiritual life.[154]

This tendency to conceive of contemplation as embodying the vertical dimension of Christianity is reenforced by a parallel tendency to regard contemplation as the true source of inner purification and hence, in a special sense, the true prelude to glory.[155]

From the fourth century on, the virtuous purgation of the mind through prayer becomes an increasingly fruitful subject for reflection in patristic writing. Palladius, for example, writing at the turn of the fourth century, describes Paul the monk's "whole asceticism" as consisting in "praying perpetually."[156] Similarly, Cassian teaches that prayer is the perfection of the virtues and the keystone which holds them in place.[157] Moreover, he describes "consummation in prayer" as "the goal of the monk and the summit of all perfection."[158]

In the Apocalypse, St. John had spontaneously pictured the parousia under the unifying image of liturgical prayer. Reflection on the purgative powers of contemplation, however, leads Cassian's Germanus to a different conclusion. Though he concedes that Sunday worship would seem at first glance "to contain all the plentitude of perfection, inasmuch as it is started and established by the authority of the Lord," still, it leads to a higher, non-sacramental form of prayer "which transcends all human sense" and in which the mind is "illumined by the infusion of heavenly light."[159]

Inner purification through contemplation thus comes to be associated with flight from sensible, terrestrial, and material things.[160] In Cassian's *Conferences,* Abbat Nilus defines prayer as the "ascent of the intelligence (*nous*) to God."[161] And he agrees with Abbat Isaac that in perfect prayer the mind experiences no images, no sound, no words.[162] And, as one might expect, preoccupation with the purification of contemplation from all earthly admixture leads logically to the distinction of levels of perfection within the contemplative ascent to God.[163,164]

By the seventh century, Maximus the Confessor is able to distinguish two different kinds of "pure prayer": one for those who lead an active life and one for those who cultivate contemplation. For the contemplative, he suggests, the signs of "pure prayer" are: being rapt into divine illumination, ceasing to perceive sensible things, receiving from God "clear and conspicuous representations" of him. For the active man the signs are: recollection of mind, freedom from worldly thoughts; ability to pray in God's presence without distractions and inner disturbances.[165] Of the two types of prayer, however, contemplative prayer is presented as the more perfect.[166] For since God transcends all thoughts and sensations, perfect prayer seems to Maximus to demand a separation from them both.[167]

The quest for theoretical contemplation as the most perfect

form of prayer entails as its logical consequence a radical de-emphasis of what might be called the "pragmatic" or horizontal dimensions of praying.[168,169] Prayer of petition tends thus to be detached from practical interests and focused instead on the graces of theoretical contemplation.[170]

The Magisterium: The Condemnation of Quietism

The earliest decrees of the magisterium which touch upon prayer are actually more concerned with the effects of prayer than with prayer itself. Thus, Gregory X in the thirteenth century and the Council of Florence in the fifteenth both insist that prayers can benefit the souls of the departed.[171] Both Florence and Trent insist on the power of penitential prayer to satisfy for the punishment due to sin.[172]

It is not until the end of the seventeenth century, however, that the neo-Platonic tendencies latent in some patristic texts dealing with prayer reach such a degree of exaggeration as to merit official reprobation. The condemnation of Quietism issued by the Holy Office in 1682 repudiates any explanation of private prayer which belittles as "useless" and "empty" the vocal prayers instituted by Christ and preserved in the Church.[173] Without forbidding the pursuit of contemplation, the decree nevertheless warns spiritual directors that not everyone is suited to this type of prayer and cautions against the errors latent in the quietist explanation of the nature of the contemplative ascent to God.[174-176]

The decree also warns that no form of prayer raises any individual to such a state of perfection that he or she is placed beyond ordinary Church discipline, the fulfillment of ecclesiastical obligations or the need for the sort of "external" worship which is embodied in the sacraments, sacramentals, or other forms of "external" piety.[177] And it condemns any attempt to absolve contemplatives of moral responsibility of sins committed in a state of contemplation."[178-180]

More important, perhaps, is the decree's repudiation of the

notion that mystical theology envisages actual progress in prayer as the one-way ascent of an ascetical ladder whose predetermined steps measure the degree of perfection of one's prayer life.[181,182] Finally, the condemnation of Molinos lays bare one of the central nerves of quietist piety when it rejects the notion that "taken as a whole, the sensible things that we experience in the spiritual life are abominable, spurious, and unclean."[183]

Papal Teaching and Vatican II

Other decrees of interest include the reaffirmation by both Pius XI and Pius XII of the efficacy of private prayer[184] and Pius XII's insistence both that external cult, while demanding the internal worship of total dedication to Christ, corresponds to the complete nature of man who is made up of both soul and body, and that sacramental worship is not merely "objective" worship devoid of any "personal" or "subjective" character.[185]

As one might expect, the documents of Vatican II pay the greatest attention to liturgical prayer. The bishops insist that liturgical worship must "express the lives of the faithful" while simultaneously manifesting to others both the mystery of Christ and "the real nature of the church" in which the human is subordinated to the divine, the visible to the invisible, action to contemplation, the present world to the world to come.[186] But the presentation of this hierarchy of values is in no way intended to deprive the liturgy of genuine impact upon the living Christian community. Eucharistic worship is a celebration of the victory of Christ which not only has as its purpose the proclamation of his death and resurrection until he comes again but also the strengthening of Christ's faithful "in their capacity to preach Christ."[187] The liturgy is not only a sacred action "surpassing all others" but even "the summit toward which the activity of the Church is directed," namely, that the people of God should "come together to praise God in the midst of his Church, to take part in her sacrifice, and to eat the Lord's supper."[188]

The bishops reiterate the teaching of Pius XII concerning the diverse functions of priest and people within the Eucharist act: but they insist that even though Christ is present in a special way in the celebrant and minister of this sacrament as well as most especially present "under the Eucharistic species," he is also present in the words of Sacred Scripture and in the worshipping community itself.[189] Moreover, they remind celebrants that their manner of celebrating the Eucharist must go beyond "the mere observance of the laws governing valid and licit celebrations." It is their *duty* as well to celebrate the liturgy in such a way as to ensure the knowing, active, and fruitful participation of the worshipping community.[190-192]

But while the bishops clearly regard the Eucharist as the apex of Christian prayer, they are careful to warn against any attempt to reduce the whole of the spiritual life to liturgical worship alone. They commend the practice of frequent private prayer and of public devotions which are suited to the liturgical season.[193] The bishops commend retreats, devotional acts of eucharistic piety, and mental prayer.[194] They regard regular family prayer as one of the marks of a truly Christian family and as integral to the religious education of children.[195] They also insist that seminarians form solid habits of regular prayer.[196] And in religious communities especially, the bishops feel there should be the conscious cultivation of a spirit of prayer.[197] Finally the bishops recommend that since the purpose of the divine office is the sanctification of the entire day, its manner of recitation should be such as to achieve that purpose, with, however, realistic consideration being given to the exigencies of modern life, especially in the case of those called upon to labor in apostolic works.[198]

The Manual Tradition

Manual asceticism ordinarily defines prayer under the metaphor either of "spiritual ascent" or of "familiar conversation." We are told that prayer is the elevation of the soul to God or that it is familiar conversation with God. The advantage of the former definition is that it insists on the element of transcendence in prayer; its disadvantages are double. First, it omits any reference to prayer's immanent aspect, to prayer's reference and relevance to the existing material universe. Second, it smacks of a certain neo-Platonic cast of thought which is dubiously compatible with a thoroughly Christian world-view.

One advantage of referring to prayer as "familiar conversation with God" is, of course, that such a definition emphasizes the personal dimensions of prayer. Its evident disadvantage is that it suggests that prayer is just like a conversation with another human being; and that, of course, prayer ordinarily is not.

Manual asceticism also teaches us that prayer is a means of sanctification. By detaching us from the creatures of this world, it unites our spiritual faculties (our intellect and will) to God, fastens our lower cognitive faculties (our memory, imagination, and emotions) on images related to God, and thus increases our faith, hope, and love of the divine. But prayer, we are told, is not the only means of sanctification available to men. At those active moments when contemplation is impossible, love should direct our deeds to God. Prayer remains, however, the normal, efficacious, and universal means God uses to impart his actual graces to men; for it makes one practice all the virtues; and it initiates one's transformation into God.

Manual asceticism also warns us concerning certain things that prayer is not. Prayer, we are warned, is not abstract theological speculation; it should, on the contrary, be practical in its orientation. Prayer is not self-centered; it is, on the contrary, openness to the supernatural grace of God.

Among the chief obstacles to prayer are ordinarily listed: inexperience, lack of generosity and of perseverance; distractions which may or may not be culpable, and the lack of a method of praying. Methods of prayer vary; but in the Occidental tradition they ordinarily consist in a list of determined mental actions to be performed as a way of disposing the soul to prayer.

Some of the chief degrees of prayer mentioned in the manuals are discursive prayer, which relies predominantly on the pious reflections of the understanding enlightened by grace; affective prayer, in which devout affections of the heart predominate over intellectual understanding; and the prayer of simplicity, in which the soul fixes its gaze on God, remains in his presence, yields itself to the action of grace, and with a simple and unreasoned faith gazes on God and loves him. The prayer of simplicity need not be confined to moments of formal prayer, but becomes a pervasively prayerful attitude of soul.

Manual asceticism also distinguishes between acquired and infused contemplation. The former consists in the active acquisition of the virtues and habitual attitudes which constitute a life of prayer. The latter is a grace received passively into souls chosen by God. The precondition for infused contemplation is the soul's passage through purifying periods of aridity in which by its painful and persistent longing for more intimate union with God in the midst of temptations and persecution, it increases in self-knowledge, in abandonment to the divine will, and in selfless faith, hope, and love.

Problems and Perplexities

This account of prayer, enshrined in the ascetical manuals, has much to commend it, but it labors under certain obvious limitations. First of all, it tends to be more "psychological," i.e., confined to the limited vocabulary of faculty psychology, rather than theological. Second, it seems at times to equate perfection and holiness with spiritual ascent from this world rather than with realistic involvement in it.

That is to say, according to manual theology, the perfection of one's prayer is measured primarily by the extent to which it engages the higher faculties of the soul and by the degree to which it renders one indifferent to material needs and goods, and detached from "worldly pursuits." Its goal is union with a God who tends to be conceived primarily under the aspect of his transcendence rather than of his immanent incarnational involvement with the sons of men. As a result, there is little mention in such a description of prayer of some of the most basic Christian concepts. There is, to be sure, concern with the supernatural order and with actual graces; but one may read an account of prayer written in traditional ascetical terms without encountering any significant theological references to Christ, to the incarnation, to the Trinity, to the Church, to the sacraments, to eucharistic and liturgical worship.

Contemporary theologians have made some attempt to compensate for these speculative deficiencies. The liturgical movement has produced an abundance of theological reflections on the ecclesial, sacramental, and eucharistic dimensions of Christian prayer; and contemporary treatments of prayer have re-emphasized some previously neglected biblical and dogmatic approaches to the problem. Von Balthasar, for instance, lays great stress on the Christocentric and trinitarian dimensions of a Christian's prayer life and has sought to articulate the speculative reconciliation of liturgical worship and of private contemplation.[199]

Moreover, at a grass-roots level, there has been discernible among American religious a growing dissatisfaction with some of the more traditional forms of prayer. This dissatisfaction has, for example, found an eloquent and admirably balanced expression in Fr. McNaspy's recent book on the religious life. Voicing the aspirations of an incalculable number of American religious, he insists that prayer should be "personally meaningful" to religious and calls for greater flexibility and spontaneity in the form and practice of personal and community prayer.[200]

Moreover, apostolically active American religious especially have been showing signs of being troubled by the rapid pace and secularity which marks so much of American life. In fact, in the case of many religious prolonged exposure to both of these aspects of American society has begun to pose a number of basic theological problems. For instance, is there any measurable practical difference between the basic attitudes of Christianity and of secular humanism? and if so, what is it? Is a religionless Christianity actively concerned for the needs of men preferable to the formalistic worship of so many nominal Christians? Is it possible to remain actively concerned for others and to preserve a contemplative dimension to one's life? How balance the affirmation that "God is other people" with its equally valid counter affirmation that "God is other, people"? How balance the pursuit of interior piety with social involvement?[201]

Such tensions and problems are not, of course, completely new; and one need not search Church history very long to discover some of their more obvious speculative sources. As we have seen, quite early in the Christian ascetical tradition, the tendency of some of the Fathers to identify prayer with the pursuit of inner solitary spiritual illumination helped to produce a polarity in Christian thought between contemplation and action, between communal, liturgical prayer and private devotion.

Of the three classical patristic solutions to the tension between contemplation and action, the appeal to authority is the most in need of historical understanding and speculative qualification. For it is theologically untenable that only those prayers sanctioned by the approval of one's superiors are pleasing to God. Nor could one argue that a religious who had, for instance, been unjustly forbidden to pray would do a heinous thing in the eyes of God were he to turn to the Father in his need. The real point of Augustine's argument that prayers done under obedience are pleasing to God is that those prayers are of suspect quality which are offered to God at the expense of one's fellow religious, who are forced to shoulder the work load of an excessively prayerful member of the community, whose personal quest for contemplation renders him unavailable for contributing to the material support of his brethren. The appeal to an arbitrator who has the responsibility and right to resolve equitably such problems in the community by establishing in concrete instances the priority of needs is really something other than seeking to justify praying merely in virtue of the official sanction which accompanies the act. For the real point at issue is the impossibility of ascending spiritually to God by studied indifference to the basic material needs of others, who in fact depend on the fruit of one's labor.

At the same time, the two other classic arguments derived from the Fathers in order to resolve the tension between contemplation and action reflect, when taken together, a truly biblical approach to the problem and constitute an interesting challenge to some of our most cherished religious prejudices. The Fathers tell us on the one hand, that prayer is itself ecclesially significant and apostolically efficacious and, on the other, that active labor undertaken from the proper religious motives is itself prayer. Those who are steeped in the ideals of manual asceticism are apt to sniff at the activistic overtones of the second of these two reflections, while the sophisticated Catholic steeped in the American pragmatic tradition is apt to balk at the passivity of the first.

In this country, belief in the efficacy of prayer, in its importance as an apostolic factor in the work of the Church, is undermined by a number of erosive forces. To begin with, educated American Catholics tend to associate such a belief with exaggerated practices like the superstitious multiplication of novenas. Moreover, the abstract philosophical conception of God sometimes popularized in the American Catholic school system, which pictured him as an abstract Absolute, incapable of active involvement in the material universe, seems to many to render prayer superfluous: why pray, if the divine response to all prayers has already been predetermined immutably from all eternity? Finally, the American cult of self-reliance and practicality inclines us to be suspicious of both contemplative prayer and of prayer of petition as a cover-up for personal sloth and inactivity.

As a result of such preconditioning, Americans are apt to find the first temptation of Christ, the temptation to self-reliance in the accomplishment of their Christian vocation, alluring in the extreme. In the case of religious, the temptation could in fact take many forms; but the two most likely ones are the abandonment of prayer and the substitution of problem solving for actual praying.

The Abandonment of Prayer

A basic selfishness, inexperience, and the lack of a method in praying are, manual asceticism tells us, among the chief obstacles to prayer. In many cases, this may well be so; but there can be little doubt that often enough it is the method of prayer itself which constitutes a source of genuine discouragement in a given individual's attempt to lead a life of prayer. A recent survey of the prayer habits of a group of American religious revealed that relatively few of those surveyed were able to pray according to the methods taught them in the novitiate and that the rest had abandoned the attempt altogether. Moreover, even though those in the latter group had managed to substitute their own personal way of approaching God for the "canned" methods of the manuals, many remained inwardly troubled by feelings of guilt at their inability to pray according to the patterns prescribed in their earlier training.

It is perhaps worth observing in passing that many priests experience similar problems in their recitation of the breviary. The purpose of breviary recitation is, as Vatican II assures us, to sustain and nourish a prayerful attitude of heart throughout the day. Priests who find little devotion in what has become rote repetition of the same book of the bible week after week would do well to seek some other form of prayer capable of accomplishing the ends that brievary recitation is supposed to accomplish but in many cases does not.

But such specific problems as brievary recitation aside, religious who find difficulty in using some of the standard Occidental methods of prayer recommended in the manuals may find that experimentation with Oriental approaches to contemplation can be an efficacious aid to prayer. The intelligent practice of yoga, for instance, can help many to inner peace and recollection. Others may find spiritual help through a balanced pursuit of Zen enlightenment. Provided, therefore, an individual is capable of preserving both his theological and his realistic equilibrium in the use of such techniques, there is no reason why such approaches to prayer should not be made available to American religious without fear of stigma or of oddity being attached to their cultivation.

Not everyone will, however, find the methods of the East congenial to his personality or temperament. And the approach to prayer best suited to the American democratic enthusiast may well prove to be some form of unstructured group prayer. Many American religious have found, for instance, the "collation" in various forms a useful initiation into a life of prayer. And the Catholic charismatic movement has already begun to inject new vitality into the spirituality of the American church.

Charismatic Prayer

For many American Catholics, the very existence of a charismatic movement within Roman Catholicism comes as a shock or even as a threat. Having grown quite accustomed to having our religion neatly structured and institutionally organized, and conscious of the abuses latent in the uncritical cult of enthusiasm, we fear the religious enthusiast as a potentially disruptive force within the worshipping community; we also suspect the "Protestant" flavor of charismatic piety. Critical reticence in approaching the more unusual phenomena popularly associated with the charismatic movement is healthy, as long as such criticism does not become itself myopically and exaggeratedly emotional and "enthusiastic." In point of fact, the charismatic movement can and has assumed a variety of forms. Like any religious movement it can indeed run to extremes; but even sacramental worship, as history teaches, is subject to serious abuse. And there can be little doubt that some of the existing forms of pentecostalism are perfectly acceptable even from the most orthodox theological viewpoints.

Most of the Catholic Pentecostals I have personally known have been people of genuine personal and theological balance. They are insistent on the need for theologically solid principles for discerning carefully the inner movements of the Spirit. Since, too, they believe that the Spirit is given to the whole community, not merely to individuals, they also insist that the discerning process should take place at an ecclesial as well as at an individual level. They also believe that normatively integral to the discerning process is solid dogmatic belief as well as vital contact with the teaching church and with liturgical and sacramental worship. What is striking about their piety, however, in contrast to that of many of their Catholic brethren, is that they actually experience spirits to discern.

A discerning, self-critical charismatic movement has, then, much to offer to the belief and piety of American Catholics. Not the least among these benefits are a lively confidence in the active presence of the Holy Spirit within the world and in the gifts he gives to men, a vital affirmation of the efficacy of prayer, living confidence in God and in the power of Christ, a love of prayer, and a conviction that it is ultimately God who must accomplish the salvation of men. All of these beliefs are, of course, already notionally present in Catholic dogma and piety. But there can be little doubt that a balanced approach to the charismatic movement can endow them with fresh vitality and significance. If too one acknowledges a strong tendency toward an unreflecting activism among American religious and that the Spirit gives his gifts according to the needs of men, one might even see in the charismatic movement a providential counterbalance to destructive tendencies to activistic superficiality in American piety. We shall return later to a consideration of some of the problems implicit in a charismatic approach to prayer and piety. For the moment, however, we merely note that there are forms of pentecostalism which do in fact offer an alternative to the more traditional forms of prayer.

Situational Prayer

For whatever the approach to God best suited to this or that individual, there can be little doubt but that there are genuine limitations in a typically "manual" approach to God. One of the chief difficulties with "canned" methods of prayer and one of the reasons why Americans are apt to abandon them rather early in their spiritual lives is, we would suggest, their lack of situational relevance. Imbued as we are with a puritan admiration for integrity and sincerity in religious practice, we are repelled by exercises of piety which smack of the artificial or the arbitrary. Also being basically pragmatic in our patterns of thought, we are pleased to find our prayer arising spontaneously from a felt need rather than prescribed at an arbitrarily fixed hour and patterned by a predetermined formula. Yet formulas and patterns are what the manuals suggest; and however useful they may be to some, they certainly cannot appeal to every American religious. Understandably, then, for not a few, the random selection each night of a scene from the life of Christ or of some passage from a spiritual writer for prayerful reflection the next morning feels "phony" or at least "canned," without both vitality and spontaneity. As a result, American religious whose only definition of prayer is derived from the manuals and whose only method of praying is patterned on the solitary meditation recommended in the manuals are tragically apt to decide that since the methods recommended in the manuals are in practice impossible for them, that prayer itself is impossible.

Then, too, in this age of the biblical renaissance, there can be little doubt that the approach to prayer typically recommended by manual asceticism smacks more of a Platonic than of a biblical cast of thought. The basic motivation of much manual prayer is to lead the spiritual novice to personal contemplation of the eternal truth and reality of the deity. Since, however, such eternal truths transcend both space and time, the situation of the one praying is reduced to a relatively unimportant status in the process of prayer. Indeed, if the day-to-day situations which constitute one's life of prayer are mentioned at all in the manuals, they tend to be regarded as distractions from the all-important business of praying. One must learn in prayer, we are told, to forget the distracting details of daily living and fix one's gaze instead on the unchanging truth of God.

Thus, the Platonic cast of mind which typifies a manual approach to prayer can through its initial neglect of the concrete situation of the one praying generate a number of problems in his personal approach to God by effectively dissociating his prayer from his vital personal needs and activities. To be sure, the manuals constantly remind us that meditation must have practical effect on one's life. After an hour of exercising one's intellect in the contemplation of the eternal truths expressed in some selected spiritual test, the novice in the prayer life must, we are told, be careful to exercise his will as well and make a practical resolution based upon his intellectual reflections. The manuals are also careful to remind one that prayer is not theoretical speculation. The warnings are well taken. But there can be little doubt that the need for them derives in part from the abstract, impractical bias imparted to prayer which is patterned on a Platonic or neo-Platonic model. One can, for instance, scarcely imagine a Jeremiah in need of the admonition that his prayer should not be too abstract and speculative and that he should, like a good stoic, be careful to exercise his will with practical resolutions before his prayer is finished.

In contrast to such an approach to prayer, biblical prayer is, of course, radically situational. It is a cry of longing to the God who saves, who is active in this world, and who sustains it and the men who live in it by his power. It is not the theoretical contemplation of eternal truths. It is a leap of the heart which is need-oriented. That is to say, it springs from a consciousness of one's finitude and of one's radical inability to achieve salvation apart from the saving action of God himself. And, on the other hand, it is rooted in an unshakable confidence in the God who is irrevocably covenanted to men in love through the atoning blood of Christ. It is not, therefore, a Stoic exercise in virtue; it is a loving response to a grace.

Biblical prayer, especially New Testament prayer, is, moreover, in the first instance, ecclesial and sacramental prayer. One can, therefore, question whether the neo-Platonic model of the solitary ecstatic contemplative is indeed the best model for a Christian to adopt in his attempt to lead a life of prayer. Indeed, the exclusively personal quest for a solitary, vertical ascent to God characteristic of neo-platonized methods of praying has in fact been at the root of most of the historical abuses associated in Christianity with the pursuit of prayer. Thus, not only has it on occasion transformed the quest for God into a flight from the material universe; but the suspicion which such a flight casts upon all things sensual and material has also led to the disparagement of liturgical and sacramental worship, to the dissociation of prayer from physical labor, to iconoclasm, to contempt for petitions for material benefits from God as unworthy of a truly spiritual man; to various types of gnostic illuminationism culminating in all of the abuses possible in the uncritical cult of enthusiasm; to the neglect or even to the denial of the ecclesial aspects of prayer.

The Need for a Model

But if the fundamental ideal, the basic model, for Christian prayer is not the solitary, neo-Platonic contemplative, what is it? The question is almost self-answering. For the committed Christion, can the basic model of his prayer be anything but the prayer of Christ? Needless to say, however, Christ's prayer took a variety of forms. At times he prayed alone; but he recommended prayer in common as well. There can, however, be no doubt that the supreme prayer of Christ, and, therefore, the most complete model of Christian prayer, is the priestly prayer he offered during his passion and death, in his final act of eucharistic worship.

But even if one is willing to accept the eucharist as the highest and most perfect embodiment of Christian prayer, one is still faced with many perplexing problems in the concrete. For what concretely is the model of eucharistic worship? And here the reader is asked to pardon what is a frank digression. But in these days of liturgical change, it is rash to presuppose anything about the concrete experience of liturgical worship. For many, that experience continues to be a stiff, impersonal exercise of formalistic piety. Rather than equate the experience of eucharistic prayer with such an inadequate model, however, the reader is asked to project imaginatively experiential possibilities of worship latent in the eucharist beyond the present revised rubrical regulations.

One cannot help but be struck by the progress of liturgical renewal since Vatican II. But there is little room for complacency. To be sure, the publication of the new missal has significantly advanced the work of rubrical reform. In the latest revisions of the Roman rite there is even an incipient acknowledgement of our need, not for new rubrics but for greater structural flexibility in liturgical worship within certain broad and rather general guidelines. No one can claim realistically, however, that these latent revisions are the final word in liturgical renewal. The guidelines can still be broadened; the flexibility still increased. There is still a crying need in our liturgical worship for greater national and regional diversity. We still, for instance, need official permanent centers for liturgical experimentation.

At the present moment in this country, one of the greatest drags upon liturgical reform is, of course, the widespread lack of liturgical formation among both clergy and laity alike. Without passing judgment on persons, one may safely aver that many American priests were liturgically educated in a tradition which insisted upon meticulous, rigid, and unimaginative rubrical obedience, sometimes even under the threat of mortal sin. It was, therefore, a liturgical formation which never really bothered to explain to the celebrant the functional purpose of the rubrics he was expected to observe blindly and to the letter. The rigid liturgical attitudes which are the product of such a formation are, of course, a commonplace; but perhaps an illustration may help to exemplify the phenomenon in question. For example, with home liturgies becoming more and more a common occurrence in many dioceses, one may legitimately raise the question whether solemn vesting in liturgical regalia originally designed for leading worship in a cathedral or parish church is quite suited to the more intimate worshipping situation of a liturgy in the home. Might not a simple stole, the symbol of priestly office, be vestment enough for such an occasion? But for the victim of the old rubrical rigorism, even such a minor adaptation in the written law is unthinkable; and he is apt to raise the hue and cry should he ever personally encounter such "abuse."

Hopefully the contemporary seminarian is being spared some of the psychological and liturgical scars and disabilities of his forebears in the apostolate. Hopefully, he is being educated, first, to an understanding of the purpose of each section of the liturgy;

second, to the purpose of the existing written rubrics; and, third, to some possible ways to adapt the existing rubrical structure of the liturgy creatively to the needs of different worshipping situations.

A Liturgical Fantasy

What follows, therefore, is only one possible approach to restructuring the liturgy with a view to such flexible adaptability, nor is it an effort to subvert the responsibility of the hierarchy to supervise the progress of liturgical renewal. It is, however, only one way of simplifying the existing Roman rite, possibly not even the best way to do it; and it is presented here simply as an indication of the variety of possibilities which exist even within the limits of traditional liturgical prayer.

If we prescind for the time from the problem of the thematic unity of a specific liturgical service, there are two basic problems confronting the presiding celebrant: What will be the order of worship for the present liturgy? What adaptations in the ordinary order of worship will be necessary in order to adapt the service to the needs of the assembled worshippers? In the Eucharist there are three essential elements to the order of worship: (1) the liturgy of the word, whose purpose within the ceremony is to dispose the community to a fuller participation in the eucharistic sacrifice by a collective reflection on Christian truths; (2) the eucharistic prayer, which is the prayer recalling and reenacting the last supper; (3) the communion, which is a personal sacramental renewal by each communicant of his faith and love and his graced participation in the death and resurrection of Christ.

At the same time, it is ordinarily useful to begin the service in some explicit and formal manner. Also, the bread and wine for the eucharistic banquet have to be prepared; and this is ordinarily and conveniently done after the liturgy of the word. Finally, the service usually needs some kind of formal conclusion. Logically, then, the eucharistic liturgy contains six elements in its order of worship: (1) an opening rite; (2) a liturgy of reflection on Christian truths; (3) a preparation of gifts; (4) the eucharistic prayer; (5) the communion service; (6) a rite of dismissal.

This order of worship is, however, only general and schematic; and the presiding celebrant must also decide which elements he specifically desires to include in each portion of the service. For example, if one applies two of the basic principles set down in the decree on the liturgy, viz., that of eliminating from the eucharistic service the unnecessary repetition of prayers whose purpose is identical and of relocating for some legitimate purpose other portions of the ritual, then the opening rite can actually be simplified down to an opening hymn and an opening prayer. First of all, the confession of sins can be easily displaced to some other part of the ritual, for example, to the end of the liturgy of the word, just prior to the preparation of gifts, where it can be introduced with some reference to the command of Christ to be reconciled with one another in repentance before bringing one's gift to the altar. It may also be relocated at the beginning of the communion service. The kissing of the altar is hardly essential to the opening rite and can when convenient or suitable also be omitted. If the prayers of the faithful conclude the liturgy of the word, the *Lord, Have Mercy* ought logically to be omitted, since the prayer was originally a response to such a litany of petition. Finally, if there is an opening hymn, both the Gloria and the entrance verse should also logically be omitted, since these were also originally intended to function in the service as entrance hymns.

Until a celebrant acquires facility in the spontaneous composition of prayers, it will be useful in the opening prayer, the prayer over the gifts, and the postcommunion prayer for him to keep a simple structural pattern in mind which he can fill with a content thematically appropriate to the occasion or to the assembled worshipping community. To be more specific, the three prayers mentioned above can always be patterned according to the following structure: (1) the statement of some fact of religious significance (e.g., that Christ has been born, has died, has risen, etc.; that God has granted the community some special blessing; that the community stands in need of some special grace); (2) a petition logically connected with the stated fact (e.g., to share in the graces of the birth, death, or resurrection of Christ; to be worthy of the graces God has given; that God will see the needs of the community and hear their pleas); (3) a concluding formula which the congregation can recognize as such and respond to (e.g., the traditional formula: "We ask this through Jesus Christ, your Son, our Lord, who lives . . . etc.").

When no music is available, the hymn may be replaced by a confession of sins (especially if the feast or season is penitential) or by the common recitation of a prayer of praise, like an appropriate psalm, the *Glory to God,* a translation of other traditional prayers of praise, like the *Te Deum,* or tasteful original prayers.

Depending on the informality of the occasion and on the needs of the worshipping community, the opening rite could even be reduced to an opening prayer, or even to a brief announcement and explanation by the celebrant of the theme of the liturgy to be celebrated.

The liturgy of the word can also be of more or less complexity according to the needs of the occasion and the worshipping community. Although the liturgy of the word is itself a prayer and should be prayerfully conducted, its main purpose is to prepare the congregation to join in the act of eucharistic worship which follows.

Except, of course, on days of greater liturgical significance, when thematically appropriate readings are in order, a community which comes together regularly for worship may find the consecutive reading of one or more books of scripture useful. For more randomly gathered congregations thematically related readings will probably be more useful.

Reflection on the readings may assume a variety of forms; and the presiding celebrant will have to decide which is more suitable to each particular congregation. Some of the possible options would include:

(1) instruction: The celebrant may undertake to explain to the

congregation the meaning of each of the readings, either before or after they are read.

(2) dialogue homily: When there are several concelebrants, they may each wish to offer some prayerful reflections on the readings; or when the occasion and makeup of the congregation allows, a general invitation may be extended to anyone who is moved by the Spirit to respond prayerfully and reflectively to the word of God. If several take part in a dialogue homily, the principal celebrant will have the responsibility of presiding over the dialogue. When suitable or necessary, he should offer clarification and commentary in reaction to the reflections of the participants and should see to it that the dialogue takes the form of a loving sharing of insights and aspirations rather than a debate between entrenched antagonists.

(3) silent prayer: The congregation may spend a moment of silence after the reading, each worshipper reflecting and praying in his own heart in response to God's word. This period of silent prayer may, when convenient, be terminated either by appropriate music or by a prayer of the celebrant which reflects the content of the reading.

(4) a meditation song: i.e., a song whose text is relevant to the reading may be sung.

(5) a litany: i.e., a series of petitions with responses which develop the important ideas of the reading can serve as a useful response to the divine word.

(6) further variety can be achieved by combining one or more of the above options. It will, of course, be the office of the presiding celebrant to inform the congregation as to the precise response expected of them after the readings.

The response to the final reading will ordinarily conclude with the prayers of the faithful, whose purpose is to express the community's renewed consciousness of its need for God and for his grace, a consciousness which should be one of the fruits of meditation upon his word. When the congregation is invited to take an active part in the prayers of the faithful by recommending petitions to the rest of the community, it is appropriate for the celebrant to begin the group prayer with one or possibly more petitions related to the readings for the day. Also, if the confession of sin is displaced to this point in the ceremony, one simple way of leading the congregation in a common acknowledgement of guilt would be for the celebrant to terminate the series of petitions with one or more petitions for the forgiveness of sin and for the grace of repentance and then to close the prayer of the faithful with the absolution normally given after the *I confess.* If the confession of sins does not occur at this point, it is appropriate for the celebrant to collect the petitions of the congregation in a summary and concluding prayer, which may be easily composed according to the pattern indicated above for the collect, offertory and postcommunion prayers.

There is general agreement among liturgists that the present rite for the preparation of the gifts needs simplification. The ritual washing of the hands has ceased to be functional and may be omitted. Since most of the long offertory prayers now included in the Roman rite for the priest's silent recitation are of dubious liturgical appropriateness, they would be better replaced by a short prayer expressing the meaning of the action being performed, viz., that this bread and wine being prepared for use in the eucharistic act of worship soon to follow is a sign of the faith and service of the congregation, or a petition to God to prepare the hearts of those assembled for the Eucharist as they prepare the bread and wine for their worship, etc.

The addition of three new anaphoras to the Roman rite is certainly a most welcome one. But the celebrant should, in fact, have several anaphoras from which to choose, each of them developing a variety of themes suited to a variety of catechetical needs. There is no reason why each season of the liturgical year should not have several such seasonally thematic anaphoras. Moreover, in addition to anaphoras written by committees there is need to engage the individual talents of gifted writers in the composition of eucharistic prayers that are less pedestrian than the available official canons. The publication of original eucharistic prayers will hopefully stimulate those officially in charge of supervising the liturgy to incorporate as many as possible of them into the official collection of church canons.

Moreover, since the eucharistic prayer is a common profession of faith, there is no reason in principle why the congregation should not be asked to join in the recitation of those segments of the anaphora which are either an expression of common belief or petitionary prayers, although the eucharistic recall of the supper of the Lord should be reserved to the celebrants as a way of expressing their special function within the eucharistic action. By allowing the congregation to assume such an active role in those portions of the anaphora which express a common profession of belief, one would also render a recitation of the creed superfluous.

There are a number of ways in which one might restructure the communion service. If the celebrant decides to begin the service with a confession of sins a variety of confessional prayers may be used in addition to the *I Confess.* The *Our Father* could then follow the confession, when there is one, as a prayer of confidence in divine forgiveness and in the promise of Christ's kingdom. If there is no confession at the beginning of the communion service, it begins with the *Our Father.*

There can be no doubt that we are in need of a new translation of the *Our Father,* one which avoids the anachronisms of the present version and which lends itself to group recitation. The following version is offered as one such possible rendition:

> Our Father in heaven,
> may your name be blessed;
> may your kingdom come;
> may your will be done on earth as in heaven.
>
> Give us today the bread we need,
> and forgive us our faults
> as we forgive those who have wronged us.
> And do not put us to the test,
> but save us from Evil.

If the celebrant chooses not to compose his own embolism after the *Our Father,* he should again have a variety of seasonally appropriate ones to choose from. The embolism may, moreover, conveniently introduce the kiss of peace by concluding with a petition related to the meaning of the ritual greeting of peace, e.g., by asking that the congregation may as a preparation for communion exchange a greeting which truly expresses their love for one another in Christ. The kiss of peace itself may, of course, be relocated at another place in the service, if that should seem appropriate, for example, after the confession of sins or before the preparation of gifts as a sign of mutual forgiveness.

An example of an alternate embolism would be:

Save us from every evil, most merciful Father, and sustain us in our trial, for we believe that you alone are the Lord of life and death and that you have sent your Son to redeem us by his blood. Strengthen us by this eucharistic feast in the bonds of holy peace so that our love for one another, which we now freely and faithfully renew, may lead us always to a greater understanding of the unfathomable mystery of your abiding and eternal love for us. We ask this through Christ our Lord. *All*: Amen

Once the kiss of peace has been exchanged, the celebrant should say some prayer or prayers whose purpose is to prepare the community more immediately for the reception of communion. The *Lamb of God,* the private prayers of preparation now recommended to the priest, and the *Behold the Lamb of God* may be conveniently replaced by a larger variety of preparatory prayers. One example of such an alternate prayer would be:

Priest: Father, Righteous One, the world has not known you; but your only Son, our Lord and Savior Jesus Christ, has known you. And we have known that you have sent him. He has made your name known to us and will continue to make it known. May, then, the love with which you have loved him be in us; and may he be in us.

All: (once only) Lord, I am not worthy that you should come under my roof; but only say the word and I shall be healed.

Another possibility would be:

Priest: The Spirit and the Church of Christ say, "Come!" Let everyone who listens answer, "Come!" For the One who is present in these words and signs now repeats his promise: "I shall indeed be with you soon."

All: Amen. Come, Lord Jesus!

With adequate catechical preparation, there is no reason why the congregation should not be allowed to receive the host either in the hand or on the tongue. The practice of receiving in the hand has the sanction of eight centuries of tradition to support it and can be a useful means of impressing upon the faithful the sanctity of the human body, which is allowed to hold the body of the Lord; the reality of the Christian's baptismal consecration, which transcends the consecration given to any sacred vessel; and their adult status in the community, since normally adults feed themselves. There might even be a possible catechetical advantage in communicating upon the tongue Christians who are not yet confirmed as a reminder that they are still destined to receive the sacrament of adult Christian living. With proper catechetical instruction, there is, moreover, no reason why everyone communicating should not communicate at each liturgy under both species. The practicalities of communicating in the cup are never beyond solution when the celebrant is genuinely interested in solving them.

The purification of the sacred vessels can, when convenient, be postponed till after the service is ended. It is also often profitable for both the celebrant and the congregation to spend a period of time after communion in silent meditation. This meditation period may often be ended by the celebrant asking if there are any requests for help from members of the congregation. The purpose of these requests should be to remind the congregation that communion should bear fruit in good works. The requests should not be requests for prayers, since they would then only reduplicate the prayers of the faithful, but requests for specific things to be done which are laid before the generosity of the community for a practical response. As in the prayers of the faithful, these requests should, when convenient, be opened to the members of the congregation. Otherwise they may be submitted to the celebrant before the service for him to bring to the attention of the congregation.

After the requests for help have been concluded, the celebrant leads the congregation in the closing prayer and then blesses them. If there is a concluding hymn, the final dismissal of the people may be postponed until after it is concluded instead of said immediately after the blessing. If the celebrant does not compose his own blessing, a variety of formulas should be available from which he can choose. For example:

Priest: May the God whose power is at work in you and who can do infinitely more than we can ask or imagine fill your minds and your hearts with everything that is noble and keep you safe until the day of Christ.

All: Amen.

Or:

Priest: May the Lord bless you and keep you.
May the Lord let his face shine on you and be gracious to you. And may the peace of God, which surpasses all that we can comprehend, stand guard over your minds and hearts in Christ Jesus, our Lord.

All: Amen.

Or:

Priest: May the grace of our Lord Jesus Christ, the love of God our Father, and the fellowship of the Holy Spirit be with you all this day and forever.

All: Amen.

The dismissal formula may also be varied; for example:

Priest: Our Eucharist is ended. Let us go and make peace.

All: Thanks be to God.

Thus the revised order of worship would ordinarily include the following elements (items in parenthesis are optional):

I. Entrance Rite:
   a. (Opening Hymn)
   b. Opening prayer
II. Liturgy of the Word:
   a. First Reading
   b. (Meditation on the First Reading)
   c. Second Reading
   d. (Meditation on the Second Reading)
   e. (Third Reading)
   f. Homily (or some other form of group meditation)
   g. Prayers of the Faithful (suitably concluded according to the circumstances with a confession of sins and absolution)
III. Preparation of Gifts:
   a. Actual Preparation of the Bread and Wine (if possible not at the altar of sacrifice)
   b. Prayer over the Gifts
IV. Eucharistic Prayer
V. Communion Service:
   a. Our Father
   b. Embolism, which introduces:
   c. The Kiss of Peace
   d. Prayers of Immediate Preparation for Communion
   e. Communion
   f. (Silent Meditation after Communion)
   g. (Practical Appeals for Help)
VI. Rite of Dismissal
   a. Concluding Prayer
   b. Blessing
   c. (Closing Hymn)
   d. Formula of Dismissal

Involved Eucharistic Worship

But we have wandered a bit from our initial train of thought. The purpose of the above excursus into rubrical fantasy was simply to remind ourselves in some detail that if we are to take eucharistic worship rather than private, individual meditation as the paradigm of Christian prayer, then the prayer experience of which we speak need not be equated solely with the highly formal and impersonal mood which often attends an unreformed celebration of the Eucharist. Eucharist worship can be a vital and deeply moving experience if both celebrant and congregation join their graced efforts to make it a truly living profession of faith.

The first thing worth noting about the humanly meaningful celebration of the Eucharist is that it manages to embody in a unified act of worship the many complex attributes of biblical prayer. It is covenant worship par excellence; the public, ecclesial reaffirmation on the part of each worshipper both of his faith and confidence in the new covenant revealed in the risen Christ and of his willingness to assume personal responsibility for the practical consequences which that profession of belief demands in his own life. It is need-conscious prayer which recognizes the legitimacy and necessity of acknowledging our humblest human needs before the Father and of associating our petitions with the efficacious and redemptive prayer of Christ. It climaxes in a prayer of blessing in which the exchange of covenant gifts between God and men plays an essential part. It is a reacceptance on the part of each worshipper of his entire religious heritage in a spirit of repentance for past faults and of thankful praise for God-given graces. It is a prayer of simple endurance, in which each worshipper unites himself to the resigned prayer of the crucified Christ. It is prayer whose sacramentality reminds us both of the presence and of the absence of God in this world. It is a priestly prayer, in which the priestly people of God unites itself in worship to its messianic high priest through the sacramental mediation of his ordained minister. It is the eschatological prayer par excellence, in which the Christian community by its sacramental recall of the inauguration of the eschatological age renews its graced awareness of the presence within it of the transforming Spirit of God and looks forward in hope to the day when it will be reunited in perfect love with the divine bridegroom. It is the supreme and efficacious prayer of the community for the graced coming of the kingdom of God, a prayer in which each of the assembled worshippers reacknowledges before God his own baptismal mission to labor for the spread of the kingdom as a sign and profession of his faith. It is, too, an expression on the part of the worshipping community of its mutual forgiveness, a prophetic sign and a cause of loving reconciliation. It is a happy prayer expressing joyful thanks to God for all his gifts.

As sacramental worship the Eucharist is God's judgment upon his people, the prophetic proclamation and the sacramental reembodiment of his saving love which challenges every man to respond with love in kind. It is trinitarian worship, offered to the Father in Christ, and through the Spirit. It is explicitly ecclesial prayer, whose communitarian dimensions are integral to the very act worship.

Moreover, it should be clear that eucharistic prayer is in a unique sense a prayer of involvement with this world and not of flight from it. It is the supreme religious expression of a common belief in God's irrevocable love-commitment to mankind, a commitment which was embodied in the life and teachings of Christ, ratified by the Father in the resurrection, and mediated to all men through the mission of the Spirit. For the Christian, therefore, each eucharistic covenant renewal demands the renewal of his active personal dedication to the work of the kingdom, to the task of realizing under grace Christ's own vision of a human community of "little ones" dedicated to a life of gratuitous sharing, unrestricted love, and atoning service.

Because it is situational prayer, eucharistic prayer arises both from a consciousness of human needs and from a conviction that God himself in his infinite love is deeply involved with the least and the greatest of our necessities, and that his concerned involvement is a model for each Christian's dealing with his neighbor. It is a prayer which is pleased to reflect upon the history of God's loving involvement with men in order to find there direction and guidance both for oneself and for the community he had founded. It is a prayer which acknowledges man's involvement with God by voicing our common consciousness of human failure and of the divine forgiveness that is ever present as a challenge to our selfishness. It is a prayer which recognizes that God's involvement with men has taken sacramental and, therefore, sacerdotal and ecclesial form, with the result that involvement with God is now impossible unless it be mediated by a concerned, loving, mutually forgiving involvement with one's fellow men. It is a prayer which sees in the actual presence of God's Spirit in this world the sign of God's continued involvement with the sons of men. It is a prayer which is rooted in the conviction that the divine involvement with men encompasses the whole of human history, that it links each moment of our lives lived in faith and love with the triumph of the risen Christ, and that it grounds our hope for the consummation of our faithful love of God and of each man, in our blessed union upon the last day.

We may conclude, therefore, that one important purpose of eucharistic prayer is to remind us of the full complexity of our involvement with God and with one another in Christ, for only in eucharistic worship are all the dimensions of that relationship sacramentally embodied.

If, then, we take eucharistic worship as the most complete and most complex instance of Christian prayer, then it is also clear by reverse logic that other forms of prayer, though perfectly legitimate, will lack of necessity some of the relational dimensions which are essential to eucharistic worship and that they will be integrally Christian to the extent that they approach their eucharistic model. Now, since eucharistic prayer demands in all of its aspects that each participant engage in involved prayer, to the extent that other forms of prayer fail to reflect this or that aspect of eucharistic worship to that extent will their degree of involvement be diminished. But Christian prayer can never become so disengaged that it ceases altogether to be involved with this world and becomes instead a mere flight to some transcendent spiritual realm, for the simple reason that when the divine Absolute is encountered in Christian belief and worship, it is encountered precisely in the form of God's absolute and challenging love-commitment to this world in the incarnation of his Son and in the mission of the Spirit. It is, moreover, a love-commitment renewed in space and time with each eucharistic act.

Any attempted Neo-Platonization of Christian prayer can, therefore, result only in its impoverishment through the elimination of its immanent, horizontal dimension. And that horizontal aspect of prayer includes: its more explicitly sacramental aspect; its situational concern; its acknowledgement of the real, if limited, value of material sensible goods; its incarnational dimension; and its ecclesial aspect. We may conclude, therefore, that any prayer of pure transcendence, i.e., any prayer which disparages or positively excludes any of these fundamental aspects of Christian prayer, is to that extent suspect.

The Purpose of Non-eucharistic Prayer

What then is the purpose of non-eucharistic prayer? Here again the Christian can turn to the prayer of Christ for the answer to his perplexities. For the prayer of Jesus was, as far as we can tell from Scripture, closely bound to his own sense of mission and purpose. It was because he felt himself divinely sent for the establishment upon earth of a community of "little ones" who would offer with him to the Father the kind of atoning service and worship which befits a child of God that Jesus prayed to the Father. He prayed, therefore, as an acknowledgement of the fact that just as the initiative for his mission had come originally from the God who had sent him into the world, so too the accomplishment of that mission, the gathering together of God's "little ones," was not a work of mere human ingenuity but the work of the Father who must first call to himself any man who in fact comes to him. He prayed for the Father's guidance in the conduct of his mission, in the choice of the twelve, in the extension of his ministry, in confronting the seeming collapse of his endeavors because of human hatred and opposition. He prayed in order to be able to confront the sufferings, disappointments, and opposition that met his effort to found a religious community based on love rather than on the meticulous observance of external religious forms. He prayed to express his confidence in the power of the Father to triumph over the malice and hostility of men. In moments of joy, he prayed in order to bless the Father for his goodness and for his love.

The individual Christian must, therefore, pray as an individual because he too is called personally by the Father to share in the mission of Christ. He must pray because he personally is called to re-create, in his own time and circumstances and to the extent that it is possible for a sinful man, Christ's own human experience of what it means to be a child of God. As God's adopted son, he must, therefore, pray in order that he personally may re-capture to the extent that he can under grace Christ's own vision of the kind of human community which is pleasing to the Father, in order that, as God's adopted son, he may find the means in the concrete situations of his life to labor for the establishment of such a community of gratuitous sharing, unrestricted love, and atoning service; and in order that as a disciple of Jesus he might acknowledge before God that the success of the salvific enterprise begun by Christ rests ultimately with the divine grace and power of God.

At the very least, therefore, non-eucharistic prayer corresponds to the felt need within each individual Christian to discern within himself God's salvific purposes in his regard. The matter for this discerning process is the individual values, the felt purposes, the personal goals, and the inner aspirations which each individual personally experiences when confronting his God as a follower of Christ and a member through his Spirit of the Christian community. These inwardly felt, personal movements of heart must, however, themselves be interpreted and evaluated. They must be interpreted because their true motivation may be subconscious rather than conscious and because feelings of profound hostility, deep aggression, and boundless selfishness can sometimes wear extremely pious masks. They must be evaluated because no simple feeling or aspiration taken in itself contains the norm, the criterion for its own ethical and religious measurement.

Now, for each Christian, the criterion by which he seeks to measure his own aspirations must ultimately be the human aspirations of God's only Son. The process of personal spiritual discernment is, then, nothing else than the effort to penetrate and to assimilate his inspired salvific vision. Moreover, both the penetration and the assimilation of Christ's vision demand an inner conversion of heart, for without at least an aspiration toward the quality of selfless and atoning love demanded of each man by the love of God, no individual can approach an understanding of the meaning of Jesus's message and the driving motives of his life with the openness of mind which Jesus himself demanded. For the assimilation of the message of Christ also demands that each individual member of the community become a visionary as Jesus himself was, that each individual member of the community learn to see himself as personally adopted to be a child of God, as called by his Son and by the Spirit to dedicate himself to the task of laboring to realize the ideal Christian community.

Finally, the discerning process which lies at the heart of personal prayer must be the graced effort to penetrate into the mystery of the person of God. That is to say, it presupposes a faith context; it presupposes that an individual has made a global commitment to Christ as the human embodiment of God and, therefore, as our ultimate historical norm both of what the Father's loving attitude toward men is and of what man in his relation to God and to his fellows is called to be. In the interpersonal context established by such a faith-commitment, any effort to penetrate into the mystery and message of Christ must take the form of one's increasingly personal involvement with a God who is himself deeply and personally involved with the sons of men.

Prayer vs. Problem Solving

As a result, individual prayer can never be mere problem solving. Mere problem solving, whether speculative or practical, is an activity which looks exclusively to immanent values. That is to say, it lacks a vertical dimension and locks an individual within himself, within the limits of his own finite, immanent experience, needs, and reflective capacities. Problem solving is the response to an objective challenge rather than to a person. Its goal is power, control over one's environment, rather than the increase of selfless and atoning love. It is the mere application of pragmatic logic to the resolution of an experienced need, not the expansion of the human heart out to the person and the reality of a transcendent yet immanent God.

Involved, discerning prayer is, therefore, the ongoing enterprise of bringing to graced consciousness the full, concrete consequences for one's own purposeful living of a personal commitment to Jesus Christ as one who is God's normative, loving, self-revelation to men. Because the ultimate Christian criterion for discernment in the person of Jesus, who is a historical reality outside of the praying believer, discerning prayer necessarily contains a theological, or dogmatic, element within it. For the mind must understand its criterion for discernment if it is to use it properly. Since, too, discerning prayer includes an awareness of one's personal fallibility and need for enlightenment, it is willing to draw upon all available human and ecclesial resources capable of enriching its understanding of the person and mission of Christ: Sacred Scripture, the official teachings of the leadership of the community, the writings of learned and holy men, etc. But because discerning prayer is situational in its origin and orientation, it approaches these theological sources from a need-determined viewpoint. It comes to them with a difficulty to be resolved, a need to be fulfilled, a decision to be made. It is, to cite one well-known example, the prayer of an Ignatius trying to decide the concrete question of whether he should in conscience as founder of the Jesuit order allow the houses of his order to have a fixed income.

Norms of Discernment in Prayer

Discerning prayer is not just activity; it involves listening as well. The discerning soul seeks to dispose itself to an inner sensitivity to the movements of the Spirit. But the discerning soul comes to prayer actively seeking and passively listening *for something.* What draws him to prayer is his concern to discover where concretely God is leading him, what specifically God is calling him to do.

Nor can discerning prayer be reduced to mere theological understanding. It presupposes inner movements of heart, personal attitudes and human aspirations capable of being discerned. For example, in the light of some of the reflections of this and of the preceding chapters, we should be inclined to approve a motive, attitude, or affection which: (1) increases confidence in God, inner peace of soul, and loving concern for God and for other men in Christ's name; (2) leads to knowledge of one's weakness, to inner repentance, and to the abandonment of selfishness, of the desire to dominate others, and of proud and arrogant self-reliance; (3) produces a better understanding and enthusiasm for one's personal and ecclesial role in the mission of Christ; (4) inspires one to share one's goods more selflessly and gratuitously with those in greatest need; (5) helps one to be open and non-exclusive in one's love and also to be faithful to one's particular ecclesial love-commitment, whether as a married or as a vowed Christian; (6) facilitates the atoning service of others in Christ's name; (7) leads to the building up of a Christian community united with its leaders in selfless labor for those in need, in its open hospitality, and in the breaking down of injustice and of artificial social barriers; (8) fosters the virtues associated with selfless love: patience, kindness, openness, modesty, thoughtfulness, magnanimity, truthfulness, mutual trust, mutual hope, etc.; (9) dispels inner darkness of soul: despair, apathy, confusion, pride, lack of purpose, fear, insensitivity to grace and to the needs of others; (10) strengthens one to inner constancy in the face of spiritual darkness; (11) encourages one to seek proper spiritual direction; (12) is compatible with moral living and with the law of love; (13) increases one's understanding of the common faith of the community and facilitates one's loving and flexible adherence to its legitimate practical demands; (14) fosters a love of eucharistic and sacramental worship; (15) discourages pharisaical legalism, the tendency to pass judgment on others, and the blind adherence to religious forms without purpose or understanding.

These, then, are some of the criteria helpful, at least for beginners, in the discerning and evaluation both of the inner movements of one's own heart in prayer and the measure of one's personal involvement with the mission of Christ.

Prayer of Involvement and Work

By being consciously and explicitly situational, the prayer of involvement could, moreover, help resolve the artificial tension which arose in patristic times between prayer and work. When one prays about the concrete details of one's own life, about, for instance, the human and spiritual development of those one meets, about the possible ways of bringing Christ to others in one's day-to-day encounters with people, about the possibility of forming a truly Christian community in the situation in which one lives and works, through promoting free and gratuitous sharing, through breaking down human and social barriers, through loving and atoning service—when the whole thrust of one's prayer is an effort to discern what God is calling one to do in the most ordinary circumstances of daily living and of one's job commitment by seeking for light in the teachings of Christ and in the graced reflections of the Christian community upon its mission, then the whole thrust of one's prayer life is toward its own integration with active labor for the kingdom. Prayer ceases to be one in a series of unrelated activities that one is expected to perform at predetermined periods in the day: it is prayer about one's day, about one's life. Even if one adheres to the praiseworthy practice of setting aside regular times for prayer, by cultivating a form of prayer which is situationally involved, not only does one gradually bring one's day into one's prayer life, but such attitudes of prayerful discernment, of petition, of praise, of confident endurance, of sorrow, and of repentance will inevitably begin to permeate one's day.

Discerning prayer which is situationally involved also helps to resolve the artificial conflict which seems to exist between active involvement in work for the kingdom and reliance on the grace and power of God to accomplish the work begun in Christ. In the first place, such prayer cannot help but increase our own consciousness that whatever we do, whatever we are, whatever we accomplish for Christ and for the building up of the Christian community is itself the work of grace within us. Secondly, no one can be actively associated with the work of Christ without coming face to face with his own limitations. Many things we can do to dispose men to receive the Spirit of Christ; but in the last analysis, only God can touch the human heart. Situations will, then, never be lacking in which one reaches the end of one's human resources—of one's words, ideas, projects—and finds oneself thrown back on prayers as the only and best resource left. To anyone sensitive to the presence and movement of the Spirit, "Shut up and pray" soon becomes a rule of thumb of the apostolate. But it must be a prayer that is genuinely confident of a response.

Moreover, if one conceives of personal prayer as situational, discerning prayer, it is easy to agree with von Balthasar's suggestion that an important function of personal prayer is to effect the gradual sacralization of the secular dimensions of our lives by providing a vital and necessary link between day-to-day living and sacramental worship.

Meaning of the "Secular"

The present demand in this country for a "secular" Christianity relevant to our times has a number of human and cultural motives. The first is the existence of a secular culture, a complex of institutions and human associations quite capable of so absorbing the interest and attention of people that they can with very little effort ignore existing religious institutions and the need for formal worship. Second, in many instances the Church has attempted to parallel humanitarian secular institutions with formally religious institutions of her own; and this practice has in turn evoked a variety of reactions. For many the very existence of such institutions is proof of a "ghetto" mentality, a flight from the secular to a closed enclave of mutual self-delusion. Persons of this bent are often inclined to embrace the secular as being more efficient, professional, and respectful of men's consciences. Others, while committed in principle to the retention of religious institutions, have begun to doubt the possibility of preserving them in our increasingly competitive and sectarian society. Still others, repelled by what seems to be the formalism of organized religion, see in secular man a healthier honesty than in religionists: secular man may be no saint, they argue, but at least he is no hypocrite. At the very least he makes no pretense in his pursuit of material goods of being religious. To add to the confusion, often the discussion of the advantages or disadvantages of "secularization" is only a theological front for a much more trivial controversy over issues of little genuine theological significance, like whether or not religious should wear habits or priests, turned-around collars.

The deep theological options implicit in the secular-sacred controversy are, at least potentially, extremely significant in the formation of the most basic religious attitudes. The order of the sacred is the order of the redemptive. If, then, the sacred has no reason for existing, then certain consequences must follow: Either man is in no need of redemption or man is in need of redemption but has already been redeemed or man is capable of redeeming himself.

For the Christian, only the second of these alternatives can hold any kind of attractiveness. But to accept it in a Christian sense is to rule out the possibility of a purely secular world. Why is this so?

It seems curious that people still exist who in spite of the abundant evidence in its favor still find it difficult to believe in some kind of original sin. Perhaps such people are James's "healthy-minded" people, psychologically and emotionally incapable of facing the malice, hostility, and selfishness which exist within themselves and human society. But that such evils exist and that they exist on a massive scale and are deeply rooted in the most basic drives of human nature would seem in any realistic appraisal of human life, undeniable.

For the Christian, the final revelation of the full scope of human sinfulness and of man's need for redemption is the incarnation, death, and glorification of God's own Son. But the incarnation seen in all of its salvific dimensions also includes a revelation to man of his utter incapacity to effect his own redemption by his own power. To be fully redeemed is to share in Christ's redemptive death and resurrection by responding appropriately under grace to the irrevocable commitment of divine love therein revealed and thus to assume one's personal role in the salvific reorientation of the historical process which was accomplished by the divine self-revelation in Christ.

Mankind has, then, been radically redeemed in Jesus, by whom we have access to the Father in the Spirit. But even though in him the full scope of the Father's redemptive plan has been revealed, and even though through him and through the Spirit the possibility of sharing in the life of God is a real one for every man, the revelation of God's love is his judgment upon the world, in the Johannine sense of that term. That is to say, it is an event which demands an active, loving response from men in this life, if the redemptive process is to reach completion.

At the same time, there is no doubt whatever, that man's every response to grace in this life is shot through with ambiguity. No man alive is complete and total master of himself. There is scarcely any externally good and holy act one can name whose motives are beyond question of being diluted and perverted either with selfishness or with subtly veiled hostility.

The secular is that dimension of human life which fails to express the quality of love demanded by Christ and which is, therefore, still in need of redemptive completion. The secular, therefore, includes all that is positively sinful as well as all that is salvifically ambiguous in human life and society. The very meaning of the term "secularity" is, therefore, an ambiguous one; for while many values of "secular" life and culture are positive human values capable of assuming salvific significance in Christ, as a theological category the "secular" must also include the world opposed to Christ and to the ideals of his kingdom. Hence, the secular may be visibly and socially embodied in actions and institutions which express either man's malice or his religio-moral ambiguity; or it may take the subtler invisible form of well-concealed inner attitudes of heart incompatible with the mission and message of Christ.

The sacralization of the secular consists in bringing it to the redemptive completion of love in Christ. In other words, the need for sacralization is grounded in the need for men to respond actively and appropriately to God's self-revelation of unrestricted and gratuitous love in Christ by laboring to found a community of gratuitous sharing, unrestricted love, and atoning service in Christ's name. To deny the need for sacralization is, therefore, to deny the need for men to respond actively to the person, the mission, the vision, and the grace of Christ.

At the same time, to acknowledge the need for men to respond to God's self-revelation in the twofold mission of his Son and of the Spirit is to acknowledge that the weakness, malice, and ambiguity which mar the life of every son and daughter of Adam presuppose that only a divine intervention analogous to the resurrection of Jesus can ever really bring the redemptive process to completion. In other words, man's need to share in the full redemption revealed and offered in Jesus grounds causally the need for the eucharistically centered sacramental system. For not only does the concrete form and structure of that system proceed from the very historical events which have revealed to men the extent of his redemptive needs, but by temporally re-embodying through the mediation of his ordained representative God's salvific commitment to men in Christ, the sacramental system remains the only sort of worship which is capable of manifesting the full relational scope of man's redemptive situation, not only by demanding of each worshipper that he acknowledge his own redemption to be grounded in an event outside himself to which he must respond and in a power other than himself which alone can bring that redemption to completion, but also by re-embodying the Christ-event and the power of Christ in the sacramental commitment of his ordained representative in the Christian community.

Far from being a liability, therefore, the "objective" aspect of sacramental worship lifts it above any merely inner aspiration of heart, any spontaneous profession of faith, any act of personal piety, or any inwardly felt gift of the Spirit. For every expression of piety, however praiseworthy and noble it may seem, retains the salvific ambiguity that attends any humanly motivated action, while the efficacy of the divine salvific commitment which alone is of ultimate redemptive importance and which is renewed in the sacramental action of God's minister prescinds from the human motivations of that minister beyond his simple will to administer the sacrament. Similarly, as Paul insists in First Corinthians, there is no attitude of heart or charismatic gift which is ultimately redemptive except that perfect love which comes in its perfection only when one has been united with God for all eternity. In this life, then, man remains, on the one hand, in need of God's constant saving action, while, on the other hand, in sacramental worship alone not only is the need for that action re-embodied in its fullness as a man moves through the process of his own personal redemption, but the divine promise of present and of ultimate redemption is, through the mediation of his official human representative, temporally renewed.

Clearly, then, in a theological context one cannot define "secularity" simply in terms of the growing specialization of human competence or even in terms of the harmonious integration of specialized skills for the general benefit of mankind and of society. In its most fundamental theological sense, secularity looks to the salvific meaning and status of every human activity, however specialized or primitive the competence of the agent. It prescinds, therefore, from the degree of technological or cultural development of individuals and peoples.

An important purpose of sacramental worship, therefore, is to provide man with the occasion to present himself in all of his salvific ambiguity and unregeneracy, with all of his sins, gifts, graces, virtues, aspirations, and needs to the Christ who sanctions the sacramental love-commitment of his official human representatives and to receive from him through their mediation the assurance that God is indeed committed to removing all traces of secularity, of sin, of redemptive ambiguity from one's life and person. Such an act is, therefore, a culminating moment in the ongoing sacralization of the world; but it is a moment within a process and one which demands both antecedents and consequences.

Personal, discerning, and involved prayer has as one of its purposes, therefore, to prepare the worshipper for these privileged sacramental moments in the redemptive process and to extend their consequences in his life. For a discerning prayer of involvement seeks nothing less than the gradual sacralization of our lives through our personal assimilation to the person and mission of Christ by deepening our understanding of the driving motives behind his mission and the mission of the community of "little ones" he sought to found. Needless to say, discerning, involved prayer may play an integral part in any individual's participation in sacramental worship. But the structured, explicitly ecclesial, and communal character of sacramental worship often precludes any extended, inner discernment of personal motives and of the quality of one's religious commitment, especially with the growing tendency in liturgical prayer to active vocal participation in worship on the part of the congregation. If, then, sacramental worship is to be more than the routine performance of a ritual, the reflective moment in liturgical worship which comes especially during the liturgy of the word needs, humanly speaking, to be supplemented by periods of personal, reflective, discerning, involved prayer.

The Eucharist is the renewal by the worshipping community of its covenant-commitment to the Father, in Christ, through the Spirit with all of the responsibilities and consequences for daily living that that commitment entails. If, then, it is to be truly a meaningful act of worship, the eucharistic action must be performed with a consciousness of the nature of the responsibilities being renewed and demands of the covenanted Christian a willingness to discern and to purify the attitudes, motives, habits, and patterns of his own life according to the ideals of Christ. Individual prayer is thus not only involved prayer, but in a Christian context it is integrally ordered to sacramental worship as its culmination and redemptive completion: that is to say, individual prayer is one of the responsibilities assumed by a sacramental worshipper in his covenant renewal as an important means of sacralizing his own life. Moreover, sacramental prayer serves the important ecclesial function of dispelling some of the salvific ambiguity which inevitably attends the prayerful aspirations of any individual.

It should be clear, then, that many controversies about the possible secularization of Christianity are posed in misleading and confusing terms. That is to say, instead of asking whether or not a particular non-sacramental institution or practice in the Church is achieving the sacralizing function for which it exists, all too often we identify "the sacred" exclusively and arbitrarily with existing Church practices and in the process lump all other possible modes of human behavior and activity together under the single category of "secularity." It should, however, be clear from these reflections that anything which actually fosters the redemptive transformation of the world in Christ can lay legitimate claim, to the extent that it does so, to being sacred. By the same token, anything which hinders that transformation is secular. Where the redemptive mission of Christ is best served by the existence of a given institution or by the inauguration of new religious practices to replace ineffectual, non-sacramental old ones, the redemptively helpful institution is sacred, however secular it may appear externally. When, however, an existing non-sacramental institution is a hindrance to that mission, it is secular and worldly, no matter how externally pious and sanctioned it may appear. And even the ritual form of the sacraments is subject to reform.

Needless to say, the precise form that personal prayer will take is an individual matter. But clearly, in addition to regular periods devoted to solitary inner discernment, prayer meetings of the sort common in the charismatic movement can be both a stimulus to solitary and to sacramental worship as well as a public profession and strengthening of one's personal Christian commitment in their own right. The discernment of the charisms of the sort commonly experienced in the charismatic movement presupposes the criteria of discernment which apply to the prayerful discernment of felt values, motives, and aspirations. That is to say, the norms of discernment which apply to the latter form of prayer apply to the discernment of charisms as well. The discernment of charisms, however, introduces an element of passivity into the experience of prayer which is absent from the discernment of aspirations and affections. Gifts like the gift of tongues or of prophecy are not developed; they are received. In the case of charisms, therefore, the discerning process demands that not only the effect of the gift be evaluated but its source as well.

Problems of Enthusiasm

In this context, Catholics involved in the charismatic movement would do well to become informed concerning the history and development of Christian enthusiasm. Knox in his historical study of enthusiasm notes a regular pattern in its development: first, there is in charismatic movements an initial tendency toward exclusivity and cliquishness based upon an appeal to inner enlightenment. That is to say, not only does the inner illumination which gives rise and impetus to the movement initially serve to distinguish those who have received it from the rest of the worshipping community, but it gradually leads to their separation from the unenlightened and eventually to the inner fragmentation of the enthusiastic movement itself. Second, there is commonly in such movements an antinomian tendency, an inclination to challenge, oppose, or circumvent church authority and to oppose the charisms of the enthusiast to the charismatic office of ordained community leaders.

Third, there is in enthusiasm what Knox calls a tendency to "ultrasupernaturalism." Knox speaks of "ultrasupernaturalism" as "the real characteristic of the enthusiast," who:

expects more evident results from the grace of God than we others. He sees what effects religion can have, does sometimes have, in transforming a man's whole life and outlook; these exceptional cases (so we are content to think them) are for him the average standard of religious achievement. He will have no "almost-Christians," no weaker brethren who plod and stumble, who (if truth must be told) would like to have a foot in either world, whose ambition is to qualify, not to excel. He has before his eyes a picture of the early Church, visibly penetrated with supernatural influences; and nothing less will serve him for a model. Extenuate, accommodate, interpret, and he will part company with you.

Quoting a hundred texts—we also use them, but with more of embarrassment—he insists that the members of his society saved members of a perishing world, should live a life of angelic purity, of apostolic simplicity; worldly amusements, the artifices of a polite society, are not for them. Poor human nature! Every lapse that follows is marked by pitiless watchers outside the fold, creates a harvest of scandal within. Worse still, if the devout circle has cultivated a legend of its own impeccability, we shall be told, in that case, that actions which bring damnation to the worldling may be inculpable in the children of light. We must be prepared for strange alternations of rigorism and antinomianism as our history unfolds itself. . . .

But the implications of enthusiasm go deeper than this; at the root of it lies a different theology of grace. Our traditional doctrine is that grace perfects nature, elevates it to a higher pitch, so that it can bear its part in the music of eternity, but leaves it nature still. The assumption of the enthusiast is bolder and simpler; for him, grace has destroyed nature, and replaced it. The saved man has come out into a new order of being, with a new set of faculties which are proper to his state; David must not wear the panoply of Saul. Especially, he decries the use of human reason as a guide to any sort of religious truth. A direct indication of the Divine will is communicated to him at every turn, if only he will consent to abandon the "arm of flesh"—Man's miserable intellect, fatally obscured by the Fall. If no oracle from heaven is forthcoming, he will take refuge in sortilege; anything, to make sure that he is leaving the decision in God's hands. That God speaks to us through the intellect is a notion which he may accept on paper, but fears, in practice, to apply.[202]

Finally, in addition to these essential traits, Knox also notes two non-essential but frequently concomitant characteristics in enthusiastic movements: (1) belief in the immanence of the second coming; (2) the cult of ecstasy leading at times to a host of seemingly abnormal psychic phenomena.

One would do a gross injustice to the Catholic charismatic movement were one to characterize it as "enthusiasm" in Knox's technical sense of that term. Knox's book is in fact a history of those enthusiastic movements in the history of Christianity which broke away from the rest of the worshipping community and from active cooperation with the hierarchy. He does not mention the innumerable instances of enthusiastic movements which remained within the Church and which have enriched its life with new religious orders and congregations and with innumerable charitable and deeply religious and apostolic works. But precisely because Knox's book deals with the history of divisive enthusiasm, it can supply any charismatic Christian with some useful negative criteria for the discernment of charisms which can supplement the more positive criteria included above for the prayerful discernment of motives and affections of the heart.

Discernment of Charisma

First of all, then, it is clear that any tendency in charismatic movement to separation and exclusivity is suspect. This exclusivity can, moreover, take a variety of forms, for example:

(1) the tendency to oppose a pentecostal "baptism of the Spirit" either to sacramental baptism or to confirmation by suggesting that those who have not received the Holy Spirit in the form of the gift of tongues or some other unusual charism are not truly graced and cannot be said in any significant sense to have received the Holy Spirit. Also suspect would be the claim that the graced efficacy of the imposition of hands practiced in the charismatic movement exceeds that of the sacraments. What is called "baptism by the Holy Spirit" is in many instances a genuine grace, but it is an experience whose consequences must be carefully discerned. If, moreover, it is truly a grace, it must be seen as continuous with the grace of the Christian sacraments of

initiation and not as opposed to them. By the same token, the prayer of the charismatic community must not be opposed to the sacramental prayer of the ordained leader of the worshipping community. Instead, the prayer of the charismatic community must be seen as supporting and in a lesser way (since the community does not speak in Christ's name in the same ecclesial manner as his ordained minister) reaffirming it.

(2) A second form of exclusivity would be to claim such a degree of uniqueness for the experience of inner enlightenment which accompanies the charismatic gifts of the Spirit as to put that enlightenment beyond the criticism and discerning evaluation of the rest of the community. If a gift is truly from the one Spirit who enlivens and inspires every member of the community, each in his own way, then, a genuine charism will be given to an individual for the sake of the community and in order to increase its love and mutual understanding, not in order to set him above his brethren or apart from them.

(3) Another symptom of exclusivity would be the demand that baptism by the Spirit assume an ecstatic and extravagantly emotional form. The sign of the presence of the Spirit is in the last analysis the transformation of a person's life in the image of Christ. It is not for men, therefore, to dictate to the Spirit of God what form that transformation must take.

Following the lead of Knox's analysis, we should also include in our negative norms for the discernment of charisms any tendency to antinomianism. Concretely, antinomianism can assume a variety of forms: (1) the claim that any gift or inner illumination is self-justifying and beyond the pale of evaluation by dogma or by rational reflection upon the truths of revelation; (2) the tendency to value inner enlightenment over Church authority in such a way as to prejudge that authority as automatically unenlightened; (3) any appeal to one's inner light as absolving one from ordinary legitimate moral and Christian obligations.

Similarly, "ultra-supernaturalism" can assume a variety of concrete forms, for example:

(1) the transformation of a specific charismatic grace like

baptism by the Spirit, the gift of tongues, etc., into a necessity for salvation for all Christians. It is one thing to be able to discern the beneficial and therefore presumably graced effects of such an experience in one's own life; it is quite another to decide on one's own just how the Spirit must work in the hearts of other men. Presumably, the Spirit is quite capable of making his own decisions in such matters.

(2) Another form of ultrasupernaturalism would be intolerance toward the moral weakness of men or to their seeming apathy toward the charismatic movement.

(3) By the same token, one should regard as suspect all intolerance of those Christians who find no incompatibility between their religious commitment and the enjoyment of the legitimate pleasures of life. One cannot legitimately invoke the sanction of the Spirit in order to transform one's personal asceticism into a puritanical rigorism binding upon all men.

(4) A third form of divisive intolerance possible in the enthusiast is intolerance of any form of religious consolation which does not derive exclusively from the inner impulse of grace, without the help of external material aids like sacraments, sacramentals, religious art, etc.

(5) A fifth symptom of ultra-supernaturalism would be the tendency to conceive of baptism by the Spirit as putting an end to one's ordinary human needs and impulses by replacing them with purely spiritual ones. One might, for instance, seek to transform a healthy recognition of the limits of human reason into a rejection of all forms of rational behavior for exclusive reliance on the inner revelations of the Spirit.

(6) In its most exaggerated forms ultra-supernaturalism transforms baptism by the Spirit in its special charismatic manifestations into an absolute assurance of personal salvation regarding those who have it as certainly saved and those who do not as children of perdition. This particular perversion sometimes results in the desire to establish a separate theocratic community in which the inner experience of the Spirit of God completely replaces the exercise of human reason and ingenuity in the ordering of society.

(7) Equally suspicious is any claim to certain knowledge of the date of the second coming.

(8) A final but very important negative criterion in the discernment of charisms is the need for extreme reticence in identifying any phenomena which might be rooted in psychic disturbance like trances, convulsions, hallucinations, etc., as clear and certain signs of the presence of the Spirit. As Paul saw centuries ago, the surest sign of his presence is not emotional upheavals but an increase in selfless and atoning love.

But even after all of these cautionary criteria for the discernment of charisms have been accepted, one still cannot simply dismiss the charismatic movement as a religious or psychological aberration. In its balanced forms, it is grounded in the belief that those who come together in a spirit of faith, confidence, and mutual love in order to pray to the Father in the name of Christ and through his Spirit can expect the Spirit of Christ to be truly present in their midst; that prayer is a time when the soul is open to the movements of the Spirit of God; that God does indeed hear our prayers, is active in the world, and will send his Spirit to those who ask him in faith, confidence, and love.

Not the least benefit of the charismatic movement is, then, its ability to restore our often waning belief in the efficacy of prayer of petition. But here again caution must be exercised lest such a belief degenerate into superstition. The fundamental ground of Christian belief in the efficacy of prayer is the resurrection of Christ as well as his repeated assurance that if we pray to the Father or to him with confidence and in his name, our prayer will be heard. But the eschatological dimension of prayer discussed above alerts the discerning believer to the fact that the divine answer to specific prayers may not come in its fullness until our own participation in the glory of Christ. Since, moreover, true Christian prayer is prayer for the realization of the kingdom in one's own life and in the world at large, there should be nothing surprising in the fact that the Father's response may indeed take such a form.

On the other hand, the kingdom is not simply a reality in the future; it is in process of realization now. Hence, one who takes the teaching of Christ seriously concerning the efficacy of prayer would expect that not every prayer addressed to the Father must await the moment of death or the second coming in order to be heard. If, moreover, God answers prayers, there must be some way of judging reasonably whether the response to one's prayer comes from God or not.

The danger in any enthusiastic movement is, of course, that it inclines one to be a bit over-hasty in attributing this or that "grace" or gift to divine intervention. Leaving aside the question of miracles in the strict sense, can we set up some sort of norms for deciding in the case of any given prayer of petition that what seems to be a response from God can reasonably be attributed to his grace and intervention?

First of all, it seems clear that any verification of divine intervention will have to be indirect. Even were God to reveal directly and immediately to an individual the fact of his intervention in response to this or that petition, the revelation would itself have to be subjected to the same sort of critical evaluation as the response to prayer. Moreover, unless one is dealing with a miracle in the strict sense, one cannot completely rule out the possibility of secondary causes, whether physical, physiological, psychological, or moral, being responsible for the experience which is being attributed to divine causality. Hence, any judgment concerning whether or not this or that event is the result of a divine response to prayer will be at best a probable one when it is the result of objective critical reflection. One can at best decide that when the circumstances and consequences of the experience or event in question are weighed against legitimate rules for discernment of spirits such as the rules indicated above, it is not unreasonable in the light of the Christian revelation to believe that this event truly comes from God.

Complex Purpose of Christian Prayer

We may conclude, then, that the purpose of prayer in religious living cannot be arbitrarily restricted to this or that specific goal. Even a superficial examination of the complexity of the motives which ground eucharistic prayer, or solitary meditation, or relatively unstructured group prayer ought to check the temptation to yield to easy generalizations in such a complex phenomenon.

We may, however, legitimately conclude that at least one important purpose of any form of prayer is to aid the disciple of Christ in his attempt to imitate his master in laboring for the kingdom by preventing him from yielding to the first temptation of Jesus in the desert. For implicit in the abandonment of prayer or in its reduction to mere problem solving is the affirmation that the work of the kingdom can be accomplished by human ingenuity alone; whereas in point of fact, the most that human ingenuity can do is either help create situations in which men are, naturally speaking, more inclined to open their hearts to the grace of God or labor to remove some of the more evident scandals to belief from the Church and from human society. But if the work of the kingdom is really to prosper, God alone can give our labors increase and bring them to fruition; and the measure of our belief in that fact is the frequency with which we turn to him in our need.

It would seem to follow, then, that the man who abandons prayer altogether either has lost interest in the work of the kingdom or has ceased to believe in any meaningful way that God is in fact active in the world, just as the man who replaces prayer with mere problem solving has ceased for all practical purposes to take God seriously as a factor in the redemptive process. In either case such a man stands before God in anything but the attitude of inner docility and abandonment demanded of one who seeks to imitate a master who lived his life vitally nourished by every word that proceeds from the mouth of his Father.

Notes

1. Ps 18:1–2;7:1;11:1.
2. Ps 6;59:1.
3. Ps 69:7.
4. Ps 140:1.
5. Ps 25:17–18,65:2;86:5–6.
6. Ps 41.
7. Ps 71.
8. 1S 1:11.
9. Ps 3:1–2.
10. Ps 9:13;18:5–4.
11. Ps 64.
12. Ps 74;79;80.
13. Ps 144:11.
14. Ps 90.
15. Ps 102;107.
16. Lk 1:68–75.
17. Ps 22:1–2.
18. Ps 7:8–9.
19. Jb 1:1.
20. Jb 1:8.
21. Jb 31:35,37.
22. Jb 42:1–6.
23. Jb 42:10–15.
24. Jb 40:4.
25. Ps 14:3.
26. 1K 11:11.
27. Dt 4:21;2K 22:13;Lm 1; 3:19–24; 5.
28. Jr 9:1–2;4–5.
29. Ps 103:8–10;Mi 7:18;Is 57: 16; Jr 3:12;Jon 4:2;Jl 2:13.
30. Jr 31:3–4.
31. Ho 10:12;Am 5:4.
32. Ps 24:6.
33. 1K 21:29;2K 22:19.
34. 1S 7:3.
35. 2K 11:17;23:1ff;Ex 24:3–8.
36. Jg 20:26;1K 20:31ff.
37. Jg 2:4;Jl 1:13;Ps 32;Lm 5.
38. Lm 3:40.
39. Ex 32:30ff.
40. Ex 32:12–13;33:13.
41. 1K 8:10–61;2K 19:15–19;2Ch 14: 10; 20:6–12.
42. Jr 15:1;Am 7:1–6;2M 15:14.
43. Jr 10:23.
44. Jr 4:19–22.
45. Jr 12:1–5.
46. Jr 15:15;17:18.
47. Jr 20:7–18.
48. Jl 1:13–2:17.
49. Is 63:7–64;Dn 9:4–19;Ba 1:15–3:8.
50. Ez 9:1–10:6.
51. Ne 9:1–10:40.
52. Am 5:18ff.
53. Ze 2:4–15.
54. Jl 2:1–2.
55. Ps 85:1–4;6; 2.
56. Ps 149.
57. Ps 110.
58. Ps 89:28–29.
59. Ps 2:8;18:43.
60. Ps 89:36.
61. Ps 46:1–3;4–6.
62. Jr 31:31–34.
63. Lk 11:2–4,13;21:36;Mt 6:9–15; 9:37;18:21–22;11:22–25;7:11; 6:7–8;18:6–8.
64. Mt 6:9.
65. Mt 6:10–13;Lk 11:2–4.
66. Mt 9:37.
67. Mt 7:7–11;Lk 11:9–13.
68. Mk 11:21–25;Mt 6:14–15.
69. Mt 18:21–22.
70. Lk 18:6–8.
71. 1K 18:36–37.
72. Mk 11:24.
73. Lk 18:9–14.
74. Lk 15:11–32.
75. Mt 6:14–15.
76. Mt 6:7–8.
77. Mt 6:5–6.
78. Mt 6:18.
79. Mk 9:21–25.

80. Lk 8:50.
81. Jn 4:46–54.
82. Jn 11:25–26.
83. Mt 14:22–23.
84. Lk 7:9;Mt 9:22.
85. Lk 3:21–22.
86. Mt 4:1–11.
87. Lk 5:42–44.
88. Lk 6:12–16.
89. Lk 10:21–22.
90. Jn 6:15;Mt 14:20–23;Mk 6:46.
91. Jn 11:41–42.
92. Lk 22:39;Jn18:2.
93. Mt26:26–29;Mk14:22–25; Lk 22: 15–20;1Co 11:23–25.
94. Jn 17:1–26.
95. Jn 17:25–26.
96. Lk 22:40–44.
97. Mt 26:36–46;Lk 22:39–46; Mk 14:36–42.
98. Lk 23:33–34.
99. Mt 27:45–46.
100. Jn 19:30.
101. Ps 31:4–5;Lk 23:46.
102. Jn 8:46;Heb 7:26–28.
103. Heb 5:7–10.
104. Jm 4:1–13.
105. Rv 6:8–10.
106. Rv 8:2–5;13:7–10.
107. Heb 10:11–18.
108. Mt 26:26;Lk 24:30.
109. 1Co 10:15–17.
110. 1Co 10:27.
111. Jn 19:12–16.
112. 1Co 12:23–27.
113. 1Co 12:28–29.
114. 1Co 11:22.
115. Ac 1:14;Lk 18:1–8;Ep 6:18–20.
116. Ac 1:24–26.
117. Ac 6:6.
118. Ac 4:24–30;Ep 6:18–20.
119. Ac 8:15.
120. Ac 13:3;20:36;21:5.
121. Ac 14:23.
122. 2Co 12:8.
123. Ep 6:18;Col 4:12.
124. Eph 6:18–20.
125. Ph 1:9.
126. 1Jn 5:16.
127. Jm 1:5–8;Jn 16:23–24;Jl 3:5; Rm 10:13.
128. 1Jn 3:21–23.
129. Heb 7:25.
130. Heb 4:15.
131. 1Jn 14–15.
132. 1Th 5:16–18.
133. 2Th 1:3;2:13.
134. Ph 1:4–5.
135. Ga 4:6.
136. Rm 8:15.
137. Rm 1:9;1Tm 5:5.
138. Ac 6:2–4.
139. Rm 8:26–29; cf. Jn 4:21–24.
140. ML 1,1674A;MG 11,441B;MG 12,120A;ML 4,521B;MG 31,244A; ML 15,1471B;33,501.
141. MG 11,549B;ML 4,521B;ML 14,-335D;14,708B.
142. ML 1,1195A;15,1471B;26,125C.
143. ML 1,1195A.
144. ML 4,540A;76,40A.
145. ML 26,47C;cf.26,125C.
146. ML 35,1896.
147. ML 77,188B.
148. ML 1,1192A.
149. MG 11,452C.
150. MG 28,264D.
151. MG 31,1216C.
152. ML 15,1721A.
153. MG 35,649B.
154. MG 35,864A.
155. MG 32,229B.
156. MG 34,1070B.
157. ML 49,771A.
158. ML 49,980C.
159. ML 49,801A.
160. ML 49,827C.
161. MG 79,1173C.

162. ML 49,839A;MG 79,1181C.
163. Nec. mon. 198;cf.202.
164. Nec. mon. 202.
165. MG 90,985A.
166. MG 90,1004C.
167. MG 90,929C.
168. MG 79,1181C.
169. ML 75,937A.
170. ML 75,1107C.
171. DS 856;1304.
172. DS 1323;1543.
173. DS 1281.
174. DS 2184ff.
175. DS 2185.
176. DS 2186–2187;2235–2218.
177. DS 2191;2229.
178. DS 2192;2224.
179. DS 2214.
180. DS 2219–2221.
181. The book in question is *Scala Claustralium* and was written under the pseudonym of St. Bernard. It is attributed to a twelfth-century Carthusian.
182. DS 2223.
183. DS 2230.
184. DS 3758.
185. DS 3843,3845.
186. *Constitution on the Sacred Liturgy*, 2.
187. *Ibid.*, 2,6.
188. *Ibid.*, 7,10.
189. *Ibid.*, 7.
190. *Ibid.*, 11.
191. *Ibid.*, 14.
192. *Ibid.*, 18,19,30,37,44,50.
193. *Ibid.*, 12–13.
194. *Decree on the Ministry and Life of Priests*, 18.
195. *Pastoral Constitution on the Church in the Modern World*, 48.
196. *Decree on Priestly Formation*, 8.
197. *Decree on the Appropriate Renewal of Religious Life*, 471.
198. *Constitution on the Sacred Liturgy*, 88.
199. Hans Urs Von Balthasar, *Prayer*, A. V. Littledale (tr.), (New York: Paulist Press, 1961), pp. 16,31–66, 94–97, 142
200. McNaspy, *op. cit.*, p. 99–109.
201. Cf. Sr. Teresa Margaret, O.C.D., "Prayer in the Secular City," *Spiritual Life* (Summer, 1968), pp. 72–84.
202. Ronald A. Knox, *Enthusiasm* (New York: Oxford Univ. Press, Galaxy PB, 1961), pp. 2–3.

DONALD L. GELPI, S.J., was born in New Orleans, Louisiana, in 1934. After he entered the Society of Jesus he studied at St. Louis University, Collège St. Albert in Louvain, and St. Mary's College in Kansas. He holds Licentiates in Philosophy and Theology from St. Louis University, both granted *magna cum laude*. He also holds a Doctorate in American Studies from Fordham University in New York. He is currently doing research and teaching at Loyola University in New Orleans.

In addition to many articles in religious and scholarly journals, Father Gelpi has published two books: *Life and Light: A Guide to the Theology of Karl Rahner* and *Functional Asceticism: A Guideline for American Religious.*